The Seasons

THE CROSS-CULTURAL MEMOIR SERIES
*Available from The Feminist Press
at The City University of New York*

Lion Woman's Legacy: An Armenian-American Memoir,
by Arlene Voski Avakian
I Dwell in Possibility, by Toni McNaron
Fault Lines, by Meena Alexander

The Seasons
Death and Transfiguration

A Memoir by Jo Sinclair

THE CROSS-CULTURAL MEMOIR SERIES

THE FEMINIST PRESS
at The City University of New York
New York

Published 1993 by The Feminist Press at The City University of New York,
311 East 94 Street, New York, NY 10128
Distributed by The Talman Company, 131 Spring Street, Suite 201E–N, New
York, NY 10012

Lines from *Markings* by Dag Hammarskjold are translated by W. H. Auden
and L. Sjoberg. Translation copyright © 1964 by Alfred A. Knopf, Inc. and
Faber & Faber Ltd. Reprinted by permission of Alfred A. Knopf. Letter from
Richard Wright to Jo Sinclair copyright © 1946 by Richard Wright. Reprinted
by permission of John Hawkins & Associates, Inc.

97 96 95 94 93 5 4 3 2 1

Library of Congress Cataloging-in-Publication Data

Sinclair, Jo, 1913–
    The seasons : death and transfiguration / Jo Sinclair.
        p. cm.
    ISBN 1-55861-056-1 (cloth) : $35.00. — ISBN 1-55861-057-X (pap.) : $12.95
    1. Sinclair, Jo, 1913–   —Biography. 2. Authors, American 20th cen-
tury—Biography. 3. Women, Jewish—United States—Intellectual
life. I. Title.
PS3537.E3514Z47   1993
813'.54—dc20
[B]   91-27010
                                                                            CIP

This publication is made possible, in part, by public funds from the New
York State Council on the Arts and the National Endowment for the Arts.
The Feminist Press would also like to thank Judith Birsh, Joanne Markell,
Nancy Porter, and Genevieve Vaughan for their generosity.

Photographs courtesy of Jo Sinclair. Cover photographs *(clockwise from left):*
the author in her garden, Novelty, Ohio, 1962; the author, age 16; the author
(seated on left), age 5, with her sister Fannie.
Cover design: Lucinda Geist
Text design: Paula Martinac

Printed in the United States on acid-free paper by McNaughton & Gunn, Inc.

For Joan Soffer
Who took me through revisions
of the book—and of life

Contents

What I ask for is absurd: that life shall have a meaning. What I strive for is impossible: that my life shall acquire a meaning. I dare not believe, I do not see how I shall ever be able to believe: that I am not alone.

Is the bleakness of this world of mine a reflection of my poverty or my honesty, a symptom of weakness or of strength, an indication that I have strayed from my path, or that I am following it?—Will despair provide the answer?

DAG HAMMARSKJÖLD
Markings

The Seasons

Some Biographical Notes on the Author

(by the Author)

"*J*o Sinclair" was born Ruth Seid in a Brooklyn, New York ghetto, in 1913. She was the youngest of the five children of Nathan and Ida Seid, Russian Jews who emigrated to America in the early 1900s.

She was three when her family moved to Cleveland, Ohio, where jobs were more plentiful for her carpenter father. Much of her life was spent there, and in the nearby countryside.

Following family and working-class traditions, she attended John Hay High School, a commercial school that trained students for office jobs. Wrong school for the girl who had been writing poems for herself since fourteen or so—rough, free-verse outbursts of frustration, anger, intense longing for "life." She was bored by her classes in shorthand, filing, bookkeeping, loved English and composition, was drawn at once to writing for the school newspaper.

Completely wrong school; not that there was ever a single question in her mind about attending college. In her rigidly traditional world, a decent child in a poor Jewish family always got a job immediately after graduating, to help with food and rent and clothes. Period. Except that this child would dream once in a while (but a quiet yearning, with none of the rage and bitterness of her poems) of going off to one of those fabulous universities she'd read about—in a flowers-and-trees city far from the barren neighborhoods in which she had always lived. Very quiet talking to herself: Sure, college probably might help, but she could do it even without those special teachers. Become the famous, rich author she had promised herself she would be someday—with money enough to help parents and to write at the same time.

Ruth Seid created her own college, via the Cleveland Public

1

Library; always the branch within walking distance of home, so that she did not even have to pay for a streetcar ride, and could carry five or six books at a time back to the house after gleaning one more library shelf. It was all free—a must for the child who had always known that there was rarely enough money for extras in life.

Her "courses" of study in library books began early, and went on all her life. As she grew older, they included real and even great poetry (Keats was nothing like her own blurts in the heart). She read voraciously, with constant excitement and curiosity, every kind of book on the shelves—soon including plays and essays and biographies of authors, but always going back to the short-story collections and novels with which she had started this education of the fiercely insistent writer.

The college-library courses were enthralling lessons about the universe outside any ghetto of street, mind, and soul; lessons about the "other people"—who lived in what she called, in some of her poems, the "garden of world." And, after a while, she knew that the precious courses would never end for her, even if she *were* permitted into that garden someday, to live and work there rightfully. She would never want to graduate, and leave her special college for the writer and good human being she wanted so fervently to be for all her life.

But there was high school to leave right now; she was eager for that kind of graduation, which naturally would be followed by grown-up life action—to go into a new kind of writing. In 1930, valedictorian of her class, the naive girl of seventeen graduated— into the Depression. So very naive: she looked at once for the obligatory job, the salary with which a decent child helps her family; and learned a great deal about that new word, *Depression*. (She had never seen it in a book.) Learned rather quickly: jobs were few, lasted briefly, and paid very little even if you managed to find one.

Much, much later, she could smile wryly at the roster of jobs the honor student searched out in the first years of what became known as the Great Depression. That period was crammed with fearfully difficult courses of rock-bottom poverty, lost homes, thousands of families "on relief"—including her own. But no smiling as that girl grew up and learned all about desperation, but kept reading her library books and writing.

Ruth Seid became Jo Sinclair with her first published short story, in early 1936. No money paid, and it was a magazine put out for the country's ghettos of poverty, bitterness, racial wars, and hatred. It was called *New Masses,* and, in all honesty, she did not want to be part of anonymous, shabby, huddling masses of people; she wanted to walk free and independent in the airy, flower-filled garden of world. But the story *was* a writing credit in a national magazine, so it felt like a little hope, even a kind of small guarantee of further publications. Yes, she would hang on to that pseudonym she had made up as one more ''being different'' for that Ruth trapped in a ghetto. She would keep using that shining pen name, but add the right credits to this first grubby one—and smash open her trap!

So it was now Jo Sinclair who was writing evenings and weekends. Days, it was Ruth Seid who found and lost the weird mélange of brief jobs: making boxes in a factory; proofreading telephone directories; doing a sort of bookkeeping in a neighborhood store that was supposed to sell spaghetti and olive oil at the front, while the proprietor handed big sacks of sugar out the back door to bootleggers. Once she was a salesgirl in a department store during the Christmas rush. Once she counted votes half the night as a clerk in an election booth.

That job was an excellent course—her first in politics—and it taught her that she wanted to be a lifelong voter. Her first-ever vote was for Roosevelt, of course, savior of poor people. And now, in the latest branch library, she began reading the city newspapers, learning as much as possible about FDR's rescue program for the unemployed.

It was Ruth who took her family off relief by using one of those programs called the WPA. The magazine credit helped; she explained the pen name, which in a sense proved she was a writer. So did her report on all the high-school newspaper writing she had done. She ended up on a WPA project called ''The Foreign Language Newspaper Digest.'' Her job was editing the awkward translations of articles into English from all the newspapers written in the languages of Cleveland's ethnic groups. She'd had no idea there were that many in her city. ''Melting pot'' in library books turned into real people, who became friends as she learned their ways.

And there was a wondrous bonus for the perennial student. Her project was housed in the main branch of the library, in downtown Cleveland—an enormous and very beautiful building she had seen once but never entered. (Too far from home for walking.) She had never even imagined so many books in one place—floor after floor, wide marble staircases between—for more beauty, so she never used the elevator. Intensely excited, she planned to stay late and investigate all the riches, use her old branch card to borrow as many books as were permitted.

The project itself was fascinating: new and complex courses in American sociology, and world history and geography. She was working with men and women who had come to this city as immigrants, like her parents, and lived in their own ghettos. But they were different; they still loved their homelands, and talked about them incessantly. Her parents never mentioned Russia. These people read their own languages in special papers, as well as the Cleveland dailies, from which they could learn English. They seemed to touch two countries at once—America and the one they had left— and obviously loved both.

The student of a Ruth listed those newspapers she had never heard of before: Italian, Hungarian, Czech, Polish, Ukrainian, Spanish. (A Yiddish paper was there too—the same one her father read at home, but he never included one of the Cleveland newspapers, as her translator-friends did. He did not read much English, had never even wanted to learn the language. Interesting variety of ghettos!) The writer of a Jo filed away her new information about foreign Americans and homelands for future short stories. And maybe a novel some day?

She liked her colleagues a lot: their warmth and overt emotions, their quickness to trust and to become friends, their easy laughter, their honest and unabashed weeping at European troubles. They did not act like any of the unhappy, always worried ghetto Jews she knew. And, one day, she decided that there must be varied gardens of world for varied kinds of people. As she listened to the accented talk, she realized that she was learning about entirely different chunks of the world outside her cramped one. These people were probably some of the "others" she had read about, but this job brought them close and real, very alive; and she knew with happiness that the horizons of the writer were widening.

Jo wrote about Ruth's new friends—contented Americans who still had plenty of room in their souls for the lands they had left. She went on studying actual people, instead of just men and women in books, and imagined a new type of garden that bloomed in two countries, and seemed even lovelier for the sturdy bridge of love between them. Wonderful how chapters of books could turn into true life. Could any ordinary university have taught her that?

One day, listening to her colleagues as she edited their work, she heard about a faraway war that had started—too near their homelands, and getting nearer all the time. Many of them cried as they discussed their families, how they were bound to be killed or made refugees by tyrants like Mussolini and Franco; and she saw the name Hitler for the first time, in several of the articles they had translated.

At home, Ruth's heart ached for her friends, and Jo began writing new kinds of stories about those weeping men and women, the war swooping toward the parents and brothers they had left behind when they emigrated. It was the closest the student had come to a war. And this one felt so different than the ones she had read about. In books you could not hear crying, or see fear for endangered beloveds. Jo wanted to write that sorrow and fear so well that her readers would be able to hear and see people in torment.

She sold one of those stories (little kids being bombed in the Spanish Civil War) to *Esquire,* a rather new and "good" magazine—nothing at all like *New Masses,* her only other credit. And they paid writers! As she looked at that check for seventy-five dollars, marvelously shocked at the amount, she suddenly remembered that this magazine had been the real reason for her pen name. Picking up the first issue in a branch library, she had read that they would use only men writers. Ah, a challenge, Mr. Editor! With much care, over a few weeks, she had created *Jo*—chuckling at the thought that it could be used by men *or* women. And *Sinclair* sounded much better with Jo than Seid. (Besides which, she admired writers like Sinclair Lewis and Upton Sinclair.) So—would the editor question her phony name?

No. But it had taken her more than two years of submitting old-type stories, and getting rejection slips for all of them, before *Esquire* accepted this new type she had learned how to write by watching and listening to suffering people. She was twenty-five when she sold her first paid story, and earned that kind of credit: a top magazine which published many of the famous authors she had studied in her libraries and used as teachers. And now Jo Sinclair was among those fabulous names! She even had the first proof that her writing was worth money, not only proper credits, if she worked the right way. New and joyous hope: could she leave the ghetto soon?

That life course turned still more hopeful as she began using this magnificent library for Jo, as well as for WPA-Ruth. During her wanderings in free time around the many departments on all the floors, she had discovered the general reference and reading room—enormous, with lots of tables and chairs and lamps for students like her. It was stocked with the finest magazines, and with newspapers from every big city—where she found book reviews, and interviews with successful authors recently published. On her lunch hour, she would gulp the sandwich from home and rush down the marble stairs to that magical room on the ground floor, study the work of writers good enough to be accepted by such magazines and reviewed in such newspapers.

Not enough time: she started going to the room after work, to spend hours enough with her new teachers of the best in today's writing. Her branch libraries had never held such treasures. The first time she read the *New York Times*—that Sunday *Book Review!*—was a revelation of glory. She felt as if she had been given a precious gift.

And the room continued to be crammed with similar gifts, as if from a god of writers. Each day, she felt inches closer to her dream garden. Wonderful sensation: as if her spiritual self were growing stronger, more courageous—the self she called ''soul'' in the poems she was still writing in bursts, between the different kinds of short stories.

That year (1938), she sold several more of those stories to two new magazines she found, that were being put out by the *Esquire* publishers: *Coronet* and *Ken*. Was paid for them, too (split the money with her happy, thrilled mother, as usual); but the really important factor was that accumulation of top credits.

Then a remarkable thing happened. The room began to hold extremely interesting levels beyond magazines and newspapers. By then, she had masked her shyness and her insecurity at being only a WPA worker, instead of a regular city patron, and had begun talking with the reference librarians. One day, she learned about grants for evening courses at Cleveland College, the downtown branch of Western Reserve University—which drew a lot of students who had to work days. Grants? That meant free courses!

The building was only a few blocks from the library. She examined it two or three times, coming early to the project; finally worked up enough courage to apply for a course in play writing. That was a new facet of writing, and she had longed to know the professional's way of tackling it ever since she'd read those dozens of library plays. Her tries on her own had been tough going. Maybe a real college would make it possible?

She was honest about her WPA job to the teacher they sent her to (a sensitive, very nice guy). He nodded with a gentle smile about her magazine credits and her pseudonym, but was much more interested in reading the copies of her one-act plays she had brought along—especially the very short one, raw with ghetto protest and frustration, that had been put on in 1935 by the Cleveland People's Theater as a curtain-raiser to *Waiting for Lefty*. (She knew the producer-founder, an unemployed actor who spent a lot of time in her branch library.)

The teacher said: "Shows talent, but a lot of the wrong technique. A play is not a short story. You'll have to learn that first off. Call me George, and I'll call you Jo. Can you make my class on Monday and Wednesday evenings, at seven?"

George became another friend, encouraged her tremendously in her work on a long one-acter she started while on the grant, taught her a great deal about writing for theater instead of for magazines. She worked earnestly on a first draft; and George was impressed enough with it to get her a second grant, on which to finish the play.

Miracle stuff happened. Near the end of the next semester, the dazed author saw *Listen to My Heart* by Jo Sinclair produced, under George's direction, in a packed college auditorium. (That *really* sensitive guy had used her pen name in the program.) A wonderful, deeply moving experience: her characters came as alive as real people when they spoke words she had written. A feeling of "thanks, oh Lord!" by the self who wanted so much to try every kind of writing the world of literature contained.

In the meantime, it was rather wonderful, too, that a "temporary" in a few evening classes had the student's status to make it possible to submit stories and poems to the school's literary magazine. Those local credits (always "by Jo Sinclair") in the *Cleveland College Skyline* made her feel more and more a true author: one who liked to sell for soul, as well as for money—and in hometown, as well as country wide.

Then, in the midst of those credits for play and stories and poems, a wry grin: hey!—here she was, getting a smattering of "higher learning" after all, for a split moment of that high-school dream about the bookkeeper going off to a great university for a writer's education. It seemed like an amusing but thrilling interval outside the thick walls of her bone-poor life.

But suddenly, that kind of life changed. The faraway war of her translator-friends came to her own homeland. The Depression dwindled, and the WPA program began to peter out, as the marching of men began and the country needed workers (especially women). Ruth left the project for a "real" job, found exactly the right one on her third try—with the help of Jo's credits—in the publicity department of the Greater Cleveland Chapter of the American Red Cross.

Such work seemed to put her on a smoother, shorter road toward the world of the "others," and she felt close enough sometimes to see open doors. She had read in many books that life is always a-changing, sooner or later; had never actually believed that until now. Now!—astounded by the indisputable proof that it *was* true, she even thought occasionally that she may have escaped from a few of her ghettos—especially the spiritual one, with its feeling of being in a lifetime prison.

This job was pretty perfect for somebody like her. It was crammed with the heart-need to help fight an extremely important war—fight not only for her America, but for the world's Jews and many others of those so-called imperfect people being tortured and murdered by a Hitler. And she was battling the writer's way, with words for weapons: carefully done publicity for the city newspapers, and optimistic stories and articles for the two national Red Cross magazines.

The war years proved to be fine lessons in life for the patriot and decent child. Though she was now living with very dear friends, outside any walled neighborhood, she was still splitting a salary with parents and seeing her family often; praying for her two brothers, off to the actual front lines, and writing them letters regularly.

This different life was as stimulating as higher college courses for both her selves. During the day, Ruth fought her country's war in the bustling Red Cross building, and, on many evenings and weekends, Jo fought her own wonderful inner war with the real writing of stories and poems. She was also studying the making of novels (a daringly new facet befitting an author in a vastly changed life), bringing home books for that course from the branch library near the Cleveland Heights house she was sharing with these closest friends she had ever had in the world. It was a time of continuing happiness—a first for her. Among other marvels, she had fallen in love with gardening, in the backyard of her home—discovered it was a perfect way of rest and replenishment after hours of writing.

One Sunday morning, in her private bedroom-workroom on the third floor (far from the activities of the family downstairs), it finally happened. Overjoyed by how well the war was going on the early radio news, Jo started a novel. Astonished (she had not planned to, quite yet), she went right on. Like many of the novelists she had studied in her library books, she began with an extremely detailed outline, a technique strange to her outside of the brief outlines for short stories—completely different in concentration and sustained work. Despite all the books she had read so carefully, she felt tremulous and unsure about this difficult way of preparing for a piece of writing. Intensely difficult, and even frightening; but she went on with the outline. She had always been a stubborn writer, especially when some kind of hope had triggered the work. This time, the devout hope came from a war being won—for a whole world of tortured people and grabbed homelands.

Slowly, doggedly, over the next few weeks, she got to the writing of actual chapters. As the war continued to go extremely well, she saw the shaping of a first draft, the true beginning of a deeply felt book. Sometimes she discussed the novel with her friends (book lovers, intellectuals), but never showed them any of the manuscript. As usual, the writing was hers alone, completely private until the work was finished. But the discussions were good, even took away some of her unsureness.

Sometimes Ruth took breathers in the garden. Or Jo wrote much easier short stories, for a different way of resting. But gradually (as if the characters and plot pulled her in), the book took over all her free time. Not even a poem for explosive curse or prayer; there was just the harsh, slogging work on that first novel. Still quite scary in her heart, but in her mind she knew that this was the most challenging, exciting course she had ever taken in her special college for the author.

It seemed to go on without any end in sight: her own war, in the midst of her country's. But an end did come for both. It took her almost three years to finish a last draft she could accept. And— double miracle—the American war was won, too—as if one victory had triggered the other. Ruth had her brothers home unharmed, and saw with gratitude that the universe was clean and full of beautiful values again, no longer tyrannized by evil leaders. Jo sent her manuscript out for a possible sale.

That first novel, *Wasteland*, won the ten-thousand-dollar Harper Prize Novel Award in 1946.

The war over, she could leave the Red Cross with a free conscience, and try out the girl's dream of being a free-lance writer. There was enough money to start. She was thirty-three when that major "life-changing-again" happened to her.

In the garden of world at last, all conceivable ghettos left behind, Jo Sinclair has written constantly. Over the next two decades, three more novels have been published: *Sing at My Wake, The Changelings,* and *Anna Teller*. A three-act play has been produced in a "real" theater. Between the big pieces of writing, new short stories and poems have been accepted (she still likes that selling for soul and money, that combination of national and local credits). By the sixties, a dozen anthologies have reprinted old stories. That meant *books* (much longer life than magazines), to add to her novels on library shelves—for oncoming students in their homemade colleges. She likes the thought of that, too: a kind of small "passing it on" to kids without money who would be as eager as she had been for those free courses.

And there are very meaningful payments to the spirit during those years of hard work. The writer has earned more awards (as if her right to live in the garden has been acknowledged often enough by the world to keep her safe in there): Best Novel of the Year—Jewish Book Council of America; Certificate of Recognition—National Conference of Christians and Jews; three-time winner, Best Novel of the Year—Ohioana Library; second prize in drama, TV Competition for Civil Rights—the Fund for the Republic; Literature Award—Cleveland Arts Prize; first Wolpaw Playwriting Grant—Cleveland Jewish Community Centers.

Jo feels humbly thankful that her work-songs continue, and that she can go on feeling that she will belong in the garden forever because the writing comes back at the right times, very like the orderly seasons of earth always come for gardeners like Ruth.

But of course there is no forever. Had she forgotten that life is change, sooner or later? Better pick up some of those library books she had studied long ago!—and read again that many once-famous authors had been subjected to these same publication silences that have sucked her in, and keep her imprisoned despite her persistent attempts to break free with new writing.

Naturally, she goes on working. By now, she knows with utter certainty that survival—for both her selves—is writing, no matter the changes in life, good or bad. This one is very bad, and especially so because she cannot figure out the mystery of why the silences began, and why they continue through months and months of disciplined work and the offering of well-done stories. Everything she sends in is rejected. Even the last draft of her fifth novel has been turned down—a particularly painful wound.

If only she could search out answers to the why. Could it be ''a time to mourn''? There had been monumental deaths in her life recently. Her mother, and then, three years later, that dearest friend as beloved as a second mother. If so, how long does a gospel season go on? (The Book never gave the exact time it took for seasons to end.)

Ruth cannot find a realistic answer for that one about mourning. She dislikes mysteries, especially psychological ones; they make clear thinking too difficult. But she asks herself other questions that might explain some of this terrifying life change. Is the writer in a creative block? No. Jo has been working steadily all along. It's more as if the publishing world is blocked—at least where she is concerned.

Grim joke! But she tries one more question. Is fame so temporary that an award-established name like Jo Sinclair has been forgotten by old editors, and never heard of by new ones? No answer—not even with slightly comforting black humor this time. It all stays the sickening mystery.

Yet she goes on with the daily writing, clutching at spiritual weapons she has used before in her inner wars (gardening, Bach, Keats, and Faulkner for sleepless nights). She even grabs at a particular weapon that had been a favorite in very rough youthful battles; starts by thinking often of certain words in that book Ruth discovered on a shelf in one of her earliest libraries. The child's first bible, her introduction to Ecclesiastes.

One day, the woman tries to renew the strength and courage that the little girl took from those words. Between stints of work, she reads them in her own bible (one of the first of the books she began buying with *Wasteland* money): ''To every thing there is a season, and a time to every purpose under the heavens. There is a time to keep silence, and a time to speak.'' And she can still smile wanly as she remembers that Jo translated "speak" into "sing."

The readings are reassuring, good for her. Except that one of those seasons does not change; and sometimes it feels as if "a time to mourn" will go on endlessly, that there will never, never be "a time to dance."

Nevertheless, that weapon helps get her through the years of near despair about the continuing publication silences. She even starts a new book, new in all ways of content and technique (as if she still half believes in those seasons of man). And then, one year—she is in her seventies—the singing begins again, but in a very different way. Life changes once more, now turns into a kind of renascence: two of her old novels are republished, are wanted in the world again as worthy books for a new generation to read.

It is a powerful, undeniable reminder that "there is a time to speak" is indeed gospel. *The Changelings* reappears in 1985 (the first publication was 1955); *Wasteland* in 1987 (that prize publication had come in 1946), by a second publisher.

Both selves of the weary survivor feel overwhelmed, unreal. But slowly, an old joy begins again in Jo's soul, in Ruth's heart, as that renascence continues like a fantastic rebirth: in 1989, *Anna Teller* (first out in 1960) earns a contract from one of those publishers. Now a favorite weapon of inner war glows like a beautiful sculpture in the spring sunlight of a new season: "There is a time of peace."

And (tasting wonderfully of the youthful writer's miracles) "there is a time to speak" goes on: in 1989 and early 1990, there are two more anthologies—out of the blue—with Jo Sinclair stories considered important enough to be taken out of old magazines and put into new books.

Is that actual singing she hears in the garden? Maybe a few more gospel words can answer that question for the writer: "There is a time to get, and a time to lose. There is a time to weep, and a time to laugh."

It is still 1990; and, yes, that *is* laughter as the singing comes true and clear with a finished book accepted: that new-in-all-ways memoir she had started in the midst of the silences. It is her first contract since 1960 for a new book. She is seventy-seven when that contract is signed, and she can give quiet thanks to all the gods in the universe for the lovely gift of this merging of old and new writing.

The whole human being has learned some important things: that forever is not necessary for survivors, that changing life can be explained calmly in the mind (there is a time to every purpose under the heavens). And she can know with that same calmness that "a time to mourn" is over.

She can even add her own new season for an honest believer in life's decreed changes: There is a time to stay, and a time to move on.

The author now lives near Philadelphia, with a very good friend. The moving-on was to a town close to New York for Jo; and yet countryside quiet, with a lot of backyard space, for the ardent gardener Ruth became years ago. Life changes, but the patterns of heart and soul remain constant. She is well into a new novel, and planning next year's garden. And, of course, there is an excellent library nearby.

Part I
The Journal of Life

Reality and Memory

*T*he first spring after the death is unbearable. Its inexorable, complete awakening. Its compulsive memories. Its intolerable mockery of beauty.

Here, of course, spring would bring the fullest grief. I should have known it, gone away to a place where I did not know each bulb shooting up its green; the feathering together, before the first pulsing, of lilac and mountain ash.

This is the countryside in northeastern Ohio, and she loved it. She gave it to me, so joyously, so knowingly, that it turned into root and home of all the seasons possible to a person.

But that first spring... It was as if I'd inherited a strange season. In a poem, I'd call it a season of new-different pain. An impossible poem: she is dead, yet these gardens planned by her are gorgeously alive. The groundhogs and the chipmunks she first showed me have come out of their winter prison again, even though she is imprisoned forever in the tree.

Nature insists, that first spring, on all of it in perfection: the gold of forsythia, the first of the fragrant narcissus, the pussy willow trees fuzzing out. And the peepers starting; pond minnows swimming in broad, shifting schools; the new muskrat holes on the dam; the summer birds coming, and the singing suddenly at the core of the silence I thought would never end.

Well, Helen was insistent, too: the house was built, completed, though the money ran out. And the one-acre pond was dug, just down the slope from the house—so we could see the wild ducks land and swim, the swallows and dragonflies sweeping in a new season. It was stocked scientifically, of course (she researched everything), the right numbers of minnows, blue gill, bass.

The frogs, snakes, muskrats, and turtles came by themselves, and stayed. Once there was a heron ("Ruthie, look!")—on those long legs. An hour or so, walking and pausing on the dam, going down to fish and eat; then the flight, spectacular, blue in the sunlight. We watched the entire scene. My short story stayed unfinished and her dinner was late, but who cared?

Once, a deer came out of the wild acres of trees and summer grasses stretching south of the dam. "Ruthie, hurry—look!" He'd come onto the dam, just stood there for a while, completely motionless before the bounding away.

Utter grace, the poem come alive, the harpsichord sonata translated into a living thing. And the city pushed another inch out of me—because Helen made it all seeable. "Look, look." She always said that—gifts—in cars, trains, in the country or city.

That first spring after her death has become the sixth. The seasons demand that the years and months stay ritual. But the demand, too, is on the changing nuances of pain.

My sister Sadie used to say to me—in Yiddish: " 'That which the earth covers over *must* be forgotten.' The old, wise rabbis said that, Ruthie." That was when Sarah J died, and I wept like a kid. And again, when Ma died; that was the bad one.

Not entirely true, wise rabbis. The gaunt kind of grief can soften, the memory gentle away from too-live eyes and smile, the special saying. Is that what you meant? But never really forgotten.

The changing nuances of grief—yes. But this sixth spring, the insistent demand is on fear, too. I keep thinking, too often: Who died?—she, or I?

There is a phrase—quite a cliché by now, I suppose: *creative death.* I've read about it so often—what happened to Hemingway, Fitzgerald, a hundred artists and composers. The drying up, the arid earth—the spiritual dying.

There are a lot of clichés. *Soul. Poem* (meaning the big writing, not just a poem). *Self* (definitely capital *S*). I know, intellectuals sneer at words like that, but these days they are my constant vocabulary. My heart calls out all the clichés—in the garden, at the desk, in the kitchen. Such: Did your soul die when she did? Did your creative Self die?

The book I was writing as she lay dying? Hasn't been published. Rewrote and rewrote; that's the fifth version my agent's trying to sell this year. Wrote another play, too. Rejected. Sent out old TV scripts to possibly new markets, sent out short stories. Rejected. Ah, who died when Helen did?

I wonder if this is my last season. The writer is a gardener: the seasons are translation for so much. Winter—death. Spring—transfiguration. Translate: rejection—death. Acceptance of a Poem—life again, transfiguration. Translate further, gardener: everything you've planted as a writer has died since Helen died. The truth, now: *are* you dead creatively?

I'm still not sure.

All I know for sure is that every bit of me has to plunge into the new season for a try at survival. I haul out all the old weapons. I run to fight the earth, still hard and heaped from last fall's rough plowing; sweat with the hoe, the rake, the preparation for seed.

It's incredible, but even in this sixth turning of the season, I still look for transfiguration in me, too—not only in the spring. Will my Poems survive? Her tree did—though one thick branch was killed this last winter. I'll prune; live wood does not withstand dead growth for too long. But how do you prune to save the remnants of a writer?

By continuing to translate, gardener! So come on, get the perennial bed in shape. Her idea: ninety feet long, eight feet deep. (''Too much work, Ruthie?'') It's roughly twenty-five feet from the screened porch, so that you can see everything from up there.

Get into it, would-be survivor. With all its old plants—gifts, exchanges, ''chiselings'' (my vocabulary: ''Could I chisel one chunk of your plant, please?''). Uncle Hugo's glads and red dahlias. Sarah J's big piece of lavender, and her Michaelmas daisies, coralbells. Neighbor Lil's Dutch iris. The ''boughten'' plants over the years (Helen's word, but how our vocabularies merge these days). And the stuff the kids gave their parents for Christmas, wedding anniversaries, birthdays; and people gave me for special days.

The tulips are almost all gone. I'd planted hundreds, massed all across the back of this bed. Moles, mainly: they eat tulip bulbs, says the *New York Times* garden section. But they don't eat our dafs or narcissus or scilla or chionodoxa or grape hyacinth, Star of Bethlehem, crocus. Those bulbs are all here, and have spread, repeated themselves in fuller beauty each year.

The house was just barely getting built when Helen planned this bed. She took me to the Cleveland Garden Center, and the lady this bed. She took me to the Cleveland Garden Center, and the lady expert there talked about certain bushes that would tie the bed together, and certain plants to relieve the eye; and Helen's notebook filled with ideas, colors, shapes of plantings. And I saw again what this woman was. I stared, again, at the wonder of dream and how to implement it, at a fine brain and sensitive heart insisting that all things were possible.

The expert suggested a Sargent crab at each end of this bed. Not too big, twisty branches, lovely in flower, and as lovely with the thousands of red berries—for birds. Including pheasants. One used to come walking, and reach up, neck stretching, to eat from a low branch. Yes, she taught me berries, too. There's a mountain ash close by, full of a different kind and color. I gave the tree to Helen and Mort ten years ago, for a wedding anniversary. It's grown full and tall.

Mort cuts the grass—down on the dam, too—but I've planted all the trees that weren't here when we came, and all the gardens. They're part of my bone, by now: eighteen years out here.

"I promise you that you'll love the country, Ruthie." We were living in Cleveland, and Helen directed me as I drove—into the blacker and blacker night. And that was a long time before she eventually found the perfect almost-nineteen acres, up high for the house, and sloping down into what would be the pond, and the acres and acres left wild beyond the dam.

In the car, I said finally: "Way out here to *live*? There aren't even any street lights. Look how dark it is." She laughed. "But darling, soon you'll see how light it is in a country nighttime. I promise you that, too."

She never broke a promise. That was an opening door, too: always to know like God that "I promise you" was something you could believe in, no matter what happened.

Then she broke one—the most important promise in my life.

No, no, don't think of that today! Just follow the patterns. Go out the first thing every morning to "tour the joint." That's my vocabulary. Like I call the chipmunk "the kid." She called him "Chippy"; and the groundhog "Johnny" (before Helen, I'd never even heard of those stories about a creature named Johnny Woodchuck). And she called the hummingbird—at the bergamot, delphinium—"Hummy."

Tour the joint, gardener. Listen. There's the pheasant. He hasn't been around for several years. Hunters? Helen used to get so furious when she saw them. "Ruthie, go out and holler. Tell them we're posted!"

She had a soft voice, always, even in anger. I was a "hollerer"—in anger, grief, frustration. We really came from dead-opposite worlds—to meet over a play in a handmade theater.

Walk, walk. The triple-trunk white birch the Weils gave us is huge—tall and broad, the branches drifting downward—complete grace, with the new "birchlets" hanging, getting ready to drop. When I planted it—five feet tall—she began calling it the three-birch. So do I now in my head, staring up its thirty feet or so.

Walk, walk. The wren houses are up, but I haven't seen or heard the birds yet. Such a singer, though so tiny. He's a real promise. He's always back, with the season. I just want to be.

There are two *small* three-birches, too. Martin's gift, eight years ago. I planted them that day he took his parents away—some excuse—and when he drove them home I had the secret trees in, and Martin bellowed in his wonderful singer's voice: "Happy anniversary."

The memories you inherit. Come on, move! Pinch back the mums—they're tall enough. To bush out the plants, of course; and you keep pinching until early July. I transplanted a lot of these from the South Woodland house, and the Shannon house before that one. City to country: rooting deeper each year, and spreading.

How complicated can a promise be? Laced through with the yards these mums first grew in, the people who added facets and layers, the children growing up and then their children calling the same name for me: "Missy! Missy, come look!" (Helen, of course: "Dear, Ruth is too informal for Barbara and Martin, and Miss Seid much too formal—they love you so. They've been asking and asking what they can call you. Do you like 'Missy'? Or is that too precious for you, toughy-*toi?*")

And I think of Barbie telling a college friend: "Missy? Oh, she's sort of our third parent."

Walk! Tour the lilacs. Were they nipped by that frost three nights ago? Can't tell yet. Our lilacs run solid across the bedroom and bath wing of the front. Taller than the house now—but that's because it's a one-story house—the second-floor storage is in the garage wing, a lot of it above my quarters. All shades of lavender here; I trans-

planted most of them from South Woodland. Around the back are
the boughten white and the French double. On the west side, outside her bedroom, the Persians—a house gift to me from a friend.
Helen loved lilac—but especially the deeply fragrant white. She'd
had two of those at the front door of the Shannon house. That scent
alone is deathless.

There's a cardinal in the ash, particularly "singy." Same lovely
song, over and over. ("He's singing 'Theodore, Theodore.' Don't
you hear that name in the song, dear?")

Yes, I do. I hear it all the way to the graves.

Three are buried on this property, but I don't tour all the graves
every day, Just her tree. Sometimes I touch the trunk of that hawthorn, or the beginning of a flower—so like a tiny rose. Examine
it all for pieces of dead wood.

On the way to the tree, stop and look at the "wedding bed"
(my name for it). Barb and Diedrick were married that year, last day
of July—right in front of the mountain ash. In April, I dug out the
heavy sod here, and made a round bed for hundreds of white lark-
spur, grown from seed. Helen's idea: "The wedding flower, *toi*. It'll
be cheaper grown this way. But—more important?—*your* hands will
beauty up Barbie's wedding. Lovely idea?" Yes, so lovely.

It's still the wedding bed—and never been wasted. Any time
I divided overgrown poppies, irises, daylilies, in they went here.
And I always sow annual poppies in this bed, and BB's (my lingo:
bachelor buttons).

South of the Helen-tree—the east groundhog family. They live
in privacy, where the mowed grass swerves into the uncut perennial rye and weeds and sumac; the ground behind their house slopes
down to the pond. If you wade through the tall growth and get close
enough, you can see the mounds—and the "front and back doors"
(Helen's lingo). I always check, in early spring, to see if the big holes
have been freshly "sharpened" (my description); that means they're
out of hibernation, and have dug out fallen earth, stones, rubble.
Last year, three Johnny-babies. (Hers—but oh, Christ, our vocabularies are one language, so often.)

The west groundhog family lives just behind the narcissus bed.
Those two holes have been sharpened, too, but I haven't seen the
kid himself yet. The east family comes out in full view of my desk
windows, so I see them at once. And I'll see the Johnny-babies come
out—get fatter and longer, become teenagers, and then big as their

parents in time to get fallen apples and sit up to eat them. They remind me of Rags. Helen's dog; though first, she was Martin's. Sealyham terriers sit up like that.

When I stand at the hawthorn, looking down toward the pond, I can see the areas where both her dogs are buried. Unmarked graves—but I know where they are: I dug, and Mort (bad back—disk trouble—he mustn't dig or push or shovel snow) covered; and then I pulled the violets and wild strawberry plants over the graves. Unmarked. Hers is marked by the tree; the box of ashes is close to the roots, deep.

Friedie was eighteen when Helen wrapped her in a blanket, and held her face to the little dog's all the way, talked to her lovingly, as Mort drove to the vet. Nineteen sixty-one. I know—it's written in my journal. In late '51, when we moved here, both dogs were fine, though Friedie was so small that Ragsy gave her hell whenever we couldn't get there in time. Sealys are too jealous, as well as tough characters. Miniature dachshunds are gentle and loving. All new to me, but my friend taught me how to be with dogs, too.

The little old one's grave is just left of the east go-down, in a small copse of woods between us and the cemetery. "Go-down" is Helen's word, of course. It's one of the two ways down—like a broad, mowed grass road—to the pond; really, to the dam, because the go-downs become the dam, which runs around that one-acre pond on three sides. Wide, heavily sodded, the dam continues into the west go-down, which is like another road leading steeply up to the part of the property where we live and garden. The fourth side of the pond is the slope back of the perennial bed—lots of trees, and full of violets and daylilies and irises I had to divide and couldn't bear to throw away. The dam is cut all the growing season; the slope, never. It grows wild, and there are birds' nests, the rustle of animals—fox, quail, raccoon, rabbit, pheasant, possum; you see them sometimes. Friedie has lots of living company.

So has Rags. Mort and I buried the chunky, white little dog almost directly across the go-down from Friedie's grave, on the beginning swell of the slope down to the pond. Ragsy loved to swim, looking wild-eyed and frantic, her eyes and nose above the water—going fast to where Martin floated and called to her, or heading for shore. On the dam, she'd shake off the water, making a loud, flapping sound with those big ears. There was always a towel waiting on the dam; Martin or Helen would dry her until she was the fat, fluffy snowball again.

Friedie was a short-hair, of course. (It was Ragsy I cursed so often when I had to comb and brush winter snow out of that long hair; or burrs, in the fall.) In our first summer here, the little dachs swam two or three times. But that was it for the timid one. Helen swam a few times. She was not a good swimmer, but she loved being in the warm water, her toes digging into the muddy bottom; and, of course, she didn't have to feel embarrassed with us for—as she put it—"being a fat lady in an old bathing suit."

She tired easily, and could never take too much sun. So she usually ended up sitting on the slope, under one of the big trees—Friedie in her lap. The kids were wonderful swimmers. I was pretty good, for a heavy smoker. Mort had never learned to swim; he'd wade around, smiling, pulling out cattails (they take over a pond if you don't keep after them). We had an inner tube, and took turns diving into it, or floating. Sometimes Mort would get pushed around the pond by one of his children, while that joyous laughter came.

Helen's laughter. I remember it the first summer—the house not ready yet, but we were there whenever we had time to drive out, with picnic lunches or dinners (Mort would come directly from the lab). I remember that marvelous laugh the day Martin (was he sixteen, younger?) decided to walk the lower wilderness part of the property, all the way to the east branch of the Chagrin River, which is the curving line of these acres on the south side. It must be about half a mile to that extremely narrow piece of the river.

Back he came, hours later—a plump, excited boy with smudged glasses and a very dirty face, carrying samples of fungus he'd found—triumphant: "Mother, the river's *definitely* navigable there!"

She and I walked as far as the river only twice. The first time, when Rags came along, I had to carry that heavy little dog most of the way home—full of burrs and weed heads, exhausted. After the second time (the second summer), it was too far and hard a trip for Helen, too, though she was fascinated by the beauty, so entirely different from the loveliness up top: wildflowers of all kinds, small or great pieces of fungus on the dead limbs of trees (Martin made many gifts out of them), rocks of all sizes and colors, a short and amazingly green kind of grass right next to that little, swift bit of river.

It was easier for Helen to walk back of the cemetery (a sliver of the river branch down there, too). It's next door to our property, not too close but we got there easily, through the tiny woods on our boundary. The first few times, we carried half-bushel baskets and trowels. For "borrowings." We had spotted a wonderful hillside sloping down from the cemetery proper, back of its rickety fence—broad, steep—down to grass and trees and that sliver of water. I'd help her down the hill, then I'd climb up, and she'd call: "Over to the left—three trillium." Or: "Ruthie, *yellow* violets. Right above your head—see them? We'll find white ones, too—I know it!" And me: "What're these funny things?" Helen: "May apples."

I transplanted baskets of stuff (that slope didn't really belong to anyone). The May apples still come up every spring, in the shady place behind our viburnum carlesi, but trillium wouldn't stay.

A few times, we wandered through the small cemetery itself. It's our only neighbor on the east, and then comes the highway. Adds an extra area of quiet and privacy to our place, and brings nearish sights of enormous old dogwood and magnolia and other trees we don't have. Our masses of grape hyacinth came from there; about a dozen had wandered onto our property, along with early, short double daffodils. I dug those, too, and planted them in our perennial bed, and Helen dubbed them the "cemetery dafs."

We would read the tombstones in that old, old place (something I'd never done in my life, and she had all over the country, and in Canada, Europe). Our tombstones: early settlers in Geauga County, Civil War dates, little patriotic tabs, family plots.

She called our place "Grave's End" for a while. I never liked the name. She thought it was fun; so did Mort and the kids. It petered out—and I was glad.

Near her tree, I can still hear the cardinal. Tireless. Forever. I'm standing very close to the spot where her ashes are buried. There are violets all around; and the orchard I planted, close by; and the three pussy willows—almost as big as trees (when I moved them from South Woodland, they were about three feet tall). The catkins are feathering out. I'd always bring in a mass of them, on a mild day in February—along with forsythia branches—to force. She taught me that a person could have the season begin in a tall blue vase, long before spring began outdoors.

She taught me so much. To label things in the garden—especially the choice, the new; the dahlias by color. The one pom-pom dahlia left of the six I chiseled is still labeled "Uncle Hugo's Red" when I put it in the plastic bag for winter storage upstairs. I use the large envelopes in which the Sunday *New York Times* arrives.

Helen was always sending away for "permanent" labels—but sooner or later, the writing wore off: snow, rain, mud. I never attached a label to this tree. According to the catalog, it's "*Crataegus Oxyacantha* (English Hawthorn), Paul's Scarlet." And the catalog went on to say: "This English Haw is a brilliant pink, double-flowered variety. A joy to see it every spring."

A joy? So I ordered it.

But didn't write out a card for it. The true label, in permanent ink that never wears off, would be:

Basilar Artery Thrombosis
Diabetes Mellitus
Age: 54

From the death certificate.

I planted her tree a good distance from the house—to give it plenty of air and sun and space to grow; but I can see it very clearly from my desk, in any season.

My God, my God, when the actual death occurs. We intellectuals! Talk, plan, use the brain—and then it turns out I didn't know a damn about the emotions when the smashup came.

She did not want a funeral. Neither did Mort, or I; and the kids had nodded quietly at the discussion. Mort and she didn't even want a memorial service. I wasn't sure about me yet. The three of us were members of the Cleveland Memorial Society. The brochure had said what we believed: "Simplicity, reverence, compassion, and reason are the values we hold to. We believe our members gain strength from simple, dignified, planned funerals which are more meaningful than is so often experienced and at a fraction of the cost."

I enrolled when Helen and Mort did—for ten dollars. But this was all when death was an intellectual plan for some nebulous future. A strange, terrible thing happened to me when Helen died. Ice and snow covered the world, and very few people were able to drive out to the country to be with us. There was a tiny death notice in the morning paper—no real obituary in either newspaper. As if she had barely been in the world. And I thought, dazed: How can it be? This woman was a tremendous force in many lives. Her brain was a marvel, her heart a real well of love, her hands always so full of gifts for the saving of souls. Why isn't there a crashing noise in the world? A weeping to pierce all hearts?

It was awful. She was dead, and not dead. She was in the air around me, the sky—though her body was ashes, waiting for the new season and open ground. Didn't I expect her to come smiling into my room and say: "How's the writing going, dear? Come take a break." Didn't I look for her, standing in the window and smiling, as I went out to feed the birds?

She floated—anywhere I looked—no matter how desperately I tried to touch her death. I tried to write it out. Facts—for the world—but really for me. I sent cards to everybody who'd known her through me—typed it out, as if to tell myself, with each card, that it was true: "Helen Buchman died—Mount Sinai Hospital—December 27, 1963—ten minutes of ten P.M."

Didn't work. Nothing did. She floated in me and all about me through the winter, into that first horribly beautiful spring. Then came the tree, the burial. And then, finally, I knew she was dead.

I leave the tree, finish my tour. Are the May apples out yet? The leaves are broadening, but no little apple at the center yet. I stare at the v. carlesi. On Shannon Road—the first house I shared with this family—the avid new gardener had just discovered sprays versus garden insects. So I dusted her beloved carlesi, and killed it—with some kind of stuff that was absolutely wrong for it.

It was one of the first things I bought and planted here. A lovely shrub. So brief a bloom, pink-white, then all white, delicate, very fragrant. The flowers never last in the house. Wilt in a day; the petals fall, white stars, all over the sink, from the window vase.

In the city, that long-ago spring, the amateur gardener stared down at the blackened foliage the day after the dusting, and cried: "My God, I'm sorry! I thought you had to dust everything in a garden with the same stuff."

Helen smiled. "Well, you'll never do anything like this again—blind." Me: "No! I even gave it extra dust, because you love it so much." She: "That's what I mean. Not blind, ever—even out of love. Plants, people—books to write?"

Does that sound smug? She never was. Or precious—or sloppy sentimental. It might sound so, to strangers, but she simply talked and loved with complete honesty—never embarrassed or afraid about showing the inside of her heart

That's so rare. Like our friendship—half in the city, half out here. But the country really began for me on Shannon. When I ran out

of gardening stints in her backyard, she started me farming on the
empty lot next door. (''Ruthie, isn't this *perfect* therapy for a writer?'')
I planted my first tomatoes there—and I'd begun my first novel. And
cukes—one skimpy row, that astounded me by the sudden, lush
growth as the vines tried to go everywhere. A half-dozen corn stalks,
a few plants of green beans—and I learned how beautiful blossoms
were on food crops. Amazing education for an ex-ghetto kid.

My education in death, too. On a tour like this, I think of that
along with the city blue jays eating the peanuts I used to put out,
and the pheasant here skittering toward his berries. So many lessons: when you're sick (flu, virus, et cetera), Orinase doesn't do
it for a diabetic like Helen. Back to insulin, until the sickness is licked.
And I remember—as a second cardinal, in some other tree, makes
a duet of ''Theodore, Theodore''—how happy she was when
Orinase came on the market, and the cruel needle-jabbing could be
stopped.

As I walk, listening to the song of the mourning dove, I remember when the first tranquilizers came, for her again mounting blood
pressure. They saved her. Again. Five years before, something called
a sympathectomy had saved her—for the day of those new pills:
a saving at the cost of awful pain and fear. Two operations—ten days
apart—cutting into the central nervous system, and tying off the
''bad'' nerve on each side. Chance of surviving the operation very
low, but no alternative in those days.

Well, she didn't die. After she came home from the hospital,
the pain was so intense that Mort and I took turns giving her the
morphine tablets every four hours, night and day. But she was
saved. So was I: to finish the lousy, endless rewrites of that second
novel. And to write the next book, and still more—only to be
smashed down by creative death after all *my* rescues. There are
rather terrible similarities.

The quail have started singing their ''bob *white*, bob *white*''—
definitely spring. So stop talking to God, or nature. In six years,
an intelligent, normal person is supposed to bury her dead, write
a new poem to prove *she* isn't dead, and stop screaming: ''Unfair!''
Look at the flowering cherry, instead, damn it. Will it bloom this
season? I've researched all the care it should have.

Education of a gardener. For years, when anyone asked what
I wanted for my birthday, I chose garden books. And the Sunday

Times garden section gave me quite a few earth and nature tricks, too (it was her idea that I read that paper, for "person and writer"). But Helen taught me the most.

"She taught me" turns out to be the most complicated piece of my life. And yet a very simple streak runs through that maze like a guiding rope: chiefly, she taught me to green-thumb things— gardening, writing, world. Because she, the whole person, was a green thumb in every conceivable way. Which means such things: innately sensitive, delicate, perceptive, utterly creative; and that people grow as freely as flowers under that touch.

To teach all that? She did. Me heading the list of quite a few. Me. This woman—who did not have the right body or enough stamina to garden adequately herself, though she loved it so—had the vision and imagination to make a gardener and country lover out of a city peasant deeply in need of stillness, time, and the beauty and meaning of earth seeping in to make the gardens of Self.

What a range of magic and fun Helen made out of my "therapy." That first tremendous area I farmed, out in front of this house: "Ruthie, how about a couple of rows of sunflowers at one end, and Uncle Hugo's glads and dahlias at the other?" Me: "Flowers mixed with limas and cukes?" She (laughing): "Goodness, what a conservative person you've turned into. Why not?"

Why not, indeed. Remember the round, formal rose bed in the South Woodland yard? Classy Shaker Heights, no less—but (money or no money) she wanted the kids to go to the Shaker high school, best in the area. Not much room for vegetables, because of the grass all over that yard. I learned about dogwood and acid food for azalea and rhododendron and mountain laurel—but not enough therapy for a second novel. So Helen suggested Bermuda onions as an edging for the big rose bed. Then we planted tomatoes in the formal, raised dining-room garden. And I trained cukes up the cyclone fence, close to the honeysuckle and Western Sunset lilies. Who knew cuke vines would climb a fence? My teacher, of course.

Out here? Yes, books and earth itself continued to be teachers, but Helen's kind of "she taught me" remained the most imaginative. For example: Dust glad corms with DDT against thrips before storing, said the *Times*. Me: "How? Each one?" Helen (after a moment): "Put them in a paper bag, pour in some DDT, close the bag, and shake thoroughly. They'll get coated. I do chicken that way for frying—with flour. And you can save the leftover DDT."

Education of a gardener—and a person. And don't forget the writer—starting her third novel in the country. They merge into the same slowly learning human being. I was thinking of how Eric Jan— Helen's grandson, Barbie's son—called her Pooh. Her children had, too. I'd never heard of Pooh and Christopher Robin before Helen. I was too busy with Faulkner, Hemingway, Negro and Depression literature.

There are so many mergings in my kind of education. I heard Mort play the Pooh songs on his Cable spinet (he'd had as a boy), heard his wife and children sing them—Christmas, summertime when Barb and Diedrick came for a visit from Ann Arbor; D was teaching social psychology at the University of Michigan by then. And Helen looked at me, smiled, her eyebrows up—as if to say: Is this really sentimental-slob stuff, as you would put it? Your eyes tell me no.

My friend-teacher. She was the kind who felt double joy when a child of hers or a student like me mastered a skill and then went out on their own. How overjoyed she was at my sudden adeptness with vases of flowers, especially the rather tiny vases she called "smalls" (for violets, lily of the valley, snowdrops, and such). These were for the kitchen window over the sink, with its narrow ledge.

There *was* one thing I couldn't learn from her—joy. But so many other things: I watched her give flowers to people who came out. I started bringing them to people in town—my mother and sisters, friends. The student experimented over a few seasons, came up with the perfect way of transporting flowers to town. One or two of Helen's wide-mouthed mason jars full of water, sitting in a basket on floor of car; prop with a brick and rags. No spills; flowers arrive as if just picked.

The joyous laughter: I put dill with flowers, and Queen Anne's lace; not only Sarah J's special "fiddle ferns" (Helen's lingo; and they did look like the top part of a violin). She: "We nonpoets know only about using asparagus fern. I bow!"

The student, still expanding on lessons: Between books, when I was broke and it was summer and fall, I brought in crops to people for their birthdays, instead of boughten gifts. Hoping they'd know I was saying: Here are cukes and potatoes, limas, tomatoes, I grew with love, with hard work—take them instead of gifts I can't afford?

Helen knew. "You can't even *buy* delicious, fresh stuff like this.

Why the sullen face?'' Me: ''I should write poems to go with the corn, I suppose—to prove that the poor farmer used to be a writer who earned enough to buy regular gifts.'' She: ''Stop that. The book *will* be published. Anyway, your tomatoes and dill are poems. At least, know that.''

I did—sometimes. Especially when she reminded me. I've always had to be reminded about things over and over. Even about friendship and love and belief. Helen was wonderful at reminding me of all sorts of things. Now things remind me of her. And of that brain, always working.

These birds who come to the feeders, to the hanging suet. Remember? Helen (experimenting, always) decided to buy whole beef suets at the butcher. ''It keeps the birds warm. It's cheaper bought whole—especially in the summer. I got this great big thing for thirty-eight cents, *toi*. We can cut it in pieces, freeze them—all ready to take out in cold weather. Smile, damn you. Warm birds in winter make writers hang on between books.''

And she thought of peanut butter—loved by the titmouse, cardinal, but especially the chickadee. And, when the birds ate through the ten pounds of wild-bird mix I'd bought—in two days—she came up with a solution. Order—from Bloom's General and Hardware Store, in Chesterland—to be delivered along with the salt for the water softener: an eighty-pound sack of medium cracked corn, five pounds of sunflower seeds, one pound of small, round, unsalted peanuts. Mix. Try.

The birds loved it. Cost: about one-third of the commercial mix. I usually paid; they rarely had any extra money in this house. Between books, when I was broke, I borrowed from my sister Fannie. When a book was taken, and I got my advance, I paid her back. It became routine. Not that I had to tell Fan about the birds. By then, my sister knew me. My teacher had taught me how to teach my sister—the city waitress in bars—to understand about gardener-poets and Soul.

In the Shannon house, once, I left Helen a fragment of what I termed a poem in those days. She'd gone to a PTA meeting, and I'd come in from gardening the small yard. I wrote her:

> Oddest of all is love—not the chain pulling at us wherever we go, but a garland of flowers—stretched out and full, by which to grope our way homeward.

I wrote it on the phone pad, standing with garden-dirty hands. Tore it off and left it on the table for her to find (and keep). I lived on the third floor by then (big paneled room, my own bathroom, the first desk in my life), and had started a book.

This year, it's my fifth novel—but nobody wants it. Where is my garland now? My "home"? Was it all in that one woman?

That which the earth covers over *must* be forgotten. Sure. But how the hell do you do it? Six years dead, but when the first spring Chippy runs across the grass, I think of Helen. When I get to the asparagus bed, I still feel the slight nausea: she loved that vegetable.

So does Mort, so I cook lots of it for him. It took me years before I could eat a little of it again. And I rarely touch a strawberry— another of her favorites.

If only I could write a poem. No, no, think gardens! But instead, I look over at her bedroom window; she'd appear there, open it wider, call: "Good morning, gardener darling. What's up, overnight?"

After a while, she had to sleep as late as she could: doctor's orders. She had a really lousy body, long long before the strokes; full of flaws, inherited from her father's side of the family. I was always out, in good weather, hours before she woke. Most of the time, I was working the back acres, so my first glimpse of her almost every morning was at that bedroom window.

But sometimes I was working the main farm, and then she would come out the front door, smile up at the sun, touch the v. carlesi or an annual poppy in the planter. "Good morning, gardener-*toi!* What's up today for dinner? For beauty? For loving eyes?"

Then I'd go in and have more coffee while she ate her break-fast. It was morning ritual spring, summer, and fall; and we caught up with whatever had happened, and the dogs came into the kitch-en. (Just before Mort left for work every morning, he'd put Friedie on his bed, Ragsy on Helen's—she was the one who had to be ca-tered to, in order not to hurt the old one.)

And I'd tell Helen what was in bloom, back and front; what in fruit; and that half the Bibb lettuce hadn't come up, so I'd patched the row. And there'd been a huge turtle sunning himself on the dock. And that I had written for three hours after she'd gone to bed last night.

I look away from that window. I study the rough-plowed areas I'll farm later on. Lots of sunflowers—yes. Including Van Goghs.

Those are the ornamental sunflowers—red and yellow singles, sunny rounded doubles—I always planted them along with the ordinary big ones called, in the catalog, "Mammoth Russian."

I love sunflowers, and especially those ornamentals. Never knew there was a reason beyond their beauty and light, until Helen said: "They're Van Gogh flowers. And you've been crazy about your Vincent for years." After that, she'd say: "Are your Van Goghs showing color yet?" Or I'd say: "Order an extra package of Van Goghs."

It was she who first discovered that the goldfinch, in particular, loved Van Goghs. Must have been the small seed. They'd cling to the heads, after the seed had ripened—the yellow males, the green females—all up and down the rows of sunflowers, making them sway. Helen: "Look! You're growing music, *toi*."

That vocabulary of hers. "Ruthie, look at Downy and Hairy at the front feeder." (The downy woodpecker; the bigger one—the hairy woodpecker.) "Mort, Mort, look—Johnny's finally awake. Ruthie, don't the dafs (or narcissus, or daylilies) need a haircut?" Which meant the foliage was ripe enough to pull up. "Martin, look! The first mouse-ear's in bloom." (Her favorite dahlia.)

Her vocabulary was kind of a poetry of the gardens. The sunflowers are up, seedlings, "with their hats still on." The green stalk bursts up through the ground, the split seed hanging onto the top of that seedling; then the first leaf spreads, pushes off the empty seed shell—the "hat." Sometimes that shell clings to one leaf for a long time—drunken looking. Adorable. Cukes and pickles the same way, only they're funnier: the seed is so small—and there sits that infinitesimal hat on the fat green seedling.

She also said that about tiny pickles that haven't quite lost the bloom yet, though the perfect fruit is there; at that time, the clinging blossom at the end of the fruit was the hat. Ditto squash—small fruits all formed, but the hat of a blossom still clinging.

Lots of very special languages. Sometimes she called our place House. She'd call me *toi* (she spoke and read French fluently). Or Joey-*toi*, toughy dear, gardener dear. Or darling, dear heart, beloved heart, sweetheart (the same endearments she used to husband and kids). Bare honest, welling straight from her heart; even for me, the ex-stranger—but not for long. This family turned into mine—my second family.

I got to like her love lingo, as I called it, as much as I did her garden vocabulary. And I finally stopped blushing when she called me something like dear heart. In my house, where I'd grown up—in my ghetto of life—none of that kind of talk, ever. And no kissing. Oh, they were good people—well, I call us illiterates in the soul—my born family. Yes, me too—until I met Helen and learned the far, beautiful horizons a soul actually owns when it's taught to walk out of prison. In my born family—no poetry. Just in me. But all choked, trapped.

That un-choking. My God, when the mystery and confusion finally are interpreted. Yes, Helen did that. Pain translated and explained, made articulate—bearable. The weeping can be music. A cello. In Helen's house, I fell in love with the cello music I'd never known existed. "Schelomo"? It felt like my own heart.

I must plant mouse-ears soon. On her birthday—if the ground is workable. I've always tried to plant something on March 24. It's a little bit like writing a poem.

That gorgeous vocabulary of hers. Because those pom-pom dahlias do look like lavender snowballs full of clusters of mouse-ears. And how those tubers grow. Over the summer and fall, all dahlias put on weight (as I used to say)—but especially her mouse-ears. After the first killing frost, when I dig them, there are always four or five for the one tuber I'd planted. I've given them to many friends, took a dozen to Northampton last spring and planted them in Barb's new yard; yet there are always enough left to lavender up big areas of the perennial bed, and the spaces between the Oriental poppies in front of my room—to take over when the poppy foliage dies back in July.

Helen meant field mice, of course. Especially baby mice—with the tiny, delicate, translucent-in-sun ears. Sometimes, in the fall, when Mort and I unrolled the snow fence (stored over the summer against the big tulip tree near the east groundhog house), there was a sudden rushing and squealing: a field mouse had built a nest of straw and weeds in the hole-core of the fence, and suddenly mother and kids tumble out, are rushing off in all directions from the unrolling fence. But sometimes one or two dazed babies lie there a second to catch their breath, and you see their ears: Helen and her dahlia, her poet's eye—so exact and sensitive.

Or sometimes it happens in the fall when you leave the wren houses up longer than usual (you're finishing a chapter of a book, or a section of rewrite). Finally, you take down the houses (the wrens long gone) and clean them out, to air a few days before storing them upstairs. You pry off the roofs of one, two, clean out the tightly packed twigs and straw and grasses the clever wren has assembled in there for the babies. Then comes the third house. You're reaming out the contents, and all of a sudden comes a squealing and dropping, scurrying. Never fails to startle me—that family of field mice. Rags often taking off after one (to no avail, of course). There, for a moment, before the last baby vanishes into the tall grass, those lovely little mouse ears live in Helen's flower.

Oh God, I must write a poem this year.

The first one I ever wrote to her: all of a sudden, it came unchoked. Un-fettered. About writing, of course. I found it in that stack she'd kept so carefully. Written on the brown envelope: "This is Ruth Seid's (Jo Sinclair) property." (As if she'd been ready to turn them over, at the right time, to those university archives she'd promised would be created some day—for every scrap of the writer.)

That poem was dated August 10, 1939.

And if this agony should go from me
And if this anguish should release me, free
The spirit from its subtle ugly ways,
Why then!—who knows what swift and birdlike ecstasy
Might move these hands,
Who knows the soaring dream this heart might take
Upon itself, and wake
To emptiness no more!

Not very good, writer-Jo; but I remember the tremendous burst of feeling that shoved those words out of the erstwhile mute.

I leave the asparagus, walk across to the long, curving bulb bed. narcissus poeticus—the hundreds I planted have spread; this broad, long curve is as crammed as the daf bed. Spring: the first inch or two of green is pushing up through the sod—heavy as it is. Nature insists: for all but me.

I stare, thinking: "To emptiness no more!" Lord, Lord. I was so full—for years.

As I look away, toward the pond, the other questions rear again: *Did* that part of me die when Helen died? But how can such a thing happen in a writer's mind? Or is that kind of death in the emotions? No, it's got to be the mind. That's where depression is, And that's what antidepressants alleviate—the despair-pain in the mind.

I can't take antidepressants: my glaucoma. But I wonder if I would—no matter how intense the pain. I've always shied away from anything that might tamper with writing (with the Me, that forced me to write).

Helen knew about that tampering business. I told her—with a chip on my young shoulder—that I would never go to a psychiatrist. How the hell did I know what a guy like that might do to the writer in me? I wonder if many actual psychiatrists are as good as she was. Would I go to one, now, if I had the money? I'm no longer that ignorant young punk.

Almost immediate answer (phony?): But why even think of a doctor? You're safe. You're writing a new book. Doesn't creative death still have a question mark in your mind? Say yes! And the gardening has started. How can you die before a book is finished? Before you cut the flowers from seeds you've planted? What kind of psychiatrist! You've got crops to gather—garden and desk. You're still not a wasteland, damn it.

Yes, that she definitely taught me. Not to waste Self—love, talent, earth and flowering, dream. And when finally I could write a novel, I asked her for ideas for an epigraph to go with that title, *Wasteland,* and the story of barren and reclaimed lives she had helped me interpret in myself.

It was Milton. My friend had read a lot of things I had missed. On a day like today, that old epigraph is again perfect for me:

And that one talent, which is death to hide
Lodg'd with me useless, though my soul more bent
To serve therewith my Maker, and present
My true account...

I walk over to the perennial bed, sit on the carpenter's bench. It was left over from the house building—and nurtured by me, repaired from time to time. It's light, and has a hand slit in the center; easy to carry it from planting area to area. Then you sit on it, tired, and have a cigarette. Or write out some of the stuff that's been roiling around in your head as you cultivated that last bed: a piece of a novel, dialogue for a play. Spring and summer and fall—the perfect seasons for starting a piece of work in your head. You garden, and then the ideas leap out, onto the pads of paper you always carry in one of the tool baskets.

Sitting here, I can see the tree. Woman into tree. And into the seasons. That should be the poem. But I can't.

I think of the old poems. I found them with all the manuscripts waiting now to be shipped to Boston University's library archives. In early 1964, I'd jammed them into the first packing case upstairs, unable to open that envelope Barb discovered in Helen's desk. She had kept them all—as if they were Keats.

There was the long brown envelope, when I forced myself upstairs to see the number of boxes full of manuscripts, typescripts, galley proofs, letters—everything Helen had insisted I keep.

And that was another tremendous difference between us. She was a completely educated, history-archives-research person. I hadn't even gone to college. A commercial high school—typing, filing, bookkeeping (yeah, but plenty of journalism and English, too!). Nobody in our family had gone to college, not even the sons, so why me? As for Helen's passionate sense of history—nuts. I was too centered on pulling this one punk out of the black hole of today—with a story or poem. She thought of young writers in the future: studying, doing research on established writers and their day. I thought only of me, me—how awful it had been to get those first things published, how rough it was to finish another book.

So of course it was she who started that collection. And the scrapbooks. "Some day, a national library or a university will want every bit about you, Jo Sinclair." I laughed, but she said calmly: "I kept the galleys of *Wasteland*. And the typescript, the notebooks, the fan mail. Upstairs—Mort brought me some good packing cases." Me: "You're nuts—it's cluttered enough up there right now." She: "Now—didn't you tell me you kept file copies of the magazines— those stories and poems you had published? And that play George put on at Cleveland College? Go find them, and we'll put them into a case and label it. I'm starting the Jo Sinclair Collection right now. And don't ever throw out any part of a book, story, play—any step of a piece of writing. That's an order, *toi*. Stop that silly laughing! I happen to know more about such things than you. And believe a hell of a lot more in you and the world. You may not give a damn about the future—but it will about you. I promise you that."

The letter came the summer after she died.

Dear Miss Sinclair:

I am sure that many institutions have been in contact with you asking that they might become the repository of your manuscripts and correspondence files. I write to say that Boston University would be honored to establish a Jo Sinclair Collection, and to plead our particular cause for these reasons.

We are in the midst of planning the building of a magnificent new library on our Charles River Campus and we hope to make this library a center of study and research in contemporary literature. . .

It is our hope to collect the papers of outstanding contemporary literary figures, house and curate these materials under the optimum archival conditions, and attract to us scholars in the field of contemporary literature. . . A Jo Sinclair Collection would certainly be a distinguished nucleus around which this University could build a great literary center. Your papers would be preserved for future. . .

Yes, her promise kept. And she had known exactly what "my morgue" should contain. The director of Special Collections wrote me the list: The manuscripts of the books in the various states; proofs; the manuscripts of stories, articles, plays; unpublished manuscripts; printed materials pertaining to the writer's career; photographs. "And, of course, as your writing continues, the Collection would grow with Sinclair additions. . ."

It was all upstairs. The two scrapbooks were still in her desk, in the living room. She'd pull one out, add clippings from book to play to book: announcements, reviews, every bit of publicity, certain letters. In the second scrapbook, more than half-full, there's an envelope of loose clippings she had not had the chance to paste in.

I did not look at any of the past-into-morgue that the university was asking for. Not then. I ran. Friends wanted me, paid for my trips: Detroit, Northampton; then, after a while, Los Angeles.

Very, very slowly, I began to think I'd live. Worked on my book (that novel manuscript went everywhere I did), opened myself to other worlds. By October, the year after she'd died, the mourner in L.A. was okay—was suddenly homesick.

And it did feel like home when I got back. Beautiful—all the familiar things in place. The groundhogs still up top—all the Johnny-babies full grown, and not an apple around for all the eating that must have gone on while I was away. The seasons merging, the way I loved it: summer woodpeckers still there, but so were the big winter ones; and Chippy was still up top, too. Hummy and the swallows had gone, but that night some of the frogs were hollering that winter wasn't quite here.

Indian summer (the first hard freeze had come and gone); cleaning up for winter was full of warmth. I'd go from working out to working in—house chores and hours of writing.

Then. What happened? Why? The first heavy snow came. Silence descended, thick. The winter season of death came drifting into all the rooms.

Suddenly—Christ!—the book was hard to write. Again.

I had to force myself to feed the birds, to tour the joint. Helen's tree had dropped all its leaves. It was lovely in its stark reach upward, but she was back—the loneliness, the need. Of course: because, from day to day, I liked the book less. Found myself shouting in my head: Finish it, damn you—then type it. You have to see what's there first, before you kick it into hell. Harder and harder to write. Until, one day (December 1964), in desperation for some kind of rescue—from the Me, from the yearning to have her back—I wrote Boston: Okay, the morgue's all yours! As soon as I have time.

Then I went upstairs and started opening those packing cases. I'd promised something; and I'd been taught not to break promises. Lights on up there, in the cluttered storage space—big as half a dusty house. Old chairs and lamps and racks of mason jars, garden baskets and tools. The first one-wheel hand plow I'd used; and the bag with the crank, with which Helen and I had seeded grass everywhere. Anytime I looked up from my creative past, I could see fragments of my physical past.

One case after another pulled out, scrambled through—and even the extra author's copies of hardbacks and paperbacks discovered, and copies of translations. And when I looked up: little Barb's dollhouse (it had been little-girl Helen's first); in another direction, my luggage—gift from Fannie for that first triumphant trip to New York. It was a little like being in therapy.

And then, very abruptly, like the crashing in of a door to a room lit with answers—in one of those long-ago psychiatric sessions—I found my deus ex machina for some possible kind of transfiguration.

It's a theater term. Greek theater—about which I was completely ignorant when I met Helen. I grew up in the thirties, and my theater writers (to read, from the library) were Odets, O'Neill, Hellman, Sherwood. I'd seen very few plays.

After I heard her say it, I looked it up in my first dictionary (a birthday gift from Mort and her); found a wonderful expression for me to learn as writer and person:

> *Deus ex machina* (L., god from a machine). 1. in ancient Greek and Roman plays, a deity brought in by stage machinery to intervene in the action; hence, 2. any character or happening artificially, suddenly, or improbably introduced to resolve a situation, as in some fiction, 3. anyone who unexpectedly intervenes to change the course of events

Here it was, staring at me from out of one packing case after another—a hell of a fated machine god. A new book could be written out of these crammed cases of my past. A new weapon with which to fight that rotten, frightening creative death.

"Anyone who unexpectedly intervenes to change the course of events." Boston University? No—Helen. Wasn't it she who'd made me save all this? And, too—so odd!—it was as if she were insisting that I rediscover my whole creative life of the past: the honors and prizes, yes, but also the rejections. Which always—no matter how awful the span of despair—had turned into acceptances. As if, right now, she was ordering me to prove that my feeling of death, today, was a phony—triggered by my emotions.

It was all like a remarkable weapon, and I felt a little stunned by the way the sharp blades were suddenly cutting through the depression fog that had been choking me for weeks.

That first blade: this was a book, all right. With quite a few angles. Because I found my garden journal upstairs, too. And the other—the diary details of her last eight months on earth I'd made myself jot down.

I stared at those two separate masses of notes I'd stuffed into a case, and titles flared at once. One was "The Journal of Death." The other, definitely, "The Journal of Life"—twelve years of me in this house. All of it: garden, the start of books, a play produced, the sales of stories; and a wedding, a child born; promises made and kept.

Back to the packing cases again. Poking into one after another, I began remembering dozens of things I hadn't thought of in years.

I had a large stack of letters from Ed Aswell. And I thought instantly: These letters should be given to the world—in my book; the rest to Boston University, for new writers. This was a great editor.

There were all the fan letters after the publication of *Wasteland*— so many of them asking for the name of a good psychiatrist in their city, or near it. (Helen, with the help of her psychiatrist friend, had gotten me dozens of names.) I'd answered every letter, had felt: My God, the responsibility a book can create.

I kept pulling things out of cases. I'd forgotten about the national prize for a TV script, the award from the Jewish Book Council of America for best novel, the three awards from Ohioana Library, the citation from the National Conference of Christians and Jews. I'd forgotten a great deal, as I'd wept and written endlessly and died over and over.

Like: Helen adored New York, and knew it backward. I didn't know it at all (born in Brooklyn, left there at three years old, back two or three times to visit cousins—always back to the Brooklyn "ghetto" so like the Cleveland one). That trip to New York with her: so many firsts for the author of a novel that had won ten thousand miraculous bucks. For the first time in my life, I had money to spend; but it was she who knew how and where to spend it.

I tasted things I had known only through yearn-reading. A Wagnerian opera—the Metropolitan looking exactly like all the pictures I'd seen. *Swan Lake,* Martha Graham's dancers. Restaurants that knocked me for a loop—French, Italian, seafood. At the Museum of Modern Art, I fell deeply in love with sculpture. Oh, I fell in love over and over. Foreign films. The stores on Sixth Avenue: old parchments, fascinating secondhand books; and I bumped headlong into the work of an artist called Käthe Kollwitz. Helen found me the portfolio of her prints, and the biography. I bought both, and several other portfolios of art ready to be framed.

Ah, what she did. Like the gardening, the cello: my heart had been waiting for Kollwitz—her etchings and drawings of mother and child, starvation, labor, sorrow. As ready as it had been for Van Gogh. Back home, Helen knew the expert in framing; and the ex-waif with money had art on her bedroom walls for the first time in her life: Kollwitz, Van Gogh, ballet dancers by Degas.

Here's something for one more blade of my new weapon: I'm holding the third rewrite of a real despair-book. I'm scanning dozens of notebooks, labeled typescripts (so many!). Carefully, I put back the galley proofs of that second novel (Helen's small but clear hand-writing as she'd caught printer's errors). Despair? But it had been published, Jo. I sat in an old chair, and started to read the poems she'd saved. It turned unbearable; I had to run. But I took those poems and the two journals down with me. Forced myself back into the old (it used to be tried-and-true) way of saving myself. Wrote page after page in the current notebook of the novel I'd started long before her first stroke—and had written during and after all the strokes. A very fluctuating safety!

That evening, the journals and poems were waiting after the dinner dishes. (Mort had gone to the living room for his usual cross-word puzzle.) My room is a very big combination workroom and bedroom. Helen had planned it for the architect to sketch, and planned the perfect desk, and the two in-a-door beds that could be rolled away behind sliding doors—creating for the day a place of books and music in which to write. The same Kollwitz and Van Gogh and Degas on the walls, plus a Beethoven death mask I'd found one year.

In my big yellow chair (bought with *Wasteland* money—picked by her to last), I looked at the possible beginnings of a new book. They were on my record cabinet, which is close to the biggest and finest Magnavox available when the prize-winning author had bought it. Jesus. Poor, rich, poor again—in money *and* in soul.

December 1964 I read my old poems. Bringing back the really poor kid in all ways, the ready-for-death punk she'd saved so long ago. But bringing back, too, the learning person. It was a long time past midnight when I got to the end of the poems and both diaries. That Journal of Life—as I had tabbed it; amazing—the constant refrain of fear and insecurity as a writer. I felt peculiar as hell: on my desk, now, a fifth novel—and the same lack of belief.

But no Helen, to change it into meaning. In those days, no matter what, there *had* been meaning to every bit of life. And it's that sudden vanishing of meaning that must be a huge part of the feeling of creative death for a person like me. Even flowers, sky and wind, birds, Chippy: they're somewhat like lies. So empty.

That winter night in 1964, I looked at the two piles of dated notes—a life, a dying and a death, and a packet of old poetry. Thought, like an odd kind of praying: Could this be some of the meaning restored? In a book?

But then, almost at once, I thought: Can such a thing possibly be written? The woman, the love between two friends, the lives so completely shared? Not sure! That such a subtle thing can be shown to the world. Which is amused or frightened by real love.

And this particular love—my God. This love that started out as the dependency of one, and then became interdependent. This love that turned into death where the poem used to be. Such a death, that took with it... No, this will not be an easy book to write. For the full loss of such a death, I *must* show the full gifts of her living. So that the world can know the beauty a few of its people possess—and share. Some of that world could be warmed, comforted, by such a story. But my God, how do I do it?

Try. Experiment—right now—start in your head, the way a book should. Start there with: "She taught me." Translate that. Not a simple statement. In fact, very complicated. But try. And after a while, maybe the deus ex machina upstairs will help. Do it the way it happened—the small and the big. All mixed up together, the way she did it, and you learned it.

Like this. She taught me how to eat asparagus, lobster, croissants, and brioche. Simple? Well, here's the complicated: How to say a word like *soul* out loud without blushing or scowling. How to say "I love you" to my mother for the first time by hugging her; the second time, a quick kiss on the cheek. Merge with: my firsts at hot biscuits, gravy, grits, and fried shrimp; the knowledge that a Southern-born woman can hate the South for its black-white stuff, but want to retain the lovin' ways and talk, the foods, the innate courtesy.

Merge it all—the way it happened, slow and fast.

She taught me earth, seed, tuber, and bulb. Honeysuckle on a fence—and a hummingbird darting to the first blossoms. Then that knowledge of soil soared toward glimmers of spiritual beauty, as she taught me how to walk out of all the kinds of ghettos I'd lived in; and—like a gardener of world—to hold many symbolic seeds in my hand, feel the touch on my senses of all the flowers a person *could* grow within the Self.

Take that word *promise*. When to say it, why not to say it. Because once you do, it's like a holy thing. She taught me that—this woman who believed so passionately in lessons that were really food for a child hungry in too many ways.

And I was. Almost twenty-six when I met her, but the child of me was still trapped, starving. The spirit can be the most intolerable ghetto of all. And follow within you, wherever you run—like your own mute, scared child-shadow.

That child knew nothing but wanted the stars; knew nothing of writing but yearned terribly to make Poems—every conceivable kind. Helen recognized the struggling, entombed, begging kid. She helped me identify both—me and my shadow.

And she taught me, finally, a tremendously important thing: that it was good to talk out loud the way your heart and guts had always talked secretly—and no need to be ashamed of such honesty. That a Self must be un-choked and un-fettered before the writer can exist.

That mute Self slowly, so very slowly, began to talk. Then, to sing. She began to write her teacher me-and-my-shadow-together-at-last poems.

Find me a moment in world today
Where I may stand in silence or in awe.
Find me a cleanness for my hands
That they may move in hard and bony strokes
Upon a wide, white space of time,
To make the first dark meaning marks.

Find me a moment of world today
In which the song engenders day
And day in turn feeds every want,
Until all hunger sings itself to ease.
Find me a passion for the mind
That will appease the bare and deathly hours.

Yes, very small stuff; but a trapped voice was being un-muffled, a creative mind partially liberated. Up until then, there had been a few poems in little magazines, a half-dozen published stories, a one-act play produced by an amateur college group, hundreds of rough fragments of poetry, and a great stack of unpublished short stories.

"Find me a passion for the mind."

She did.

By teaching me the ways of a world I had never touched beyond reading about it in free library books. What a mélange of things

I had never known in my ghettos. How to write a check and balance a checkbook. How to buy good clothes and shoes. To travel, tip a redcap and hotel maid and cab driver and waitress. She introduced me to fresh crabmeat, bouillabaisse, tossed salad with wine vinegar and olive oil dressing; Lake Timagami and Montreal and Quebec; some of the stars and gutters of a city like New York.

She taught me that a person should have her own towel and washcloth. How to use a cloth napkin, fold it into a silver napkin ring (engraved with the initials of her grandmother; mine had never used even a paper napkin; nor my parents, either). How to help myself to a platter passed by a maid. All about a salad fork, a dessert spoon, a tiny oyster fork, a slender silver knife just for butter. How to set a table, make a bed properly. In my parents' house, we had remained very much like peasants.

God, what a stunning gamut of things I learned. To show love without fear, embarrassment, cynicism. To accept a kiss given in affection. To be free enough to leave my mother (my trap, my beloved cross) and come to her house—to that third floor on Shannon, so clean and quiet, removed enough from the rest of the house and the world so that I could write out the slowly clarifying dream.

The things that distorted child-woman of a Ruth did not know! She taught me how to watch her children grow, how to accept their love and love them—and recognize their fine minds and hearts. How to accept her husband's friendship—and prove mine for him. To know, in all my finally undistorted emotions, that I had two families now; my own—to understand and to acknowledge at last without shame—and this one, hers, which had adopted me with such eagerness. She taught me to want them both, and to know in all honesty the place of both in my heart.

Note: Regarding a phrase I call ''pass it on.'' She helped so many of my own family—through me: through the magical ways of one person getting strength and awareness enough from another to be able to give some of it away . . . A beautiful, never-ending gift to get, and to give. Because I saw that such gifts are often passed back—or on to others (yes, like pieces of divided plants). It turned out that my little shy peasant mother liked to be kissed. It happened that I was able to cry when my father-I-thought-I-hated died. It came to be that I really wanted to walk with my sisters and brothers in any street of the world, with affection, the shame (for me, for them) exploded into the phony ghost it always was—but the maimed child hadn't known that.

What lessons. Slowly, they went on and on. How to shake hands, on meeting a person; and "how do you do." And Bach, Rilke, Kazantzakis, Vivaldi, Christopher Robin; art museums, cathedrals and shrines in Canada, my first Reform Jewish temple. Picnics in lovely, quiet parks. And how to offer a loan with grace. A good lawyer—to help buy that house for my blood family after the big money came; to write me a will. A will! Something out of a book about rich people. No? Helen: "No, dear. Something for all people who think of tomorrow and the people they love."

More? This. She taught me to take life out of the library books— and to live it. First the Self, then the writer—and eventually they merge. Me and my shadow, again.

No, not easy to write—it won't be, and I know it. To tell the world what one human being is capable of doing for another? I have to say it this way: that woman un-ghettoed me. With me, *ghetto* takes in emotions, family, creativity, sex, religion. It is prison, double-locked gates on Self. When Helen reached out her hand, I took from that dark stranger-place only the dream and grope of the choked poetry. The rest of the chains I left. After a while. A long, long while.

That fantastic, quite miraculous "she taught me" went on—big and little, simple and complicated. The arts, avocado and watercress and French endive; and she had my cavities filled by a dentist who said he'd wait for his money, and she got me my first real physical examination—and paid for it. I entered that sum in a notebook, too, but didn't have to write out the fact that I never again would shrink from the idea of a man's touch in such circumstances, after her stern but patient translation of the importance of medicine to a body, no matter how confused the psyche. And, in 1946, after that prize money, I paid her back the doctor's fee. Paid the dentist, and my sister; paid off all the other debts incurred on the way toward the smashing out of prison of that waif who could finally buy her own typewriter.

Waif? Yes. And, essentially, with all her great heart, Helen was a gatherer-in of waifs. I learned that, after a while. By then, she had taught me that a strong, whole person can have love and strength enough for husband and son (eight years old) and daughter (ten) and a divorced, sad father and an arrogant, wealthy (but so needy, too) mother; for her husband's two old aunts and uncle, and many friends (often, lonely men and women). And plenty left over for a punk whose talent she'd sensed.

Strangers saw a fat, homely, rather short woman. She was the most beautiful person I've ever known. She taught me that, too: that the true, the never-fading, never-changing loveliness is the spirit.

She had a very direct gaze—blue eyes, large, crammed most of the time with word-expressions. She was myopic, couldn't see across the room without her glasses; her eyes were extremely beautiful.

So was her love of life. So was her sense of humor. I had read about that kind of laugh—full, joyous, so honestly and loudly amused. To actually hear it was marvelous. Yet her voice was always soft. And she woke smiling and eager for life every morning. I woke dark, bleak. It was her smile that turned into the real morning sun for me; the ordinary sun had never worked.

Clothes? She didn't give a damn about them; the less money spent of Mort's always-small salary the better. Though, of course, she had some "good" clothes—for concerts, PTA and civil liberties meetings, the few trips. Beauty shop? Big laugh. But her hair was always fresh, combed and brushed. Naturally curly, brown—no hair spray. No perfume; a delicate cologne, sometimes. Lipstick, when she was going out. No commercial manicures, but nails clean and shaped by herself. Such good hands—small, but such a strong, warm handshake.

World, world, see her. A lovely vase was much more important than a dress. A flower, a fine book, a new recording (*Songs of a Wayfarer* was one of the first I saw her get excited about)—and to hell with jewelry, or an expensive coat. And this was a woman who had grown up in wealth, where luxuries and exquisite taste in clothes and jewels were very much a part of life. But this, by God, was a woman who'd married a guy with not much money—for love. She made all my youthful library books come alive—out of choked dream stuff.

Yes, she was beautiful as a human being. How else can I say it? Her heart, and the sensitivity and quickness of her mind. And so beautiful her deep interest in the world: politics, trees and animals, racial issues, theater and movies, food, the blind, refugees, artists of all kinds, children. Beautiful, her feelings so freely shown. Her tremendous capacity for friendship.

Christ, how can I write this person? Quicksilver, clouds, warmth, and brilliance so merged. Well, take just her honesty. In my kind of ghettos, people were afraid to be honest—even if they knew how (rare). That honesty in Helen scared me, at first. I was afraid of how it was smashing me open, cutting through all my insides, making me talk out all the secret pain and fear. But I long for it now. I miss it so deeply.

Honesty. And about imperfections, too. After we became real friends, and I, the "ex-patient," was strong enough to be her spiritual equal, she shared with me the truth of her failings and her hurts, her own maimed childhood—the scars that made some of her as human and little as I was; and yet those scars had helped make her the perceptive rescuer of people. She gave me that part of her honesty only when I was able to take it (and she knew the moment that would be possible)—and then I could understand why and how I'd permitted myself to be saved by her. My guts, my instincts, my confused heart must have known that there were bridges between us—wonderfully strong, wonderfully delicate, and beautiful.

Helen was no angel, but that was part of the honesty, too. She never lied about the fact that she was extremely proud of her mind—which she herself had fashioned into a formidable weapon, out of the child's very good head to start with. (It *was* magnificent, and anybody who knew her admitted it, even those who disliked her—and a lot of people did.) She was very envious of beautiful women. She was so intolerant at times that I was amazed: of Republicans, of organized religion—Jew *or* Gentile. She loathed communism and fascism almost fanatically, and even the idea of Zionism: to her, a kind of ghettoization. She was a forceful, dominant woman, and one hell of a lot of people resented that.

Me, too—at first. That was before I learned that it was real strength, and that many people needed and wanted that part of her. And that it was another weapon she had created out of her own need (her parents a mess, her childhood quite tormented at times—despite the money and culture and real class). And *that* was quite a lesson to the peasant-punk who'd always thought money and class could do anything. But that was another bridge, too.

She didn't dominate me. Well, not for too long. I was—as she said with a smile, after a while—just as strong and stubborn as she. That made us better friends—after we left the doctor-patient arena. So did her faults. It made us more equal—that taking her down from the angels.

But how really different we were. Take the way she walked—

always as if she were looking up, and that erect carriage. I looked down—hunched shoulders, most of the time. Say it symbolically: one was geared to the stars, the other to the ditch she was always afraid she'd fall into. Helen was hope—every inch of her. I was despair. It made for a devout friendship; I had needed those stars all my life, and it was her nature to point them out. To say, with that marvelous belief: "Look! Of course you can touch one."

That evening we'd met; no, she was no mystic, or mind reader. She knew a little about me before she saw me. My play writing teacher and she were good friends, but she green-thumbed the rest.

Dr. K (she called him George, too) suggested I go over to investigate this amateur drama group called Contemporary Theater. Told me Helen's name, that she had started the whole thing. Then said: "You know, they might want short original plays like yours some day. And, anyway, you may learn a lot about actual theater—they have some good, experienced people Helen has latched on to. I think you might like her. Mort, too—her husband. Fine people.

I went, forced it. Always, in those days, I was scared of the world outside. Shivering away from a stare, what I thought was a derisive laugh. Unable to feel that I belonged anywhere. Those were the chips on my shoulders, and the mask of tough babe. It was 1938, and I was an editor on a WPA project. Helen's group was working on its first production: *One Third of a Nation*.

The evening of May 25. God knows why, but there I was. Fate? That's a word I used to scoff at, but I know enough now to step back from "I know." About anything.

I stood at the back of the big room in this old house they had rented, in mid-Cleveland, near slums and business; and watched a lot of people buzzing around, some rehearsing, some working on scenery and costumes, or cleaning up the place. After a while, she came across the room to me. (Much, much later, she told me she'd seen me the moment I'd come in. That both George and she had wondered if I would come.)

She talked—about theater, my short plays, this play—did I know it? Yes, of course, I said at my toughest (I'd read about it). Naturally, I knew about Federal Theater—wasn't I on WPA? She smiled, and I got my first glimpse of those direct eyes, the deep warmth. She toured me around, showed me backstage, scripts they were reading for the next production, introduced me to people. I was—

in my heart—excited, but fought it. After all, how could *I* be in such company?

When she phoned, a few days later, and asked me to lunch, I went. God knows how I forced that. Because not only was I painfully shy, but I thought I didn't like her. She was too "goddamn fancy and high class," too articulate, too sure of herself, too rich. I didn't know it then, but the phony dislike must have been fear, too—of that complete honesty; it really sort of radiated from her eyes and tone of voice. It scared the hell out of me. Plus: she was entirely different from anybody I'd ever known.

So was her house, in classy Cleveland Heights—art, music, all those books, the lovely vases and lamps, carpeting in both the rooms I saw. I drove to all that class in my shabby secondhand car that my sister Fannie had helped me buy because I couldn't bear the idea of riding streetcars or a bus (I always thought people were staring at me—my short hair, my "different" way of walking, everything about me). What a confused, emotional mess I was. But that Helen-difference (the complete opposite of my life, my home, my family) drew me powerfully, even as it made me angry and more frustrated.

And that lunch! Awful—and wonderful. A pretty, young Negro maid served us (uniform). Beautiful dishes and silver, tablecloth, linen napkins. Shrimp salad on Bibb and watercress, Southern biscuits in a basket—wrapped in a huge damask dinner napkin to keep them hot (I found out all these details later). Everything: the ghetto child in a frightening but wondrous fairyland. The beauty of everything filled me with excitement—and, of course, anger. But then, in those days, anger was my disguise for so much: the desire for life, the fear that I'd have to die of longing unfulfilled.

I watched Helen intently, mimicked every move she made with fork and butter knife, the breaking of a biscuit. I listened with amazement to the casual, friendly talk between an employer and a maid. I'd never heard of pewter (the sugar and cream). I didn't know that you don't fold a napkin after such a meal, but crumple it and put it...

Oh, God, the beginnings of the education of a ghetto kid. It reminds me, in retrospect, of the girl who went two or three times a week to the branch library, and read her way through every shelf in that big room—scanning even the books she didn't take home. Yes, Old Lady Nature has her cute little ways of putting survival in your path. That kid, that young woman, had longed for years to be a member of the real world—was sure she never would make it. And, in retrospect, I *do* know why I went to Helen's theater— and to lunch in her home. The same ambivalent struggle in me between wanting to die and yearning to live. The seesaw in the person and the writer: and sometimes the death trap seemed to close in—but then, at once, the other piece of me fought like an animal on the edge of its waiting grave. To write a poem or story, to crawl toward a possible rescue like an evening college course—or one called Contemporary Theater.

How can I tell that day, that luncheon? The more uneasy and excited I felt, the more arrogantly I talked (when I said anything at all). But, after a while, I managed to really look at her. That smile—so tender, so full of a strange kind of recognition, and of so many other things I simply sensed; I finally smiled back. I admitted: "This is the first time I ever had real Southern hot biscuits. Your maid make them?"

Helen: "No. I do all the cooking. Did you like the biscuits?" I nodded. She: "Will you come back? And meet my children?" I'd met Mort at the theater. "And bring me a play or short story of yours to read, please? I'd be so flattered. Would you—if only for more biscuits?"

We both laughed—and it was good. It turned out that not only did she love theater, but she knew a lot about writing for it. She'd written short plays at the University of Michigan; one, a prizewinner. Her one long play, written after she was married, was about somebody named Moll Flanders (naturally, I'd never heard of her). The Cleveland Play House had given it a reading, but nothing had come of it. Nor of her three children's books, which her kids had read over and over, and adored. I learned something else—and was stunned: she didn't really care that nothing had come of any of them. Other things were much more important than writing. "I'm not you," she said. "You're a real writer. I happen to know the difference. And I respect the real thing—with all my heart."

Jesus. Nobody had ever said anything like that to me.

Sure, I came back. And soon, what that ignoramus-me really began to learn! Not much money in that house, no, but all the music I knew nothing about: baroque, chamber music, harpsichord, cello, sonatas. Mort played, the kids played (that boyhood piano), but

Helen only listened, sometimes sang along. Learn, learn. That a maid was very cheap during the Depression. That Helen had taught herself to cook (and she was wonderful) only after her marriage; and taught herself how to cut every corner there was in making money stretch. She even canned fruit (by the case), put up tomatoes and dill pickles. She shopped for produce late Saturday, bought for half price the stuff in the store the man would have to throw out by Monday if unsold. I saw a woman use her brain and imagination to make one dollar buy a great deal, indeed. The kids had music lessons, dancing lessons when the time came; always, proper clothes. And a million dollars' worth of kisses and love and care—and books.

How I learned. That the joyous woman was not strong at all, her body a really lousy one, and her back was bad (weeding and making beds particularly painful); that the cheap maid was damned essential. That the house had been bought only after Helen had inherited money from her grandmother. Every penny of it had gone into home (that thing of life so important because the child and young woman had lived in a luxurious house that was never a home). And it was not classy—but a sturdy brick house with plenty of room for simple wants.

Later, I made a much better thing in that house than a maid; this friend's work was not only for free but for happiness. This friend was fiercely insistent on paying back for the thousand gifts—unpayable, of course. I was the physically strong one, who finally knew her strength in a hundred other ways; a new person, who had learned how to give as well as take. I gave a lot, with all my heart. Including the gardening, for I had turned into a lover of earth and plants—now that I knew so much about the new bloom all over my newly freed earth of soul.

And what a freedom! I wrote before and after I cultivated the roses and pruned the mums, or ran the sweeper over all the carpeting. And I read all about Oscar Wilde in prison, and knew all over again how confused and ignorant and fearful my psyche had been before Helen. I tried classic Greek theater (hard!—she had to explain plenty), got introduced to Strindberg, Ibsen, Pirandello. They were all in that wonderful library, along with the Pooh books, her own and Mort's kid books—and you name it in novels, poetry, essays, criticism. But that was later, after I'd learned so many, many new things that it was like going to college, after all. And continuing, at all times, to learn a very big thing. Me—my insides.

The poverty kid, smashing open spiritual doors left and right—starting to look up for the first time—toward things like stars, horizons. Would I have written a first novel anyway, with no Helen in my life? I wonder. It was she, not I, who believed so fervently that I had a book in me. Ready for me to want to do it—when the last door came open.

She opened it.

Of course, she didn't; she got me to open it. And all the other doors. The good psychiatrist always gets the patient to do it. The good gardener feeds and waters, prunes exactly right—and then the tree soars, the vine suddenly is loaded with fruit.

After that first novel, she'd say: "Write me a book, Ruthie." Remember? Nobody else, before or after, said that to me. God, the utter promise in a remark like that.

Remember, damn it! Not only the grief, but the whole, full, rich thing. Tell it. All the strange, beautiful chance and rescue, and the vanquished death in me, the released Poems of me.

We met; and almost two years later, I moved into the house on Shannon Road, and inherited a second family. Contemporary Theater was over, and WPA was over, and I had found a decent job. Yes, she even taught me to know that my small talent could be used for a thing like public relations—and that a person like me could write one-act radio plays and stories and articles for her boss, who turned out to be the American Red Cross, which used my stuff nationally. And we were at war, so even the local news releases and speeches I wrote seemed important to me.

Nothing like that comes quickly or easily. It took a while for the "she taught me"s to catch up with that punk she had recognized and acknowledged despite the disguise. It took a while to soak in enough of this woman who had frightened me, and excited me in my head, and then made my heart glad it was full of Poems. That heart had never been glad before.

Write it! She was a rescuer of people in need. And I saw, after a while, that I was not the first, nor would I be the last. And that was very good to know, too. Nor did she specialize in the needy. The word was *people*—and when it wasn't help she was giving, it was only love. She taught me that, most of all, over the years: what you can do with "only love."

*

That book I started in my head, in December of 1964? It's still only in my head.

Today, this year, I find myself thinking with my entire being: Helen, somebody, let me—with only love? Let me write, live? They're the same for me.

It's time! For that book, for me to walk out into this new spring and feel not death but some stirring of transfiguration.

Today—But Mostly Yesterday

*I*n this very early spring of 1969, her tree has come to life. But the Helen-book begins very slowly, sporadic notes; I think I'm afraid to actually start. The rejections—how they've piled. A mountain of pain.

Nobody knows about that pain flaming from each rejection, the depression continuing even during the new half-possibilities that drag you back to the desk for one more try. It's writer-pain, of course, but it takes over the whole person. Helen knew—always put out her hand. And isn't that part of the intense loss in this death? And she knew how hard I worked. Now nobody knows one more thing—that in my writing is my only meaning; and when that meaning seems to crumble, it's a terrifying sensation of dying.

Oh, Christ, Christ, go touch the tree and start her book. Why should that belief she gave you fade? It was so strong and clear. Touch! The tree is alive, even if you feel you aren't. So is the other world, I suppose—clamorous, full of rush and people. This one I live in is almost pure silence. Mort goes off to work, and I do the house chores, read the paper—all about that other world—tour the joint. Birds, the wind in the locusts and tulip trees, the peepers. They're all oddly part of the silence. Sometimes, even her little radio on the kitchen hearth seems to thicken that quiet.

Helen was a talker, a laugher. Rags was a barker. Friedie was a weeper. All of those cut silence. And I miss the children achingly sometimes. Once, the girl of the house practiced Clementi and Beethoven for hours. And the boy—Mozart, Debussy. Or he sang, at the top of his gorgeous voice, especially in the shower.

Silence is beautiful, of course, and as deep-rich necessary for spirit as Helen always believed. But now I know something else:

it's beautiful only when it has boundaries of great patches of life sound. I should write a poem about how silence can change; from peace, in which to work or read or think, and from inner strengthening respite, to some kind of isolated well into which memories keep dropping like stones—without a sound.

And the novel, that got finished long after she died? Didn't make it—in noise or in silence. First time in my writing life. So frightening: yes, sometimes it's as if—with her dying—a secret ingredient of the writing had died. And yet, she never even read anything of mine until that first draft was finished and typed. We just talked about it. How could its failure have anything to do with her death?

Well, maybe it doesn't. Maybe it's just a "bad book." Every writer is entitled to at least one, they say. Then why did I write it so many times (and why did the publisher go along with my ideas for rewrite)? Why do I think my heart was in it, and still is—and that my heart's ready to die?

Nature makes survivors of plants and trees, birds, woods creatures. What about some people? Is it Old Lady Nature, the real ringmaster, who whips me up to the packing cases full of past proofs of survival? Is she really that interested in helping me fight creative death? Oh, I need that whip today; touching the tree hasn't helped.

Careful, now—make it a good try for survival. Go through the latest case: manuscript notebooks, four different rewrites in typescript—but no galley proof, oh no! Study the stuff—so you can have some kind of comparison between this apparently dead book of today and one of your novels that seemed just as dead in the past—but *did* come to life.

• • •

This fifth novel—my God. I wrote and wrote. Endless, years. But I did finish a first draft. Typed it. Discovered with shock and complete disbelief that I had a typescript of 1,502 pages. Knew that I must have been in some completely crazed labyrinth while I'd been writing most of it.

And K—the editor who'd been so full of admiration and excellent criticism re *Anna Teller*—had resigned from my publishing house. I was pretty worried about that, too.

Ah, but the old ambivalent patterns? Two or three days of despair, then I attacked that first-draft mass of words. Cut and edited as honestly as I could. Worked—with all of me. Then did a final typescript—in triplicate, of course. And no Helen to stack paper and carbon, no indeed. Finished in December 1965. Five years and one death later (mine hadn't really started yet). The book was now, titled "Three Women," and was 1,273 pages.

It could very well have been a kind of insanity—because, even then, I thought: Well, lots of long books are published. And maybe *they* will think it's good?

So I sent my novel to New York—original to editor, first carbon to agent. And fed the birds, shoveled snow, cooked for Mort and me, kept the house clean. Tried to sleep—tried to believe Helen's way—even tried to start her book.

Nothing worked out.

From my agent—to this effect: Can't believe it—reads as if you had typed your notebooks and written out the continuity between episodes...drastic pruning necessary...no discipline...realize the grueling work and enormous thought, but where's the professional writer? Et cetera.

She's an honest, good agent.

The editor? Impossible, she wrote—in three pages of variations of why. Plus: Hate to slam all this...utmost reluctance...my respect for you and my realization of all you've been through.

An honest woman, who has admired my writing for many years, and who had very much wanted my next book. So (I thought instantly) they are both telling me the truth. And the shout of pain exploding all through me was: Helen! What'll I do?

But she wasn't in that house, and the crying chair wouldn't work without her. That was how creative death started in me. Not when Helen died, but when my book looked as if it had. Now I had both of us lost. I remember thinking: I must be so sick. Why didn't I know how bad the book was? Or even how long it was going to be?

Dig deeper into that packing case of rewrites and years: one day, a week or so after those letters from the New York market place, I opened my carbon copy of the rejected manuscript, began reading it, studying it. I made notes; a hundred changes—both those letters of detailed criticism in front of me. On and on—working like the professional I was supposed to be. Then I wrote a careful six-page memo to my editor (carbon to agent) on what I wanted to do, and why I thought my book should not be thrown into the garbage can.

On February 3, 1966, a phone call from my editor. Roughly as follows: Your letter hit me so hard! So unlike most writers. *Respect.* For your conviction, your belief in your people. Yes, I want to see the book when you've rewritten. Keep me posted?

From my agent, to this effect: Memo superb...salute you for tackling the rewrite, but honestly I thought you would...Let us discuss it...Respectfully.

And the letter, following the phone call, from my editor had words in it like: Tremendously impressed...courage and spirit and strength to react as you did...all here united in hoping...

Courage and strength? Don't make me laugh. The ambivalent-me is simply—again—fighting death. Nobody but Helen would know that. So I touched the tree and went to work. Wrote and wrote —most of the time in acute depression. The following February, I sent in the revised version.

My God—miracle? Suddenly there was a contract, an advance— though the correspondence told me there was one hell of a lot of further revision ahead. But a contract! I was a writer again—I was safe again. And I could pay my sister a big chunk of what I owed her.

Now, now!—I'm part of a new season. I start the rewrite; I work my guts out. I try my hardest to be objective. And I think, with gratitude: I'm safe. The book was wrong—it wasn't me.

In September 1967, I sent in the fourth version of my novel— now titled "Approach to the Meaning" (sure, Eliot). It's shorter, tighter—that I know. But is it better?

I waited. (Christ, what that kind of waiting does to you.) And gardened—hard. Touched the tree often, every day. And waited (another, different kind of waiting) for a poem to come into my heart. It didn't.

End of the month: The current royalty statement and check for *Anna Teller*—$62.78 less agent's commission. An old book still alive? That comforts me. But it's a kind of weeping comfort—not strength.

October: I put the garden to bed for the winter. Hung the feeders. And waited (by now, no belief). On November 10, I got my "no." My agent broke it first: They're rejecting...she had fresh readings all over the office. All agreed that the book still does not come off...do you a disservice to publish it...

Five days later, my editor wrote me her "no" and why—with great kindness, "reluctance, and admiration for you as a writer, past and future.'' And I was to keep the advance against royalties ''in view of all your expenditure of creative energy and time.''

There are all kinds of dyings possible. But the next day, automatically, I did the professional thing—a letter of thanks for her time and effort, for her generosity (I'd already spent most of that advance).

Inarticulate Mort's eyes were full of sorrow and pity. And yes: Helen's death came back, overwhelmingly. The grief and loneliness, the intense need to see her, to hear her voice; it was all raw pain again. It was as if this devastating rejection had dynamited any span of quiet bridge I had tried to build between that December in 1963 and the one catapulting toward me now. And yet, incredibly, my head went on working. What is this stubborn nature-survival thing that's so cruel and powerful and not to be fathomed? You want so terribly to die—and that secret thing in you fights with every weapon you can grab or create.

Such weapons—all in the mind: But if I kill myself, that would be a waste of her, too, wouldn't it? Spring's coming—hang on, for the seeds to plant. It's impossible that I can't write anymore; damn it, if Helen were here she'd *tell* me that; well then, listen to her as if she is here! But—is this proof that I'm dead as a writer? I'm almost sure of it, but...

Almost. One of the Old Lady's most cynical gifts of taunt-weapon. It stayed in my limp hands during the weeks and weeks of depression, drinking. Almost—that's like a tree that looks dead, and yet you're not positive. After you've pruned away all the dead wood, down to the bit of green remaining, how do you know whether or not it will survive? That kind of knowledge takes time. And sometimes you have to wait until...

Ah. Suddenly—as in a new spring, the pruned tree leaping up an inch into further green—another Poem appears.

A local theater outfit in Cleveland wanted an original play. There was even two thousand dollars involved: a play writing grant—half given if the outline was accepted by the committee, the other half if the play was produced. Several people I'd known for years in that group phoned: ''How about it? You've been threatening to write us a play as soon as you had some extra money.''

Hey! Suddenly I'm working again. Weeks, weeks; then finally, the outline is accepted (wrote it three times before the committee said okay). My heart lifts to the old song: I'm writing something new—I'm safe.

It's February, and the catalogs are arriving. Order your seeds—in between big chunks of dialogue. At your desk, look out the window: the snowdrops have pushed up. Come on, feel nature as teacher again!

So the play gets written.

Well, all right, the first draft is much, much too long, and a first draft of a play is bound to be full of junk, of enormous rewrite spots; but the core, the essence, the meaning? Won't it be there for perceptive theater people? Oh, sure, the subject is touchy, too: the theater is part of a big Jewish outfit and you've been told that the "Jewish content" is extremely important—and delicate. But let them see it now, even in this rough form; then we'll discuss, argue, hash it through. Then I'll write a dozen more drafts if I have to.

Aha, guess what, dear deus ex machina? The play is turned down. Cold. What's the difference why? And it continues to be true: your heart doesn't burst, it just feels as if it did. And your head doesn't stop (that's the most exhausting), no matter what: drinking, sleeping pills, reading, movies.

Your head, your head. It tries stubbornly for awareness, even in the midst of any kind of blur you're tossing at it. You try to remember all the things you've read about writers going stale —having to rest, replenish. Sure, like depleted soil. Nature orders it.

Nature? Her survival whip started to lash at me. Suddenly—as in the phony vigor and rallying that sometimes fevers the patient with strength just before he dies—I start trying anything I can think of. A letter to that top agent who was in on the production of my play at the Cleveland Play House: Remember me?—if so, want to read my too-long, very rough draft of a new play?—plus eight TV scripts?

While I wait for an answer, I go on. Get in touch with a new theater group in Cleveland that's putting on "strong, different plays" (I'd met the director a few times); offer and send—when he says yes eagerly—two short plays for a possible "meaningful evening" in theater. They're old, but they were prizewinners nationally at one time—too controversial in those years for TV production (I'd adapted them to the stage long ago).

But the Old Lady can be a real bitch of a liar. Nothing worked for the struggling patient. The agent: Don't send the play; too long in its present form for me to read now. (Intellectually, I knew that meant: Cut and edit right, then possibly I'll read it. Emotionally, it was a rejection.) Same agent, after a three-week silence: No to these scripts, but our TV department thinks you are very talented, and should you be in New York would be glad to meet with you. (My head knows that the market is very different these days, and that the key words are "very talented." But emotionally? Another rejection.)

The local theater: So sorry, not for us. (Their next production was one of the "theater-of-cruelty" plays which had had an extremely successful run Off Broadway. The direct opposite of my kind of writing.)

I hole in—no people—the way I've always done when I'm scared about writing, depressed. She used to un-hole me; gently, or sternly. This time, I'm badly scared. That creative death looks and smells for real now: will the actual, physical death *have* to come? But it's the writer-death that haunts me, whatever I try to do. (A new book? Why? How? You're finished.)

● ● ●

It haunts me today, as I look at the other packing cases Helen had insisted I fill—and try to figure out the right comparison book to prove something very important: can old promises kept burn bright enough to light up a new one?

The two cases full of the first novel-makings? Wrong god from a machine to look for here: not one word of this book had had to be rewritten. All was hurrah for the writer who had copped the country's top literary award.

Another case: yep, there sat the right deus ex machina, grinning slyly. I dug into the history of the crashing failure of a book—the legendary second-novel disaster. Pulled out piece after piece. And started remembering much that I hadn't thought of in years. The fear, the weeping—and that beautiful guy, Aswell, so involved in this book. Helen? Part of the time in the hospital—then convalescing at home.

As I counted the different versions I'd had to write of that novel,

I thought: But this did come alive. *Can* old promises be renewed? Perhaps in this way of comparison—because, after all the despair, here were the galleys, copies of the actual book—hardback, paperback, French translation.

While I scanned those galleys, I thought of the thinking Helen-invent for final typescript: she'd fix paper and brand-new carbon—a whole boxful—for the three copies, stack them like a careful hill of threes; the first in one direction, the next pointed the other way, and so on up. All I had to do was reach and type. Then, when I was almost through the pile, she'd take what I'd typed and remove the carbon, sort the copies, prepare the next batch of threes for me to continue typing without having to monkey with mechanical stuff. That wonderful believer—who always promised that if you worked hard enough any star could be touched.

Go on, recreate that promise. Examine the proof of how the dream of that second novel came out of its coma, and lived.

• • •

October 1947: The new editor at Harper's most eager to read the manuscript of your novel, "Sing at My Wake"—please rush.

Note: Edward C. Aswell, my editor at Harper's, had left for McGraw-Hill by then. My contract gave first yes or no on the next book to publisher, not editor, of course.

Longer note on a different next book. Also on the kind of man Ed was. While he was still at Harper's, I sent him a novel titled "The Long Moment." It was a complete rewrite of a kind of book I'd written in 1930, a kid just out of high school, and called at that time: "Now Comes the Black." Changing neighborhoods—white into Negro—I'd lived in two of them.

Ed asked me to come to New York; told me, with his infinite kindness, that the book was immature, poorly written. That the novel to follow *Wasteland* should be a fine book—for my sake as a writer. That he knew I had many good books in me. To take my time—not panic because of the success of my first novel.

Which is exactly what I'd done. Panicked—and dug out an old carbon and notes (all I had left of that youthful hash). I came back to the hotel from Ed's office, said to Helen in a fury of tears: "Christ, what a coward I've turned into! Why did I do that?" Helen: "You know why, coward-*toi*. Let's go home. You're so lucky—Ed's a great

editor, who loves fine writing, who believes in you. Just as much
as I do. (Smiled.) Now—I have a question, dear: got another book
in your head?''
    Yes, I did. The people and story of *Sing* had been in me for years.
The day after we got back from New York, I began to outline a new
novel.
    Helen had that carbon typescript of "Now Comes the Black"
bound. "For your archives, writer dear. And, you know, you're going to rewrite this novel the right way some day. So a lot of students will want to see this young-Jo version. And please keep 'The
Long Moment.' They'll also want to study that.'' Me: "You crazy
dreamer. Archives—Jesus!'' She (calmly): "Wait and see, scoffer.''

    November 1947: Harper editor, to this effect: The book is
lousy...sorry...delighted to work with you on a new project.
Me: "My God.'' Helen (calmly): "He's crazy. I read that book—
it's good.'' Me: "You're not an editor!'' Helen: "No, I'm not. That's
why you're going to phone Ed.'' Me: "Why? He'll probably say
the same horrible...Jesus, that letter certainly made me a punk.
Listen, what's the use? All right, I'll write Ed...'' Helen (dialing
operator): "As soon as I get through to him, I'll hand you the
phone.'' Me: "Helen! What'll I do? I just want to die—that's all.''
Helen: "You won't. You've got a book to rewrite.''
    Read on—letters. Ed was "greatly excited at the prospect of see-
ing your new book.'' Another: one of his most hardboiled readers
had been told to drop everything and sit down with the manuscript.
"She has no patience with pretenders who don't know how to write,
but she has immense respect for those who do. You have commanded her respect.'' And he was about to read the manuscript.
    Helen: "See? I don't care how hard you have to work. 'You have
commanded her respect.' '' Me: "I'll never be able to rewrite that
book. I worked my guts out in it.'' Helen: "Yes, you will.''

    In December, a long letter from Ed—definitive criticism, almost
four pages of it. Ending with:

> ...perhaps to you not too cheerful a letter. But the chief feel-
> ing is, as I said at the beginning, that I believe you do have
> in this manuscript the makings of a good novel. Therefore, the
> letter is engendered by hope. But I don't minimize—nor, I

think, do you—the amount of hard work that still lies ahead of you. I am genuinely interested in this...

Helen: "What a tremendous editor. That's *great* criticism. And what a sensitive, perceptive, lovely man." Me: "Listen! Lovely or not, I'm going to have to write that whole goddam book over. From scratch—that's obvious. I can't! I'm too tired." Helen: "You'll be much more tired unless you start. And by the way, you don't have to take every word of Ed's as gospel. Study his report. But figure out your ideas, too. You respect him? He respects you. And *you* respect you! Even though you don't think you do, right now."

Kissed me, took my hand and led me through the kitchen to the stairs up to my place (servants' quarters for some once-upon-a-time rich family), pushed me up the first step. On South Woodland, those quarters—over the garage—were perfect for a writer: bedroom, workroom, private bath, view of treetops and sky.

It was awful. But I started. The next day, I went another inch. And by the first days of 1948, I was at it in earnest, working toward a completely rewritten outline. From Ed, words to hearten: "Your letter gladdened my heart. We shall work together again—and that's why."

On March 16:

> ...and I have carefully read the revised opening chapters of your novel; it seems to me, Jo, that you are on the right track. I find very little in these 98 pages to question...I am pleased with this new beginning and you certainly ought to be, too. I want very much to see more, and I leave it to you whether that will be when the whole revised draft is finished or at some point before that. It will depend, I suppose, on whether you feel I can help you by reading parts of the book as it goes along... My very best to you, Jo—and cheer up! You are going to pull this off yet, and don't let anybody tell you differently.

Helen: "Amen, *toi.* Go write me a book."

April, May, June, July: The dafs and the tulips bloomed. I dusted the roses, planted those Bermuda onions around them—and was able to laugh at the idea. The Western Sunset lilies along the fence opened, and the hummingbirds came. In early August there were cukes hanging all over that cyclone fence, and tomatoes were ripening.

Mid-August 1948: Finished. Telegram from Ed—so pleased. Then a letter, begging patience—just back from vacation, behind in his work, but "no dust will gather on this manuscript, I assure you." Followed a month of anxiety. But Helen and the gardening took care of the author.

September 16: No, not yet:

> ...and the revision shows definite improvement. But there is still a great deal more work that needs to be done on it before you will have a book here...I think you first have to be very clear in your own mind what it is you are trying to say in this book...Now, don't be discouraged, Jo. You are trying to do a hard thing. A second book is always harder than the first and it is harder still if the first is very successful...Again, and I underscore the point, don't attempt too much. Nobody can help you much in this. It is something that you, and you alone, must work out for yourself...I feel, as I have all along, that there is a book in this material. I'll help you to the fullest possible extent, but please don't have exaggerated ideas about what an editor can do. He is only a guinea pig through whom you can make a preliminary test of your success in communicating whatever it is...

Then came plenty of detailed criticism. And me: "Jesus, I can't, I can't! He wants another new book." Helen: "That's not so. Please study Ed's letter and his associate's report. Dear, he wants a *fine* book. But fight them on those things you want. You're the writer." Me: "Some writer!" Helen: "Ruthie, that man respects you. Your talent. Or he wouldn't spend all this time and thought on you." Me: "I'm tired." Helen: "I know, dear. How about hoeing the devil out of the rose bed? That'll help."

By November, I'd started another rewrite. Of course. What else was there to do? Do you throw pieces of yourself out?

Nineteen forty-nine: Helen was in the hospital—the sympathectomy—when I finished the rewrite. Nights, mainly—after I'd come from the hospital visit. When she came home, I was reading proof on final typescript. She wanted very much to help with catching typos; I let her, hoping she could forget some of the pain that way.

The revision was sent to New York in July 1949. I was damn tired, inside and out, but the new season was in full swing; I went out with the rake and hoe, for my convalescence, while Helen tried for hers in the house and on the patio.

August: I drove her to the Cape for a different kind of convalescence—still in pain and weak, but the doctor had given his permission. An uncle paid for the trip (and we even had a lovely day with Martin, in summer camp close by).

Dig deeper in this same case. There's another Poem lying inside: swimming and then sitting on the beach in Provincetown, while her friend rests in the cool house across Commercial Street, it happens. The writer's mind opens again. What a marvelous feeling!—that first slash of a new piece of work in your head.

I wipe the water from my hands, take up the pad of paper and pencil (in a beach bag now, instead of in a tool basket at home). And the play bursts out. All of a sudden, three characters. Part of the plot. Obviously, it's all been hiding in me for years.

By the time I got into the house, I was full of fragments of scenes, a possible second-act curtain. Helen smiled and smiled. "Oh, darling, how I love to be in on the beginning of a new piece of work. And a play! Do you have a title yet?" Me: " 'The Long Moment.' (Grinned.) Borrowed from a novel by Jo Sinclair that was dead wrong. If Bach and Vivaldi can borrow from themselves, me too!" She: "For Karamu?"

Of course. It was a play about Negroes, for Negroes, and I'd written about them in short stories (as well as in that first immature novel); grown up and lived with plenty of them—in three different neighborhoods. Two good friends were Negro—including my dear, sick Virginia. Some of my favorite loves in writing?—Richard Wright, Langston Hughes, Countee Cullen. One of the first stories I'd had

published told of an old Negro and an old Jew in a street based on
my childhood area of town. (I didn't get paid for it, no, but five
anthologies picked it up—over the years.)

As for Karamu House—that social settlement in Cleveland that
had become nationally famous for its theater and arts—I'd wanted
for a long time to write for those talented, unpaid actors, many of
them good as professionals. The closest I'd got was an article about
the House, published in a magazine called *Common Ground*—which
had brought me into warm contact with the directors.

The play grew, along with Helen's strength. By the time we left
the Cape, I had a good working outline and several scenes blocked
out. On the way home, Helen: "I've got my eye on Broadway.
Karamu can give you a good showcase production." Me: "Hey, you
nut, are you starting with the stars again?'" Helen: "I'll never stop."

A few weeks over the garage, and a first draft is completed.
Helen: "*Toi*, this reads extremely well. And you a novelist who
writes too much! There's a lot of drama, suspense. The kid's very
appealing. But isn't Molly a little didactic? People will resent her,
I think. Especially men." Me: "I'll see when I rewrite." She: "Let
me read you this one long speech. Out loud. Dear, a play tastes
so different when it's talked. The director's going to fight you on
at least this one speech of Molly's. It *is* a speech, dear." Me: "What
director?" Helen: "Leave that to your agent?" Me (laughing): "Set
your own commission." Helen: "I have. Four seats to opening
night." Me: "As Ma would say: you—are—crazy."

And the novel? It's September, and here comes a letter. Damn,
damn! But:

> . . .and so I think the book is not yet ready to go to press.
> And, looking at the matter from your own point of view as
> an author, I think you would be well advised to have one fi-
> nal go at the manuscript to revise it in the light of certain sug-
> gestions I want to lay before you. Our combined opinion is
> that in this draft you have improved the book immensely but
> that further improvement is still possible and even necessary
> to make it the fine book which it ought to be and a worthy
> successor of *Wasteland*. What you have already accomplished
> here seems to me so important and so encouraging that what
> still remains to be done seems minor indeed in comparison.
> And I shall say one thing further and I believe it is the thing

you want most to hear: that if after considering our sugges-
tions, you feel in accord with them and are prepared to make
them your own and carry through the final revision which they
indicate, just drop me a word to that effect and I shall be ready
at that point to offer you a contract for publication without waiting for the final revision to be done.

Helen: "Ruthie! Congratulations. Oh, that beautiful man. I love
him." Me (sort of dazed): "I do, too. He knows what this contract
means to me. Proof—finally." She: "He knows a great deal about
you." Me: "Helen, why am I always so unsure of my writing!" She:
"Dear, I think you're afraid your readers won't get the point. You
don't trust them enough." Me: "Trust them, or me? (Heartsick.)
What the hell's the matter with me? It *must* be the Me who's getting in the way of the writer." Helen (wry-gentle): "Did I do such
a lousy job on you, *toi*?" Me: "No! I just continue to be such a damn
mess." Helen (quietly): "Going upstairs to work?" Me: "Damn it,
I'm sick of this book. Do you realize how much more work's involved?" Helen: "Yes. But with a contract offer. Did I tell you we're
having biscuits and shrimp salad for dinner? Special for a rewrite
day."

After a minute, I laughed. Went up and started the revision (saying to myself: Dear Lord, kind Lord, gracious Lord!).

The contract came, plus: "All my very best to you, Jo. I'm very
happy about this."

Helen: "So am I! How's the second draft of the play coming?"
Me: "By itself—nights. Days, I'm a crappin' novelist." Helen: "What
a marvelous schizophrenic life. Your psychiatrist is thrilled, dear."

The publisher's check came. I wasn't broke yet—gave Ma a wad
of extra money with the cukes and tomatoes I brought in. And wrote
and wrote on the revision. The play did sort of write itself.

November: Finished the third draft of the play around three one
morning. Had Virginia check it from "a Negro viewpoint." And
Grace, from "a sociology-universal viewpoint." Passed both—and
neither one of those women would phony up a test like that. Talked
to the Karamu directors (phone), sent them a copy of the play. Helen
had a lot more copies made (Mort's office—for free), and started a
whole nutty battery of queries going by mail—and I thought she
had really gone crazy when she got the addresses of actors for pos-

sible lead roles (Jose Ferrer was one). I shrugged. I had a novel to finish, said with a laugh: "Hey, agent, let me know when the Theater Guild wants in."

Helen: "You'll be the first one I tell, dear. What's with the book?" Me: "About another week. Then that damn typing again." She: "Let me know when to start stacking paper and carbon."

December 8, 1949: My dear Ed handed me another sock in the jaw—gentle, but it hurt:

> ...much impressed by the job you have done. Even though you did not go down the line and accept all of our suggestions, the general effect of the book in its present form is now much improved, and your theme greatly clarified...worried about the length. A book of 511 MS pages will almost inevitably have to be over-priced, and I am afraid that a high price will present a serious handicap to adequate sales...I intend to take the MS home with me and spend several days in seclusion with it...discover ways to shorten or condense it somewhat. Be of good heart, and do not allow yourself to be in any degree troubled. This is a book we are both going to be proud of.

Me: "God damn it!" Helen: "Stop hollering. Wait for the man to do his job. He wants a fine book. So do you."

• • •

Dig a little deeper, machine god with the sly grin; pull some more stuff onstage for that proof I need so desperately today. This far down, the case holds two contracts: one from McGraw-Hill (fifteen-hundred-dollar advance), the other from the Cleveland Play House. Quite a lesson there, too: I got a hundred dollars—from that repertory theatre; and even though it's one of the oldest and best in the country, the red ink predominates.

Yep, Karamu had turned down "The Long Moment." Helen (angry, cold): "That polite crap is for the birds. I don't know if they're afraid to put it on because of their stuffed-shirt board—or if it's just too controversial for scared white directors. And don't stand there with the word *rejection* smeared all over your poor eyes!

This is not going to stay a rejection. Take that from me.''

The packing case turns up a lot more: the correspondence with Audrey Wood. Yes, Helen picked up the phone and called one of the top play agents in New York (Tennessee Williams, among other clients). To my amazement, Miss Wood did indeed want to see a copy of Jo Sinclair's (author of *Wasteland*) play, if the Cleveland Play House was producing it. And the case holds extra newspaper clippings of the first announcements and publicity: pix of playwright, director, actors; the reviews.

I sit there remembering the promiser, the keeper of promises, the believer. Helen: ''To hell with Karamu. I happen to know a few people at the Play House. They're always looking for good scripts—if you can get to them. Let's see. Mac ought to direct this—he hasn't had a new and different script for a long time.'' She meant McConnell, the head of the theater. Me: ''Are you completely nuts?''

So the Play House took it. And Mac directed—wanted to. Helen: ''And it's time we buried that word *rejection* that throws you for such a loop. It's a long, long time since your emotions told you that your father and the world rejected you. Or did I *really* do such a lousy job on you?''

Me (and I had to laugh): ''The job wasn't lousy. The patient just continues to have big fat spurts of needing crutches. Hey, the Karamu big shots are going to be sore, I'll bet.'' Helen: ''I'll bet! Especially when Mac borrows some of their actors. Because the Play House just ain't integrated yet—remember? And maybe you'll help break *that* little barrier.''

• • •

Read on: *The Long Moment*, a play by Jo Sinclair. World premiere. Opening April 5, 1950, Brooks Theater of the Cleveland Play House (their small experimental stage).

Read on into the next year: A three-night stand at the Saint Martin's Little Theater, Harlem (Audrey Wood, agent). A one-night stand at Fellowship House, Cincinnati (the college gal who played Molly in Cleveland went back to her hometown with her social worker's degree, and got them to put on the play, she doing the role again). ''It was a packed house, Jo! Enclosed, reviews.''

Raves. Helen pasted them into the scrapbook, along with the local publicity, and Brooks Atkinson's review. Yes, he of the *New*

York Times. A fluke: he was touring repertory theaters, and was here during the run.

Read on. From the *Call and Post* (local Negro weekly): "Theatrical Circles Hum with Talk of Inter-Racial Play at Cleveland Play House. Theater Uses Mixed Cast in Sinclair Play...This is the first play to be produced at the Play House using Negroes in major roles."

The *Cleveland Press* (afternoon daily): "Jo Sinclair's highly controversial play will be greeted tomorrow evening by an entirely sold-out house. In fact, there is a waiting list from there to downtown. Author Sinclair, whose real name is Ruth Seid, several years ago won the Harper Prize Award of $10,000 with her first novel, *Wasteland*. Her second is scheduled for publishing this year."

Young Reporter: "Why do you use a pseudonym for writing?" Me: "When I first started trying to sell my short stories, I wanted to make *Esquire*. At that time, they were taking stories only by men. I thought of the Jo—it would fit a man or a woman—and the Sinclair sounded good. So, ever since, I've been using that name." YR: "Did you make *Esquire*?" Me: "Twice. And three articles sold to *Ken*, two stories to *Coronet*. All three were owned by the same outfit." YR: "Fascinating!" Helen: "And true. Reputation established slightly, you go on with the name." (Her cocked eyebrow said to me: See?—he didn't even flicker when you said Jo would fit a man or a woman. Page Freud!)

Okay. It's opening night. Audrey Wood's in town. So's Herman Shumlin, producer and director; Audrey had given him a script to read, and he was interested enough to fly in to see how a showcase production came off. (And, feeling unreal, I remembered kid-Ruth reading his name as director in all those library versions of Hellman plays.)

Unreal night, altogether. I remember only spots: lots of applause, both my families there, all my friends; author and director finally being dragged onstage for bows. Sitting in a downtown bar with Audrey, Helen and Mort, and Fannie—waiting for the morning paper.

Fannie (so happy): "Just like New York!" Not exactly. First review (dean of Cleveland reviewers—the one Audrey paid most attention to): "Jo Sinclair has a great deal to learn about playwriting, but she has an instinctive sense of drama...inexpert and faltering in terms of theater, and strong and moving in terms of human

character and conflict. I was genuinely stirred by the play..."
Audrey: "Not bad, for a first play. Let's see what I can do in
New York. But plenty of rewrite and hard work, Jo." Helen (laughing): "You've got the right customer. She's rewritten this latest novel
for Ed Aswell four times." Audrey: "Good experience for theater!"

Both afternoon papers had more or less the same type of
reviews. I was really happy about the editorial in the Negro weekly: "With the opening of this play, a new chapter will be written
in race relations in Cleveland...Bringing together a cast of inter-
racial proportions signals an approach bordering on the theme of
'practicing what we preach'...And the turn from use of dialect and
casting of stereotyped impressions of Negroes..."

Helen: "Ah, that really pleases you." She always knew. Did
anyone else? Even Fannie, who loved me dearly: "My sister's a big
shot again! Wait'll Hollywood buys this! Let it get to Broadway!"

It never got to Broadway. See Brooks Atkinson, the *Times* of May
22, 1950:

> ...her first play. She is not alone in hoping that it will not be
> her last...In a makeshift evening of playwriting, she pokes
> into several of the darkest corners of race relations...And in-
> teresting and vivid situation, with many ramifications. But, un-
> fortunately, *The Long Moment* is rough and strained
> apprentice-work, and seldom achieves the flow and unity of
> a work of art...This does not alter the fact that Miss Sinclair
> has stuck a pin into a sensitive area of American life...

Helen: "Damn him. There goes a New York production." Me:
"I don't care. Honest. It was such an exciting, marvelous...And
hey, babe, I made the *New York Times!*"

And the novel? On and on and on. Weeks, months, correspondence, minor revision over and over. Then!—end of nightmare, September 28:

> ...So you can now relax, dear Jo. It seems to all of us here
> that you have done a really remarkable job of final revision
> ...Congratulations!...Within the next few days the manu-
> script will be ready to go into the works, which means that
> it won't be too long now before you will be getting proofs...

Me: "My God, is it possible?" Helen: "*My* congratulations, dear. And that's the understatement of the year. I saw you do it." Me (rather dazed): "You said 'I promise you.' Do you *ever* break a promise?" Helen: "Never." Oh, blessed laughter of relief.

Galleys—in December. They come in two sets, every morning, special delivery, to be checked and corrected, sent back as quickly as possible (author keeps one set). Helen sometimes reads aloud from the galley, I check the manuscript—with which I'm so familiar; she fixes errors on both sets of proof—in case we need my set for page proof. Sometimes I read aloud, from manuscript, for a change of pace.

There's one of the real excitements of writing: reading galleys on a book soon to be tossed at the world. It's not like theater excitement, at all. This is sort of a quiet feeling, a kind of respite-time. Though it never lasts too long before you start jittering about the next book. The next? My God, can I ever write another book!

Didn't take too long—and then Helen (coolly): "What are you waiting for? Go out and feed the birds and squirrels. Walk. Got your pad and pencils?"

Yes—in my jacket pocket. She knew, all right. How brief the respite of stillness between books. How the anxiety, the compulsion, the mixed longing and fear start again—and mount. No peace. It's as if that writing, that "proving" over and over again that you can, is the only meaning you've found for yourself in life. The only real safety.

I sloshed through remnants of snow after filling the feeders and putting peanuts down for the squirrels and jays. Spring was in the air. I could smell it, see the first bits of green at the base of shrubs. We were still on South Woodland—though the property in the country had been bought, and the preliminary steps of building had begun.

When I came in, Helen said: "Coffee? That was a nice long bird-feeding. (She poured.) Story, play, novel?" Me: "Novel. Not much yet. A few of the people. One kind of high point—but pretty shadowy yet." She: "Not bad, for one tour. (Smile.) Want to drive out to the new place after lunch and walk around—think about your new book? Plan where you'll transplant the lilacs, mock orange, roses?"

Dig deeper. Publication day—local reviews, raves; national reviews, mixed. Me (grimly): "Doesn't look like the smash of the year, does it? Where's that damn, son-of-a-bitching great book I keep feeling in my guts! And I'm practically broke—already." Helen: "Pardon me for not weeping. You want to write literature? Get used to your attic! (Laughing.) How about a few short stories—for dirty money? Be glad to turn agent again, *toi*. Now that the professional thinks the market can't take tears."

Yes, here are the letters from Audrey (stepping out in all honesty, after quite a few tries): no possible movie sale for *Sing*; this year, the market (including magazines) is sure death on anything "downbeat."

But here's a letter from Ed:

> . . . and we have just succeeded in placing the French rights with *Editions de Flore*, dear Jo. True, the advance is small, as French advances are apt to be: $200 against royalties of 8% on the first 10,000 . . .

Helen: "Ruthie, how wonderful—I'll read it in my favorite language! (Laughing—*her* laugh.) Two books translated into French. That first novel into seven languages. Not bad for a 'ghetto kid who never went to college.' " So, of course, I laughed, too.

Almost at the bottom of the case—dear Ed, friend-editor:

> Congratulations on Mrs. Buchman's sale of the short story to the *Saturday Evening Post*. Let's hope it is only the beginning, for I know very well that you must be worried about money. No doubt it is very fine to give writers the hackneyed advice that the proper way to write is to live in a garret and starve to death. Certainly some very fine books have been written under those conditions, yet I wouldn't call such conditions ideal, and I don't believe there is any necessary connection between starvation and great literature. I am reminded of an anecdote that is told about Sinclair Lewis when he was a student at Yale. He went to Professor Tinker and confided that he had an ambition to write.
>
> Said Tinker, "Then you will starve to death." Lewis replied, "I don't care if I do." "In that case," said Tinker, "you will succeed."

Helen: "I absolutely love that man. Honey, let's send him a snapshot of your awful garret—where you're starving to death!"

● ● ●

I pile everything back into the case, feeling very tired. On the way down the stairs, I think: *Was* that a kind of proof? I did get *Sing* rewritten right, published—though I was positive I never would. And a play written, produced. (Ah, but a great editor was still around. And a great, stubborn, brainy believer and promiser.)

I sit in my chair; next to me, on the record cabinet, are the two journals, the packet of poems. The next book. Possible?

Uh uh, don't! What would be the point of crying? She isn't here—and this is the wrong chair. All those other smashing blows? I'd be sitting in that chair next to the leather table in the living room (phone on it). Shannon, South Woodland, here—only the chair was re-covered yellow in this house, and the springs finally tied. It was always sort of my chair; it's straight, and *fits*—to read, to talk. And to read the mail—including rejections. Helen named it—very tenderly—"the crying chair."

I wasn't crying: I was staring at the thick wad of pages I'd labeled the Journal of Life. And I had a sudden memory of a July day, the first summer in this house. Very hot afternoon. I was cultivating—with that one-wheel rotohoe she'd found at the Farm Bureau.

Helen and the kids were still discovering things about the place: certain wildflowers, the different kinds of birds and bugs, the toads, garden snakes, the newly arrived frogs and turtles.

After a while, they brought over a mason jar, with several flying insects (I was working on the baby limas): did I recognize this bug?

No. But not even Helen had; she who knew so much about nature's creatures. Martin had caught the bugs, put them into the jar, carefully covered the open top with wax paper (holes for air). We all studied one of them, at the bottom of the jar: pink head—a dot in the middle; long body, very narrow rim of gray, lots of feelers.

Helen: "We must identify them. Got to know our thousand tenants!" Me: "Or charge them double rent."

Much giggling from the kids. Helen's eyebrows up, until I said: "All right, let's go. I know what you want."

We all piled into my car, locking the dogs in the house, in

separate rooms; and I drove us to the Garden Center, in Cleveland. And the mysterious tenants? Fireflies! By daylight, no flaring torches, of course; an who ever notices an unflaming firefly? Lord, we laughed. So did the Garden Center expert. Helen told her how beautiful her suggestion of Sargent crabs had turned out—and this pleased her very much. Then, for a while, we wandered in the Fine Arts Gardens, looking at the gorgeous seasonal trees and bloom, at the swans and mallard and goldfish in the lagoon. Looked up, north, at our lovely Art Museum; looked up, east, at Severance Hall (the boy was planning to audition soon for Robert Shaw's choral group, which sang with the Cleveland Orchestra).

On the way home, I treated: "To make us all feel not quite so dumb—about daylight fireflies." Double-dip ice cream cones. And we licked and ate and laughed; and they talked, all the hour's trip home. There, the boy released our fireflies.

That evening, we sat on the porch in darkness; Helen had turned off even the lights in the house. Watched the air delicately afire, split seconds of firefly flash, off and on, off and on—everywhere we looked. Barbie said, "Oh, Mother, how beautiful." And went to kiss Helen. Martin: "Isn't it *spectacular*, Pooh?" Mort (laughing): "Anybody recognize the ex-prisoners?"

● ● ●

The memory went away. Helen stayed.

Very abruptly, I went to my desk, took out pads; large for outline, small for notes. Brought the two journals, the packet of poems.

At the large bookcase-cabinet that Mort had built for my South Woodland servants' quarters, getting a fresh pack of cigarettes— turning, lighting up—I stared at my desk. Vases and pitchers crammed with sharpened pencils, with pens. Everything looked ready for the start of a book. Was I?

Helen had planned that desk like a real green thumb. It's in the east-south corner of my room, a four-window corner: I can see the perennial bed and the slope, the pond, to my right; in front of me at the desk, the orchard and cemetery and fruit trees and the seasonal east groundhogs—and her tree. A desk specially carpentered and attached to the walls by the Amish workers who had built our two fireplaces. Done to her careful figures and rough drawings, translated by the architect. She had "measured" me sitting down, for both levels: the lower, for the typewriter space; and the top level, on which I write first drafts in notebooks. That top level flows, west, a section of beautiful wood over five feet long and almost two and a half feet deep—where notes can be spread out for chapters and left for days, where paper can be stacked for a final typescript.

The desk is beautiful. So's the whole creative dream she believed in and created this desk for. Dreams. Fireflies and laughter.

Thinking, as I came back to that desk: Is there enough of my heart left to write a book about Helen, for Helen?

Sat down, picked up a pencil; all I could think was: No publisher waiting. First time since *Wasteland.*

All right, what *is* waiting? A new season—the only sure thing I know. And a new book to write—the unsurest thing I know.

I looked out, at the tree, at the faint greening of a new season of spring all around it. I started to write.

Levels: Ascent and Descent

The carton of seeds is open on the utility room counter. I always check through my carbon copy to make sure the entire order has been filled. Then I let the packets air in the open carton, until planting time. Once I said to Helen: "Funny. Dill is the only seed I know that smells like the crop-to-be, right in the closed envelope." She: "Yes—wonderful! And the crop is so beautiful. No wonder you've taken to using it with flowers in vases."

But of course it's essentially for dill pickles. I loved Helen's kind, even before I raised most of the makings myself. Out here, they were even better. I'd pick a half bushel of our tiny, perfect pickles, and cut large bunches of young dill; Helen would start the canning within an hour. Makes a difference—that timing.

The dill smell is bombarding me today. Hurts. I left quickly, took the packets of pansy and viola seed out to the garage; they'll go in soon—they like cool weather. Helen's new seed every spring: two, this season. Yes, you carry on rituals.

In the living room, today, another one. The pussy willows and forsythia I'd brought in weeks ago, to force. Plenty of great branches for my friend, too; I cart them into town in a bucket of water. And, these years, I'm taking in vegetables and flowers again.

I kept thinking of those rituals as I went out. It was forty degrees, sunny. Nice—but the dill smell was still in me deep, haunting. I could not go to the tree right away.

This time of year is between-seasons: the first green starting, but the birds still to be fed. Chippy, yes, but no Johnny yet. All in order. Eternal, permanent. But does the Old Lady know how perilous the heart is? In there, permanence can shatter in a second

79

—for no reason that makes sense.

What *is* permanent? When I fill the peanut butter feeder, the chickadee flies a few inches above the pot and spoon. He's never been afraid of me. Every year, he comes. Yes, a permanence. I have a large piece of beef suet in my basket. The feeder in the chestnut is still pretty full, though well nibbled. The one in the mountain ash was emptied in one gulp this morning by an owl—as I watched inside, trying to write.

I'd never seen an owl get that close to our house. He came first to one of the east locusts, just back of the perennial bed. I hadn't realized they were that big—sitting. Flying, they look bigger. I kept watching; he kept sitting in the tree. Then—so fast—he flew directly to the ash feeder, took the big lump of suet right out, and plunged to the ground with it. Wonderful. He sat there, looking around constantly. Maybe five minutes. He has a great, translucent-looking tail when he's on guard that way.

Then—bang abrupt again—he took the suet in his claws, flew away. To the sycamore near the east go-down—for a second; then away toward the cemetery. What *is* permanent?

I replace the owl's snitch, and remember the Leonard Baskin owl on the Smith campus—when Eric and I biked all through there. I love that bronze sculpture. (First time in the country, Helen—about the owl's cry, so new to me: "Listen. He's saying: 'Who cooks for you-all?' Darling, can't you *hear* those words? Tune in your new country ears.")

A Downy comes to nibble at the replacement-suet. Two cardinals are in the east crab, waiting for me to fill the seed feeders and beat it. All right, kids, I'm leaving. Tour the joint? The dill smell's gone out of me, so I start with the Helen-tree.

It seems to focus the entire property today. I look around; how the place has changed. Like: it's a little too soon, but I can visualize our perennial rye grass blue in great patches with violets. What a stealthy spreader that plant is. To think that I had to bring our first violets from behind the cemetery. Now they're everywhere. They take root like magic—and keep spreading. Mort's mower has probably helped with the seeding. And the wind, the birds.

So changed. Several of the fruit trees have died. I never did learn how to prune dwarf fruit trees, so they grew big as ordinary ones. Of course, we all ran out of time and strength. Mort even stopped spraying the trees, after a while. They're beautiful, anyway—bloom, shape. And groundhogs don't mind wormy apples.

I touch the Helen-tree a second, then walk. Most of this property has been left wild. How right she was. She knew what bird song and sky and wind and snow can do within the spirit. Knew about leaving much of the land to be the property of wildlings. To be owned, in great beautifully shapeless areas, by the skunk cabbage, marsh marigolds, cattails, the goldenrod, and Queen Anne's lace and Indian paintbrush.

A long walk; then I go up on the porch for a sit-down cigarette. It's a bit soon for Mort to bring the furniture down. The last time I was upstairs with my Boston morgue, I brought down the wicker chair and the little, round wood table I've always used out here; and set out some ashtrays.

You can see so much from here—especially now, before the trees have leafed out. Even most of the pond—so glittery in the sun. This porch is screened, all ninety feet of it (to match the length of the perennial bed, she said with a laugh); door out is near Martin's bedroom, way west. And you can see a lot from the kitchen windows right back of my chair, and from the huge living-room window. "This is really our front yard," she said.

The regular front door, facing the road, was rarely used. Almost everybody still comes into our house the garage way, right into the utility room. And there's another door, at the back wall of the garage, that leads directly to my back hall, bathroom, and bedroom. Utter privacy when I wanted it—come and go as you like, without having to use the regular house doors; that was Helen, oh yes. We'd open the front door summers, for air. And to stand and look out at the planter, at the morning glory rising out of the earth there.

It took me a couple of seasons to come up with that idea: train the vines (which Heavenly Blue seedlings turn into) up on tiny stakes, and then onto the green garden tie I'd staple all over the solid area of redwood wall north of the two small side living-room windows—those green ropes carefully looped, as I tried to visualize where the vines would leaf out and the hundreds of glories bloom.

I skipped three years of putting in that mass of blue-blue glories after her death. But then, suddenly, I needed it again. Last year, that wall of blue was breathtaking, every morning.

And the front yard? It's in perennial rye now, and Mort cuts it, but the first eight years or so, I had the main farm out there—

between the three-birch and the line of maple trees I'd planted close to the road, but plenty of grass all around it. People (including my blood family) said at first: "Vegetables in the front? Crazy."

Her idea. And a good one. Our private life was definitely at the back. But aside from that, I could've said to those people, did you ever see anything as beautiful as straight rows of vegetables and brown, fluffed-up, weedless earth between green and blossom and fruit?

It was too much, in the long run. No, Helen was no angel; she was overambitious, reached very high, and tried to encompass as much as possible—even with gardens. She (and I went along for quite a while) wanted to grow and taste and look at everything we read about. And I should have been writing part of those days—instead of farming for six hours at a stretch; and, in harvest season evenings, helping to clean vegetables and shell, shuck, cut, freeze, and can—because she got so tired I couldn't bear to walk away.

She fought me: "Go write, damn it!" But I fought her back—and won. And what Ma called the "crazy farm" out front? Beautiful.

But then even I got tired. Though I didn't complain until I saw how exhausted she was getting. I knew her: when finally I hollered about *me*, how tired I was, and where the devil had my writing gone; of course she ordered me to cut down, to farm only on the west side—a few small areas we labeled the "back acres." And we sowed rye grass where the big farm had been. She: "If you ever want to get back, we'll plow it under. After all, rye is green manure. It'll replenish the earth."

I never got back. But I packed the back acres with family favorites. Including plenty of Van Goghs and Russians. I simply stopped raising enough food for five or six families.

I can hear the radio on the hearth (the small sink window is partially open). A Mozart piano concerto. Yes, some things return to permanence. Music went away from me—for too long—but it did come back. I'm so grateful.

Music. Well, a person is a kind of instrument, too. And whatever voice or song lies within is dependent, so often, on a teacher. And, of course, the person-instrument is always different. What fashioned this particular one?—or who? Where was it created?

The second movement of the Mozart. I think: How can an instrument go mute again, after so many years of singing? Her kind of teacher should have left permanence in an ardent student like me. I look around the porch; bare, I can see too much. My eyes pick up the long line of tooth marks on the wood right beneath the east wall of screen. Rags. She used to sit on the glider a lot (often with Helen). Somebody would come around the corner of the house—a stranger who'd been invited to fish, or a new visitor—and Ragsy would fling herself off the glider and bark her head off, bite at the wood as she ran back and forth.

There are similar marks in the living room—the wood baseboard and sill under the big Thermopane window on the north (that matches the one on the south wall). Rags used to sit up in front of that great sheet of double glass, on her broad Sealy bottom, and watch birds, or rabbits. Then a car might pull in, somebody walk toward the house, or a dog come up the driveway—and Rags was demolishing the enemy by barking, biting all up and down the width of that window. The marks are grooved as permanent as the voice: "Ragsy, stop that. Now you be a good dog. That's a friend."

I had to get off the porch. The music was turning into the wrong memory. Very hard to handle, suddenly. Come on, fast!—and keep walking, looking. Okay, gardener, what's to do? Too early to cultivate the perennial bed, or unhill the roses. Too soon to drag out the two rain barrels and roll them up to the right downspouts. Keep going. The asparagus bed. What a mess—never got round to cutting down last year's fern before the snow flattened it. Too busy with a novel rewrite, sure.

As I looked, half planning the coming chores, my heart sank: the recipe-with-the-hearts had rushed into me. She dictated it in bed. The strokes hadn't begun yet, but those rather frequent sicknesses when I learned how to cook were undoubtedly the slow, insidious prelude.

I was helping everywhere I could. It was easy—simply a matter of time, which she had always saved for the writer. The cooking, however, was completely foreign to me; and I had to have blow-by-blow recipes for anything I was to fix for dinner. I wrote them all out, sitting on her bed: in paragraphs, with commas and semicolons.

Helen (tender laugh): "But darling, asparagus is so quick and simple. Do you really need a recipe?" Me: "For everything! Am I a cook?" Later, she looked over my stack. But she drew the hearts only on the directions for cleaning and cooking asparagus. Here and there, all over the sheet, as if saying: Oh, silly beloved scared-in-the-kitchen-too writer. Not to trust yourself with even this?

Why am I mourning her so much today? Is it the new spring? Or this book that's starting to grow in me?

I get over to the bed where I usually plant potatoes. Do I even want to, this year? Mort doesn't care that much, and potatoes take plenty of time away from writing. So why even think about buying seed potatoes? Pattern, ritual, that's why. And she loved home-grown potatoes. Especially the Katahdins, with their "gropplers."

That's her word. It means the little potatoes you grope for, inside the hill of earth piled up around the plant. You gropple for them, said she. The early reds and cobblers never make gropplers. It was Helen (that curious one about everything) who discovered that those tiny potatoes were right under the surface of the hill, waiting to be nipped off, scrubbed, boiled in their jackets.

Come on, come on, keep going. Let her be quiet laughter here, not this rawness of loneliness. Walking fast, I get back to the tree. What a blank stare I'd get from a shrugging world if it heard me say: "Woman into tree, save me?"

Do I really need such a symbol? But I believe in trees. "He who plants a tree loves others besides himself." I believe in that, too. I've planted a lot of trees. Do I still love others? These depressions, this fear about creative death, the awful preoccupation with self—does that mean I don't love others?

Impossible. Like a tree, a Poem is for others. Written only for me, it's worthless. Is it okay to talk to a tree in your head? (The playwright trying out dialogue for size.) Or does that make me a kind of a nut?

Why isn't it okay? said the tree. We're very good friends. I'll ask you something: do you still think she broke the big promise?

She couldn't help it!

True, said the tree. And that was the beautiful but mortal woman. Fighting to stay alive, battling back so many times—no doubt battling also not to break that impossible promise no person has the right to make to another, because nature decrees—

Shut up, I said quietly. To the tree, to me. (No, it's not a play, after all!) But I stand there, remembering. Does my heart still call it a broken promise? My head knows better, but this heart is a poet's heart, too. In Greek tragedy, the enormous promise is broken only by the gods.

I did believe her. It was during all my fear over that second novel. When, finally, I came up with a publishable book, I said to her: "My God, what would I ever do without you? Don't die before I do! Don't do that to me!"

Oh, Helen. Believer in the soothing of hearts so terribly in need. She: "I won't. I promise you."

I leave the tree, pass the dogs' graves, walk the east go-down to the dam: first time since last fall. The pond is clean; no algae yet. Water clear enough to mirror the past, to reflect the greatest thing that woman did for me. Yes, we'll have to call it therapy. Though both of us—especially she—knew she was no psychiatrist.

How important she was to my coming out of that other kind of dying—so different from today's sense of creative death. Oh, she had to lead me—and the entire me struggling like a wild animal to stop her, to stop my own fearful self. Though, in my heart, I didn't want to stop—and she knew it.

The thing about Helen was that she was not afraid to tangle with the soul. Her own, or anybody else's in need. She'd had a lot of spiritual (as well as physical) pain in her life, though I didn't find that out until much later. Nor did I find out for a long time that to really feel other people's pain, it helps a lot to have experienced some yourself.

She also had the kind of daring that imagination and awareness, plus knowledge, can create. Therapy for a talented kid, whose potential was trapped in a kind of awful prison. Stare into this pond and *know* what she gave you.

Helen was not a psychiatrist; no degrees, no official qualifications. But she'd had a lot of courses at college, and had worked closely for a long time with a very astute psychiatrist. She'd studied a great deal in the field—was still reading the current professional papers when I came along. And she knew something: I would never go to an actual psychiatrist, but I needed a doctor desperately.

Tremendous courage; because she also knew, in every detail, how dangerous it was to monkey with a messed-up soul. (And mine was a ghastly confusion of anger, shame, longing to live and to die.) She knew that it could all be pushed into deeper damage—possibly, permanent. But she knew one more thing. That a person like me *would* die—in all ways—if she did not find her real roots in the world and in her art. Person *and* writer had to be freed.

Two things were vitally important: she believed in herself—and in me. And in courage (yes, she knew I had it, too). I found out, much later, that she had asked her psychiatrist-friend if she could and should do it. He: "Yes, if you can take it—you know enough. If she won't go to a doctor, try it. She sounds dangerously ill. Don't hesitate to ask me anything you're in doubt about." (She did, often.)

My psychiatrist was a green thumb on this perilous mission, too. First she made me a friend—lunches, dinners, the kids, Mort; comfortable in the house, in the yard. Comfortable with her—and that was a hell of a big step. Because I was still half-afraid of that direct glance, that open way of talking, the warmth and people-love I did not trust. But she did it the right way. Only after I was able to accept all the friendship and trust in that house—only then did she promise.

She waited me out—and then, when I finally was able to admit that I'd wanted too often to die, and yet, God! how I longed to live the right way, she promised to help me. That promise was not broken. Nor the promise that I would understand myself, my torment of a family and background, my personal world I thought so wrong and real-world-despised. Nor the promise that I would be able to write about what was stifling my entire being.

A rusted instrument, a prisoner, a maimed and dying waif—call it what you like, but put it on record, stage center: she rescued the human being, and helped release the song.

After the therapy started, I came to her every morning at nine. She had already sent Mort and the kids off—breakfast, lunches packed—cleaned the house, phoned her other needys. I never knew what all she'd already done; when I arrived, she was smiling and quiet, completely unencumbered: friend, then doctor at the exactly right moment—when I walked down into her silent, spotless recreation room as a patient.

Tortured patient—crawling inch by inch onto a new, strange level of Self: fearful, fascinated, deeply in pain much of the time; but learning (slowly!) to dig for all the sacs of poison, learning to vomit them up by talking, by beginning to understand.

Hard! For one thing, I was terribly afraid of what would be disclosed to me—and yet I wanted as terribly to know. Ambivalent-me: I fought her, often. So it was all almost impossible, at first. But she helped; she knew some of the sources of the poisons, or suspected their hiding places. It was I who had to find them, to talk—

but a word or a phrase from her, a question, could often set me stumbling in the right direction. After a while. Sometimes. Very hard work. Sweat, silence, a sudden blurt. After a while, tears. But (not that I knew it until long, long after) it was exceedingly hard for her, too. That sensitive woman was completely aware of her patient-friend's hurt and self-disgust and bitter, shamed confusion. Her own pain was her pity for the tortured human being she was forcing out of a maze. And she knew, every moment, how fragile the screen around danger was—how easily it could shatter.

Very strong, that Helen. But so was I; and I fought her almost every inch of the way. Like a cornered ghetto rat, I suppose. Emotionally, I felt she was killing me with these new facts she made me dredge up about myself, family, world I loathed, writing I couldn't get out right. Emotionally, she was my enemy—breaking me to pieces.

Awful period of time. Real levels—most of them the intense hurt and fear of the beginning truth about a Self.

It was a lot like living in one world down there (the past, mainly, and the past of my whole family), then coming up into her kitchen; and then going: my car, the street, the now. Another world, another level of spirit. Often, for hours, I couldn't focus on which was the real world. It helped to phone her (she said never to hesitate to call—day or any hour of the night) when I got scared, away from that downstairs room of battling truths. Mort understood completely; she had assured me of that at once.

Cornered, fighting rat, but I was fighting the wrong enemies—and she was the only one who knew it. The ghetto kid lost. But really won, of course. And a long time after that year or so of therapy, when we had become close friends, and I was at last giving as well as taking, Helen and I were able to laugh together about that ghetto kid label I'd pinned on myself. But I couldn't laugh then—at anything. I had to learn how to cry first; had to learn that weeping was not necessarily weakness, softness (the two things I'd fought all my life), but could be for hope, too.

God, God, what she taught me in those days. Probably only a poem could say it: that it was okay to break any trap of life—you had the right, as a human being. That it was okay to accept help of any kind—in acute need. That you *wanted* to walk out of any prison devised by man or nature. That you could learn how to walk among all the kinds of people outside those walls, head up: you had the right, child of nature and of world.

Sound easy? Wrong. When I say "she taught me" in those days, I'm talking about life out of death. What many call a cliché.

But break that cliché down into all its beautiful complications. You learn the first inch of pride in yourself. You learn how to walk like any human being—then you know how to begin crawling as a writer. You learn to accept the real world, and the trapped love you always had in you for that world you thought you hated. Only then can you write with love about it.

Friend, dearest friend, I say to you now with such love: I wish you didn't have to die.

I walk halfway around the dam, my head clamoring with accusing questions: Is a person un-choked so temporarily? Wrong, wrong! Where did I leave the poetry I felt so intensely after she taught me to free myself?

Because the singing did start. A kind of miracle of communication came—even upstairs, in the actual world, so different from the downstairs harsh, digging communication that was disclosing the past-as-truth.

This happened: my level of today lost its fogginess, became the reality, became un-choked into freedom. That was very slow, but it happened. A rusty instrument did begin to shine rather silvery; the reed was tender-new and sensitive. And the new Self practiced joyously, earnestly, like an eager musician. Often, I'd leave her notes after the daily sessions—when she'd sit me down in the sunny breakfast room with a cup of coffee, and casually go away for a while until I was breathing again. It was her way of creating a bridge of stillness for me, so that I could walk back into today with some comfort. The bridge between worlds; that inner world I had just left, and the one I had to go back into when I left this house.

Ghettos. You crawl out, eventually; and up, slowly, to higher and higher levels. Like so: that house of Helen's was always full of music. Not in my parents' house. We had an old, floor-model, wind-up phonograph that my sister Sadie had bought years back— before she was married—and left for us. Nobody but I played it. At fifteen, sixteen, that's where I stood and wrote Sundays, evenings (before dragging my folding cot out of the closet, and going to bed).

The records at home? A guy named Cantor Rosenblatt singing

"Eli Eli" and "Kol Nidre," and a few Yiddish folk songs. A record with arias by people named Caruso and Galli-Curci, singing stuff called "Rigoletto." Oh, and we had "Beautiful Ohio." I still remember the *feeling* of the music in my body, after I'd wind up the machine and start it, lean on it and write.

Later, after therapy had taught me the magic of wanting to know more about family, roots, generations spanning the ocean, I got my sister to talking. How bright Sadie's eyes became in the aging face as she told me of herself at twenty, going to hear Caruso at the Met, in New York, fifty cents for a Saturday matinee. She talked of herself and my family in Russia, too; and the first ghetto in America— my family in those rotting Brooklyn streets, then in Cleveland. And again, way back to my grandparents in those Russian streets and shacks. And the daily downstairs sessions I'd had with Helen took on added flesh and bone. Strange hearts I once had raged against became familiar, full of a different kind of meaning rooted in the living warmth of why they came and how they worked for bread, and why and how the hardness and fear begin in people.

Ghettos. My God, the songs that came bursting out as I walked into liberated country. More and more complicated ones became easier to sing. The sudden awareness—and it *is* a singing—of how deep a reserve of strength and love I had. Enough for both my families, for friends, for writing, the chores of living. The word *help* in proper perspective: you have enough for so many people, and from the heart now—not from the maimed emotions and their confusion of false motivation for such help you used to give to mother, sisters, kid friends.

Ghettos. They're finally gone, though you'll never, never forget how it was in that other world, on that other level. But when I was living in the house on Shannon, at last—and two years had gone by, and three—the most marvelous rooting occurred. Holidays, for example. Thanksgiving Day, Christmas Eve, and the Day itself. What a rootless ghetto into universals, what an ever-deeper growing downward, too, to match the leap up; down into earth so rich that the flower becomes a perennial. Back each year, no need to replant.

And birthdays? Helen and her family made them laughter, loves, gifts selected with care to fit a particular kind of head, heart, soul. Birthdays in Helen-land were a special cake (you didn't even know you had a favorite), and the foods you have begun to like so much. The ritual birthday dinner became fried shrimp and grits, hot biscuits, tossed salad, and that three-layer dark chocolate cake with mint-chocolate icing—and candles to wish on, of course. The wish? Always the same: Let me write a good book, God, please!

Then you yourself made little rituals to fit the ones she gave you: always do some writing on your birthday, and on New Year's Day. Symbol stuff. Later, I expanded the horizons: on Helen's birthday, some writing, and try to plant something. Same movement of the heart.

Living there? Being there? It was like getting born again. In my own house, "Ruthie's writing" was sort of a laugh; from my father, a shrug like a jeer. In this house, a woman and man and children respected my writing deeply.

She'd pulled it off: rescued a badly disturbed person. Rescued, and much more: opened her to life, the meaning of friendship and love.

I continue walking around the dam. Those two muskrat holes are fresh; Mort better fill them. No frogs yet, or turtles, snakes— too early. I come to the wood dock that Diedrick and Mort and Eric repaired last summer. The water's still winter high, but the dock is clear of it. I walk out to the edge, sit there.

Yes, this is a day to think: That which the earth covers over *must* be forgotten. But will Old Lady Nature do that for me—ever?

I look up at all that house glass reflecting the sun. The Old Lady—Jesus. Sometimes, in flashing sunlight, when grass is very green and flowers in full bloom, a bird flies fast toward the green and color seen through those sunny windows, and smashes itself against the thick glass. It falls to the ground, into the ivy. Sometimes dead. Ah, but sometimes it lies there quivering, blood on its beak; you leave that stunned bird alone, and in a while it flies up. And away—a survivor.

I can see a piece of my room from this dock. I visualize the desk, the makings of a new book. The Journal of Life, the Journal of Death. They'd have to merge—definitely. Become the Journal of a Soul. Wherever I've crashed, blood on my heart, will I fly up again? Do birds call it transfiguration, too?

Still staring at that visualized desk, I think suddenly: Could my Helen-book be, finally, the obituary I missed so bitterly while she floated until the tree was planted and her ashes buried? The real obituary of a woman and the lives she touched and made truly alive? Doesn't an obituary have to contain the living ways and deeds, too? The living past? If thou wouldst know the full loss and anguish a death can create, know first the full riches of the person alive. My head aches. I'm thinking of my books, published—and that last novel, still in limbo. I'm thinking that any publication and prize and citation always seemed twice as wonderful because of her happiness and excitement and pride. It was as if I were writing half for her, sharing it all. Like the gardening. Now I write for me only? Plant and harvest for me only? Impossible. Never did before—once the rusty instrument cleared.

And the new book—has to be written alone, unshared?

No. How can I possibly be alone, writing a book like this?

I walk up the west go-down, and toward my desk. The life and joy and seasons, and even the tears, were both of us. Is the death? That's what I'll have to figure out; and maybe the new book will help me do it.

It's spring, the season of beginning life. And Helen and all her people in this book will be very alive, at first.

Yesterday—Long Ago

I was running out of money; it was the time between my second and third novels. *And* our first real planting seasons in the country—those wondrous years of 1952 and 1953.

Helen had several of my short stories out. And, of course, I'd started on the old money-anxiety cycle (customary between published books)—smack in the middle of all that spring excitement. The wheelbarrow—full of tool baskets and hoe, cultivator, rake— came with me anywhere I gardened, but when I grabbed for the pad and pencil out of a basket, it was for suddenly flashing stuff on the new novel, not notes for short stories and possible quick money.

Isn't that why I started what turned into the farm journal? I knew I should get a job, probably—even though Helen refused to take any money whenever I was broke. But I couldn't bear the idea of going into town every day for meaningless work, away from this independent life as a free-lance writer I'd been given by the gods. So I came up with the idea for a possible column for one of the Cleveland newspapers. Country and town stuff, gardening, writing, my ideas on sky and corn and books. I started the notes, thinking vaguely: Soon as I have something good, I'll get in touch with an editor (I knew several). Have a *salary*.

Those could-be job columns were quick scrawls (and I'd obviously added to them, because there were garden tricks and knowledge it took us several years to learn or test):

Get in such: me in love with garden stuff though I was born and bred in city streets. Stress entire seasonal gamut: nar-

93

cissus and tulips going into poppies and beans, roses, tomatoes. Get in ''permanent'' beds for thrilled new-country folk:
asparagus, rhubarb.

City kid growing potatoes for first time: Mrs. Moody, my
old friend in Shaker Heights (I call her Sarah J, for Jane, and
she loves it, and I love her, and she loves her little old-
fashioned flower garden), begged me to grow them because
we would love those new potatoes with our own peas, in cream
sauce. So I did, and brought her plenty of both. But at home,
we like peas separate—just briefly steamed, then drained and
lots of butter; and the small potatoes boiled in their jackets—
butter, salt, and pepper. Wonderful. Skin fine as silk. And how
about okra as a vegetable (Helen being born in the South,
where it's eaten by black and white alike)? And okra mixed
with corn and beef and all the hundred vegetables for a marvelous soup almost as thick as a stew. Freezes perfectly, too.
Use Helen's recipe?

Another batch of notes:

Detailed stuff on the birds who love to eat sunflower seeds
out of the still-growing heads. Constant flights—constant singing. Me and all the details of brand-new flowers, crops, trees.
The first time I saw a bloom on a tulip tree—and that wonderful squarish leaf. The real delicacy of aspen leaves quivering
in the slightest breeze (exactly like you've read it in books).
The gorgeous white, kind of peeling bark on a triple-trunk
white birch. Describe the pheasant: come spring, almost too
gaudy to believe. And the incredibly fast, low take-off of that
heavy body.

This batch; it must have been an August when I sat down to
rest on the carpenter's bench—because the food crops were starting:

Wouldn't city readers be interested in corn? Hilling the row
against summer storms, or the stalks will fall like nine-pins.
And those really beautiful tassels, silks. The rustling sound
near harvest time—wind music. Stake tomatoes, even though
there's plenty of earth around to let them ramble. Cleaner fruit;
less rot, because they hide under the straw mulch. But pon-

derosa (or beefsteak) tomatoes must be mulched; the heavy, huge fruits would break a stake. Might describe one of our favorite summer sandwiches: Jewish rye with caraway, mayonnaise, slice of ponderosa, slice of Bermuda onion, salt and pepper. Wow!

Another page:

Use only rotenone to dust vegetables—safe for eaters. But you can't dust off a tomato worm. Pick off (*if* you can find the big, cleverly camouflaged bastard), and feel nausea at its sheer ugliness. Step on him—hard—and walk away. The countryside *is* a fight. Used aluminum strips to scare off birds: they go for blueberries, strawberries, cherries; blackbirds and crows uproot the tiny corn seedlings (to get the half-germinated seed, I suppose). What a sight, early in the morning—the whole row of yesterday's delicate light-green seedlings flat and limp. The aluminum strips simply made a nice song in the wind for them to eat by. So Helen researched about the corn, came up with a crow repellent. Got coal tar in it—smells awful—and the black has to wear off your hands. Takes twice as long to do a row, too—seeds stick together in the old coffee can where you've soaked them. But it worked!

As for berries, Helen's wonderful head figured that out. Cheesecloth—by the bolt. Go into detail on wrapping it around the whole blueberry bush, tying carefully so birds can't slip in. Can't do it around a whole cherry tree, though, so we never have any—sweet or sour.

The cheesecloth on strawberries: spread the cloth, pull the bolt along, over each row of matted berries—cut to size of length of row. Use bricks (left over from the house building) to weigh down cheesecloth on both sides of rows. What a Helen-invent! But what hell on the picker's time: you move bricks away on one side of row, toss cloth toward other side. You pick—hours! Then bring cloth back over the wide row, replace bricks—so no bird can sneak under, no wind lift even a bit of it. Gorgeous berries—no bird eats first! End of season: roll up cheesecloth, store (good for several seasons before rains rot it, or winds tear holes).

I would have had pretty mixed-up columns:

When corn is exactly ready to pick, enter the groundhogs. Who eat a lot of those beautiful ears and leave the cob and husks. Thanks! Plant Heavenly Blue morning glory on the feeder stump outside the writer's desk windows. Blooms until first freeze, though the beauty draws the eye away from notebook too often. Note on stump: it's part of a dead tree, about five feet tall, and I found it over the slope, and Martin pounded it into ground. Bark on it, looks like it grew there. For early fall, nail a sunflower head on top, and keep replacing (chipmunks and birds empty *that* dish fast!); for winter, a seed feeder.

Use 5–10–5 fertilizer for vegetables, bone meal for flowers. Best thing is well-rotted manure (for everything), but expensive as hell to have delivered and spread. (We could afford it only once—and, at that, I did the spreading. Saved five bucks.) Watering: don't use outside taps unless there's a prolonged dry spell. Use rain barrels. And we do have heavy dews in the morning, mists at night. Helps a lot. Water costs money. We're poor. Get it?

Freezer (we have biggest and best possible—double door—bought at Farm Bureau—much cheaper): not only is it perfect for all our vegetables, quick jams, extra meats, but for those city things we like and can't buy out here in "goy" territory. The real rye bread and rolls, kosher hot dogs, bagels. Even lox—if you can afford it.

A dog like Rags: outdoors, she leaps like a ball. Sits up and eats cherry tomatoes (loves them): up to beg, down to actually eat—splattering seeds all over the place. No, dachsies don't like tomatoes.

Get in: the lousy market for short stories—more and more mags going under, and less fiction being taken by those left. Plus this one writer's emotions at rejection. Plus this: my sensation when I scan a published story of mine in a mag (but especially a published novel). In print, it always looks different, feels different, than the manuscript version. Better, yes—but they're never "the dream" I wanted to get out of my guts. Funny!

Here's a page I wrote much later:

A possum (God, they're repulsive) comes to the ash. Eats bits of suet which have fallen to the ground. Exciting, in a rather grisly way—first one I've ever seen. Two days later, a raccoon. In broad daylight! That mask of a face—I've seen it only on the road, at night. But all these ugly or charming "people" are a pain in the neck to country lovers without much dough. For example, last week, on Friday, the possum (must have been) stole suet and holder out of the chestnut tree. A dollar fifty for that redwood holder! I looked for more than an hour, but no luck. So Helen came up with a free idea: take a meshed potato sack (five-pound size), fill with a whole beef suet, hang out. Birds eat through the mesh.

So, one winter morning, looking up from my desk work, I saw the possum climbing the ash and reaching for the potato sack (hanging on a bent clothes hanger I'd rigged up). Out I roared, plucking a hoe from the garage wall. We glared at each other, as I poked at her and hollered: "Get down, damn you!" She wouldn't budge for a while, but I won—toppled her off with the hoe, chased her.

When I came in, Helen was standing at my bedroom window, laughing her head off (my hollering had drawn her). "Big, brave mortal. That possum practically thumbed her nose at you.' Me: 'Babe, the more acquainted I get with Old Lady Nature and her jokes, the more I wonder who's going to win.' Helen: 'She will, dear. She always does.''

Last note for a newspaper column that never was:

Royalty check today: $152.38. Six month statement: 459 books sold, 319 returned. God damn it. Is that fair? I worked *years* on that book. Why can't a writer make as decent and regular a living as a carpenter? I work just as hard—and a hell of a lot of evenings and weekends, too.

And this nuance:

Does a carpenter ever get anything to equal what happens to me near the end of typing a final draft of a book in triplicate?

(After the first typescript, then the cutting and editing.) My fingers get what I call psychosomatic. The little ones refuse to reach for the proper keys—and I holler at them in my head, and they do reach—letter usually comes pale, and tummy feels a wave of nausea. Doesn't that alone rate a few bucks regular as a workman's wage? Not to mention the book itself, which ain't easy to create!

Last note because Helen sold "I Choose You" to *Collier's* for eight hundred and fifty dollars and I took a deep breath. (No job necessary!)

ES is now fiction editor there. Used to be at *Today's Woman* (where Helen sold her several stories), and they've had quite a correspondence going ever since. Not with the author—not one word—but between her and my "agent." Cute?

I put the "possible job" in mothballs, but went on making notes; somehow, I was in the midst of a farm and garden journal and I liked the idea.

So—enter a real journal: story sold, I asked Helen what I should give House, instead of the agent's commission she always refuses. She: "No! I'm tired of you spending in one gulp and then starting to curse about money again." Me: "Threat: tell me, or I'll buy the wrong thing." Turned out, then, that she'd longed for one of those burning bushes we had on Shannon. Euonymus alatus: the kind with the beautifully different, corklike bark, and the foliage that turns red in the fall, until the whole bush seems to burn. Then the leaves drop; leaving berries for the birds, of course. So I bought two, because I love e. alatus, too.

Now, into the real journal: the days of a growing season—oh, wonder and glory. They filled and overflowed with trees planted, new vegetables tried out, the stuff to dust, the lilies and poppies and other "talls" to stake, the second planting of beans. . .

How did I ever do all that? Sometimes I was out for five or six hours, at hard, slugging labor that made me fall on my face in bed instead of reading that mounting pile of musts for a writer. But I felt okay about it: the notes for my novel grew longer and more detailed in the tool baskets.

Marvelous. Roots, anywhere I looked. Spiritual roots, in addition to tree and shrub and flower. And I, the eternal searcher for roots—I felt them tugging in my bone, floating like lovely rainbow water lilies in my blood.

But what a physical rooting. We kept all the carbon copies of the seed orders. Always sent in February, because by then the heart is weary of winter. And besides, you get a discount for early ordering. My God, what we ordered to plant, or for Mrs. Marous to raise in her hotbeds for us!

First, though, it's early spring; Helen and I sowed grass everywhere, taking turns at grinding the seed evenly over the freshly plowed and disked earth. She found the sower—a stout cloth bag with a crank—at the Farm Bureau, of course. Conferred by phone with the county agent, found the best cheap mixture of seed for our kind of unmanicured lawns: perennial rye grass, mainly, mixed with some Kentucky bluegrass and some clover. It had to be cheap—we had enormous areas to cover, plus the dam.

March: It was nippy, and we wore jackets and boots. Grass seed—and laughter. And how she walked—fast, head up; that's in all the grass we sowed.

March 12: First marsh peeper—in the night! Helen very excited. Well, me too.

Early May: The triple-trunk birch (balled and burlapped) in. The dwarf fruit trees in—twelve of them: Helen's "orchard." And the two Chinese chestnut trees (one east of the house, one west). Then the free red maples.

Ten of them—at the front, rather close to the road—as an eventual screen between Fairmount traffic and us, when they grew up. Helen and Mort had gone for a walk, discovered the stand of little maples—way back; no owner's name posted. So I took them home.

No, those maples weren't planted until the next spring. It's just that the entire, exciting melange of trees, shrubs, farm, and sky rolled together in me those first two planting seasons like a giant avalanche of happiness, merging everything.

Merging. Well, then, skip to fall for a moment—bulbs.

Early September: I planted mixed crocuses around the base of the three-birch. Helen: "So we can look at them from the front window, even if it's too nasty to go out and see them in person.''

Bulbs. God bless them and also damn them—if you're poor in money though so rich in soul. I prepared the ground (hours) and planted about five hundred narcissus—after driving two hours to my friend Jini's place and digging them up. (I got some peonies there, too, and Oriental poppies.) Narcissus poeticus: a long curving bed (Helen's idea, of course). Bloom every late April—that graceful, tall white flower with the heart of yellow-and-reddish. You can see them out Helen's bedroom window.

Bulbs—Jesus. A friend of a friend of Helen was selling her house in Cleveland Heights. We drove in, and I dug up hundreds of King Alfred daffodils. Helen fed me sandwiches and coffee and cigarettes all along the hard work; and, at home, brought me iced coffee while I was sweating over the new bed I had to dig before planting. Crazy!

But how beautiful that bed turned out to be. The dafs spread as eagerly as the poeticus. Just west of the bedroom wing—so Helen could see them the minute she woke up and came to the window in May. She (joyous): ''I've never, never had enough dafs and narcissus—*and* enough to give away to other beauty-pigs, and still have enough left for a country landscape. *Toi,* thank you!''

What else? My God, that perennial bed. Slowly, I filled most of it with chiselings and gifts. How the devil did I do all that—and then the gigantic farm planting? Long, long poem—that's how.

And fascinating, each new poem of the countryside: it's like learning to see and hear brand-new in life. Quail—soft colors, lovely soft shape, running in little groups. The brown thrasher runs, too—but differently gaited, and all alone. Bank swallows, in hot weather, skimming over the pond, close to the water (eating bugs?)—pure grace. The talk a cardinal makes besides the song itself, the beautifully funny talk-song of a hummingbird, the actual ''chip-chip'' of Chippy, the ''bob *white,* bob *white!*'' pushing sweet liquid into the air, the marvelous, loud song of that tiny wren; and the most poignant singing of all—the mourning dove.

No, you don't learn it all at once; the mounting seasons grow the poems in you. There's the tree toad, heralding the fall. The wild ducks—the sound in the air, far, closer, suddenly over the pond and then in it—four or six of them swimming in formation, diving. You can hear them next morning, sometimes, and know they're still renting there.

And then! Suddenly, all the firsts are over, and Eddie Puzder comes with the plow and disk; and the old, hackneyed thing you've read so often is absolutely true: black, silken earth, velvety under blades. No time for nothin' now. Here comes the farm.

And Mrs. Marous (Ma called her our "farmer lady") has raised flats and flats of stuff for us from those seeds. You drive miles to pick it up (time, time), but what plants—and so cheap, this way. Including three different kinds of pink, less acidy tomatoes (Helen had researched the seeds out of the U.S. Department of Agriculture, impressing the hell out of Mrs. M—who hadn't seen a pink tomato since the old Acme disappeared off the market). And—Jesus—artichokes.

Me: "Are you as crazy as Ma says? That thing grows in tropical countries." Helen: "This kind is supposed to grow in Ohio. Doesn't it sound like fun? And it's a perennial, *toi*—no replanting. And everybody in the family but you loves artichokes."

New country people—we're completely nuts. Eventually they ate a few small ones, not very good, before we finally had them plowed under because they were such a headache: I had to mulch them over the winter, and that one row of artichokes screwed up the spring plowing of the farm.

Mrs. M's white, fragrant petunias and mixed annual dahlias went into the planter Helen had got the Amish to build: just outside the two western living-room windows. Red brick, running fourteen feet long, two feet broad, and deep deep (Martin and I had to cart twelve wheelbarrows of woods earth to fill it!). Ah, but how gorgeous.

Note: I planted a flat of 125 kohlrabi seedlings the first season. Helen fixed them according to her grandmother and mother's recipe (you even use the greens, chopped), a dish we all loved, and it froze well, too. But those two babes had maids! Grandma's recipe for all that blanching and chopping (even though we ate a lot of the kohlrabi sliced raw, with salt—wonderful!) was a killer.

At one point or another, I named that rotohoe the one-horse shay. It was terrific. Or both of us in action were. Up and down the twenty-eight rows (sixty feet long) of that first main farm. Not to mention the back stuff: four kinds of peas, early corn, five kinds of lettuce, two kinds of spinach. You get peas in on Saint Patrick's day, if earth is workable (the first spring it was—never again). The planting's not too hard, but you have to weed by hand. And the tall peas need trellis support. And the picking is awful. You even raise snow pod peas; and they're delicious. But pretty soon, everybody (including visitors) is helping to shell—and to blanch—and to fill freezer boxes with those thousands of sweet, hellish, beautiful peas. And the novel goes down the drain again, of course.

After a fashion. Because, sooner or later, I always sat down for a rest, and made pages of notes on tool-basket pads of paper.

March 24: Helen's first birthday in the house. I started another ritual. Planted pansies (plants) as a surprise. In the big redwood bucket Sarah J gave me last Christmas. It's got a heavy carrying rope—and of course I filled it with woods earth from down below. Giant Swiss (many of them in bloom)—bought them in town the day before. Sat the loaded tub at the edge of the planter coping—all very secret, because that one adores surprises. Early morning, stuck a tall stake in the earth of the tub—card attached with red ribbon: "Happy Birthday to a Pooh—a pot of different kind of honey—made by The Gardener." Pretty sappy-sentimental? Sure. But let's face it: the ghetto kid is quite dead!

Okay, the farm. Sunflowers, two rows, on the west boundary. On the east, one row of dahlias (didn't chisel enough from Uncle Hugo, so I finished out the row in potatoes); and next to it, mixed glads.

That farm list, started by Helen, was to be a permanent record. Leave it to the gal who believed in archives and order: in the garden, the kitchen, the button boxes, story sales for her friend; even the drawer of the sewing machine table, with dozens of different colored thread, each spool on a nail. Mort had driven those nails in at her direction, so that the fine seamstress could select the right color instantly. God, how she taught me. And helped me in the garden—as much as her lousy body permitted. But the brain was never lousy.

Let's jump to the marigold-zinnia bed for some of that brain stuff. From the first spring, always the same—except subtract an old marigold and add a new type. Or ditto new-old zinnia. The bed in front of the screened porch, all across that distance, the seeds mixed, so that the yellows and oranges of the marigolds are massed and mixed with the gorgeous zinnia colors—seeds planted thick on both sides of the big center patch of bergamot (chiseled from Sarah J, who called it bee balm). That patch was there to lure hummingbirds—that little one's favorite food of all the garden flowers.

Of course (Helen), we planted the bergamot there so that we

could see Hummy from the porch, and from the kitchen table. We did, too—often in twos and fours, or tangling in the air over a fresh mass of red bloom—and sometimes (rare) even sitting for an instant on the cord I'd put around the bed, looking to me like a small green cigar, of all things. And if you're quiet, on the porch, you can hear him humming as he hovers (besides the sound of those speedy wings).

The way of that marigold-zinnia bed. Helen: plant the seeds so thick that no staking will be necessary—the flowers will hold one another up. I just hammered in some outside thick stakes and used cord around the boundaries of the whole bed, so that wind and rain wouldn't flop the flowers onto the grass.

I prepared the bed: digging, fertilizing, then hoeing and raking fine the earth. Then came the Helen-mixing of seed. She appeared with kitchen dishes, and how I laughed as I watched her use a soup bowl for the mixing of both kinds of seed; and then she had sauce dishes for the four separate beds she called "pies."

Like so: she divided the planting area into four pies, and drew lines with a stick to separate them. She measured out the mixed seed into the sauce dishes—equal amounts—her eye as excellent outside as it was for seasoning and grammar inside. Then she scattered the seed, one pie at a time; and I covered (wheelbarrow full of topsoil), and tamped down the half inch or so of earth with the hoe blade. And watered (rain barrel): what I called "pasting down the seed."

It was she who had come up with the idea of those two rain barrels, to sit under the downspouts (one on the south side—close to the flowers; the other on the west—for crops). At the two regular spouts, going from gutter all the way down into the earth, there was a short spout, about halfway down, and turn-off gadget—to direct rainfall from the regular into this special one, which poured the rainwater into the tall steel barrels. When they were full to brimming, turn the flow from the short back into the regular downspout. She had read about it somewhere, and had sketched a picture of it. The workmen looked at the sketch, at her smiling face, said reluctantly: "Good idea."

She had Martin make covers for the barrels (free—Mort's lab) out of leftover plywood, with square holes for under the short spouts. Keep the water clean, keep Chippy or field mice from falling in by accident. That Helen-invent saved quite a bit on electricity to run the well—any anyway, the barrels looked so "country" (stained the color of the house by Mort).

Note (important one): Of all the gardening, the marigold-zinnia bed was the one job we always did together, from beginning to end. It was pure Helen-and-Ruth. And it had music in it, always. I'd move her little white FM radio out to the porch table for the whole job.

Item: Though the May 1 planting of beans was frozen out, the seven dahlias in the perennial bed weren't touched. That's when I found out that frost skips. A whole bed of pepper and squash can go limp and black in an early or late freeze, and, three feet away, the cukes are still okay. The front lilac go black in a spring freeze, and the side and back lilac stay perfectly fine. I could kill the Old Lady sometimes. For those limp lilac florets alone.

Early May: Planted sweet Spanish onion (plants)—back acres (plus the yellow onion sets for cooking). Bought them early at Bloom's when I drove up to Chesterland for more tomato stakes. Couldn't resist—even though Mrs. M was raising a whole flat of Bermudas for us. Helen laughed so hard. "Now who's crazy?" It *is* catching.

Week later: More dahlias into perennial bed. Tall ones—purple, white, mauve (to blend with the mouse-ears). Gift: neighbor-Lil brought them over—plus some Dutch iris.

Merge with the farm—everything mingled, after all: corn planting. Two rows each of earliest to latest, including Evergreen and Country Gentlemen (first white corn I ever ate—marvelous). Helen: "At last—enough corn for a *whole* season, for real corn-pigs!" (My God, they eat five and six ears at a time. My God, again: I started to do the same. It's easy—with perfect ears, brought in at the very last minute—the water already boiling. And *never* put either salt or sugar in that water.)

Item: All the Bermuda and Spanish onions stored very well over the winter—in old onion and potato mesh bags we'd saved—hanging on nails all over the garage walls (poem, for sure!). So—no point in putting in yellow onion sets any more: the sweets are good for cooking, too.

The cuke bed and pickle bed—half a row to each. Sure, they're different. News: you can eat pickles very tiny, besides dill them; but cukes have to grow out their full span or they're bitter. I'll have to mulch the row with thick straw against weeds—before the seed-lings grow tall enough to fall on their faces and start making like vines. But thin first, to six plants a hill, says the packet. I over-planted, of course, in anxiety that some wouldn't come up. They all did, and then I wasn't secure enough to thin properly. (Quite a comparison between pruning cukes and cutting a book!) Result: a labyrinthine mat of vines, *thousands* of pickles—and then, later, of cukes. Live and learn, gardener-writer.

Same day—late afternoon: one row of okra, and nine heads of red cabbage. Helen makes a marvelous dish of sweet-and-sour red cabbage: Aunt Hattie's recipe. She wonders if it'll freeze, cooked. (Answer was yes.) It sometimes makes me smile: Mort's two aunts and Uncle Hugo, very wealthy, live together in a beautiful house in Shaker Heights (and the old gent has a shack and a lot of acreage not too far from us). Anyway, I've taken to calling them Aunt Hat-tie, Aunt Amelia, and Uncle Hugo; and they seem to take it for grant-ed. I also took to referring to the old girls as ''the Aunties''—and eventually the rest of the family called them that, too. I rarely see my own aunts and uncles, in town. This two-family deal is peculiar as hell.

Day before Decoration Day (northeast Ohio's planting deadline in case of late spring frost). Got in the delicates—six eggplant, six sweet peppers, three hots (for my Hungarian friend). Same day: twelve Early Wakefield cabbage, twelve early cauliflower. Also planted six Copenhagen cabbage. Helen got the seed because Sarah J adores those pointy heads, hasn't had any since she was a young woman because you really can't buy them in the store. We liked them, too. They're a more delicate, very sweet cabbage—particularly good for slaw.

Jesus, beginner's luck! Everything I touched turned into three times too much harvest. We could've gone into business. Helen toyed with it—because of my no-money—but Mort reminded her the zoning law forbids any business in this area. But leave it to her. At the height of the harvesting, Martin and she took cukes and to-matoes, by the basket, and sold them to our grocer in Chester. So it all came to a final $11.86—at which point we burst into hysterical laughter.

June: Planted two rows of Katahdin groppler potatoes (turned out to be our favorite, and Sarah J's). One row of winter squash (acorn and butternut), one row of mixed summer squash—including zucchini. Live and learn again: summer squash, once it starts, is awful in number and gets boring to eat, and there aren't enough people to give them to. You can store winter squash. And the butternut looks lovely with Indian corn and strawberry popcorn and gourds on the kitchen mantle, or on the long redwood porch table. With boughten bittersweet, of course. Both Helen and I adore it.

On and on: do everything a gardener is supposed to do—and it shall follow as the night the day? I wonder. I should be filling the blank pages of notebooks for a novel. And who—for heaven's sake, who—is going to eat all these vegetables? But Helen wants it this way. Well, don't you? Yes, but—so much? Well, in a way, I'm paying her back, no? And paying for my bread and room, too. Haven't given her a dime for board in how long?

Note for a journal page of laughter: Ragsy always helped us pick berries. Sat up, straight as a fat white soldier, at the side of a row; made a polite little whine-noise if she wasn't given part of a berry one minute after she'd eaten the last one Helen or Martin had shared with her. I'd start laughing—and to hell with time lost.

July 1: My birthday—as well as late cabbage and cauliflower planting. Okay, symbolic stuff: I (sort of) started the outline for the novel. And when I told Helen, she (jubilant): "Thank you! And *toi*, beginning next year, I'm having your family here for your birthday dinner. *I* know how to start symbolic rituals, too."

Ah, period: all the planting's done. Amen. Can I rest now, Lord, and write that book?

Hell, no. Though any time left over goes into those tool-basket notes. That is, time left over from cultivating, weeding, using the one-horse shay; and thinning bean and okra and lima seedlings by hand, weeding between plants. Down on your knees, farmer. When you stand up, writer, the day is shot again.

But the absolute worst is ahead. All of a sudden, harvesting begins. First sensation: My God, I'm raising actual food—what a thrill. But then, mounting sensation beginning to taste a little like horror, as the first beautiful tomatoes and cukes, pickles, beans, turn into oceans, into bushel after bushel brimming with red and green and yellow.

And there's the constant fight to pick the peas and beans before they turn tough, to dig the potatoes before worms or rot. Or field mice: I found a family of them halfway up a row (their hidden nest filled with straw they snitched from my mulch pile)—and they scurried away, and I dug up two hills of half-eaten early reds the little family obviously had been living on. Wonderful! In the sunlight, the babies' ears definitely Helen's mouse-ear dahlias in flight.

But back to exhaustion: there are sudden gluts of everything, including wax beans and limas (Fordhook *and* baby, of course). Everything practically at once, naturally. So everybody sits on the porch evenings, shells and snaps, cuts French style, fills bowls and bowls for freezer boxes. Or fills jar upon jar with pickles, with tomatoes. Far into the night. Including the gardener. Weary!

However, note for a truly joyous July page in the journal: The lily centifolium is blooming outside her south bedroom windows—three huge flowers on one stem. White, particularly fragrant at night. I gave it to Helen for the anniversary of the day we met. A joke between us—but we always exchange little, cheap gifts on May 25. To me, still the greatest moment my life ever sucked in.

New summer-fall ritual: I washed a lot of cherry tomatoes (stems on for "pretty") and put them into a beautiful bowl for porch eating. Better than candy or nuts. That's in my journal—along with: "My God, we've *got* to cut down on the farm. Or I'll never write a thing until winter. Helen, do you hear me?"

And this, in my (second season) journal: "Mort's still jobless, and Helen's eyes are starting to say good-bye to the House. I *can't* sell a story (she can't—she's trying it, again, to save me time), or think of any way to get a big wad of money for them until this damn novel gets finished (years?!)."

Several pages go on with that sudden Mort-disaster:

> Finally came up with an idea—very small stuff money-wise, but makes me feel better in a psych way. Fannie is working as a waitress in an Italian restaurant, downtown (Mrs. G, proprietor and cook). So, yesterday, I sold to Mrs. G eight bucks' worth of tomatoes, eggplant, green peppers, cabbage. To her sister-in-law (works there): two bucks' worth. It meant hours of picking, then driving all the way to downtown Cleveland, but I did feel better. Until Helen refused to take the money. I lost my temper, rushed out and bought nine bucks' worth of meat. "Freeze it—or throw it in the pond. The

remaining buck is for the gas I used."

By then, she was laughing—*her* kind. So I had to laugh, too. Helen: "*Toi*, you're insane." Me: "Take the money, you dope—you're much better at bargain food than I am." Helen: "Ruthie, the time. And Ed's waiting for that novel." Me: "God damn it, my soul's important, too, isn't it?" Helen: "God bless your soul. I love it." Me: "Cut the schmaltz. It's like glue around here. Unstick me—I got things to do!"

A week later: Drove in to Ma's for Friday night Sabbath dinner, and made the trip count. Aside from stuff for the family, I sold to Mrs. G and her sister-in-law ten bucks' worth of tomatoes, carrots, eggplant, green beans. Fannie is hysterical with laughter. Ma is sore: "You're working like a peasant!" Sadie thinks I'm nuts. No, it won't pay off the mortgage, but I don't feel quite as black inside. And hey, God, snap me up on this book, okay? *That's* the kind of dough Mort and Helen need—and soon. Please?

(I never told her about the journal. Probably a very private thing in my guts, no? Yes.)

Ah, hallelujah! Early October. Radio: "Frost tonight, away from the lake." That's us. We tore out, and Martin and I picked everything in sight. Helen: "Be spurred: fried green tomatoes tonight!"

Live and learn—again: an Indian summer came, two days later—as if there'd never been a freeze. God, the country: each season is really blessed with a different kind of beauty. Now, leaves starting to turn, and the air beginning to flame and color like museum art. Never before realized how burning-bright sumac becomes in the fall. The fairy-tale colors of turning leaves on trees—each color so different—sonnet, ode, trio, full symphony. And, of course, this kind of balmy fall is perfect for the cleaning up of garden and farm, getting it all ready for the spring sure to come again. Time to pull up all the frost-blackened garbage, cart it away to the pile far from the house and well hidden behind a stand of trees. Time to dig up dahlia tuber and corm for drying, labeling, storing.

Yes, live and learn. For example, the Oriental poppies (foliage withered in July) have sent up fresh, short green clumps of leaves: next season is already here!

And now? The sunflowers. Oh, my God. Because of course we

sentimental, amateur farmers think we can raise our own seed for our own winter birds. We saps! My beloved sunny Mammoth Russians turn out to be torture when the seeds ripen and I try to get them out. The Old Lady really glues those ripe seeds into the heads. I gave up on the shelling when my hands took to really aching. Thereafter, I cut the heads off after the seeds were ready, and spread them around, a few at a time to prolong our fun, on the carpenter bench and under the ash; and nailed them to my feeder stump. Humiliating and laughable: we could all see Chippy shell the heads with the greatest ease. Birds, too: blue jay, nuthatch, tufted titmouse (Helen calls him Tufty-T), cardinal. Me: "Yep, the Old Lady takes care of her own—and to hell with big-shot mortals. Right?" Helen: "So right, *toi*."

Now? Ah, take a deep breath, gardener turned writer again. Most of the cleanup is over. There's a little time sailing out of the country-in-fall. For a novel. Even for rather regular entries in the journal. Not every day—just when the spirit or nature's actions or creative triggering moved me.

October 14: Planted about five hundred tulips, three solid rows at rear of perennial bed. Many of them dug up from South Woodland and cured (before that, from Shannon). Many, gifts; some, boughten.

October 17: Virginia is back at Saint Vincent's Charity Hospital—another heart attack. No wonder she grows more cynical about life or fate or what-not, though she remains the devout Catholic I've known for more than twenty years. Originally, we met on a tennis court, but writing was our bridge. V used to write very good poetry, but hasn't for a long time. Damn it, what happens to people? I wanted her to write a book about her family. One grandfather a slave, one grandmother Indian and French, plenty of white blood in the family; mounting to class: her mother a teacher before she married a lawyer and politician in Detroit; her sister, Suzanne, a teacher, still in Detroit. V: "You write the book. One thing this world doesn't need, baby, is another nigger book by a nigger." I *hate* it when wonderful people get exhausted in the soul. Interesting note: from fine social worker to crack police officer—V changed jobs for money, to help support widow-Ma.

*

October 21: At 2:15 P.M., *I started complete outline of a novel called*
"The Changelings." (Amen, amen!) I've done a great deal of frag-
mentary stuff, and fat notes on plot and theme, but this is it. My
first novel in this house. That screams a lot, Ruth! Helen says she's
going to find the comparison fascinating—this and "Now Comes
the Black." That first amateur book (can't even call it a novel!) by
the kid, on which this novel is somewhat based. She reread it last
week—the typescript she had bound. Now she's going to reread
that next version, "The Long Moment." Not me; those oldies would
depress me. But to her it's all "growth, new perspective, literary
history." What a woman is my friend, Helen!

Further (undated) garden-life journal entries by the writer-back:
At my desk: hordes of red-winged blackbirds, massing and feeding, east; ready for migratory flight? Shades of spring. The redwings
were the first sight and sound (pure rust) those months; right after
the marsh peepers and the crow songs. Now, fall: crows are caw-
ing out this season, and the redwings are leaving, too. God, do I
love country stuff.

The mums are starting. We still have three plants of the Koreans,
from the Shannon yard originally, and Helen is so pleased. Me, too,
talking of symbolic roots!

Barb's birthday coming up. I sent her a cheap but rather nice
edition of *Sonnets from the Portuguese.* Then came whining to Helen:
"Damn it, I want to buy my people gorgeous, expensive presents.
I'm sick of tight money." Helen (that rarely cold voice): "The book
is enough. Barbie will love it. Why do gifts from you have to cost
a lot?" I tore out of the house, furious.
When I came back in, she was baking Barb's birthday cake. It's
always a tall, fluffy angel food—from scratch. We smiled at each
other. Me: "I'll try harder. Okay?" Helen: "The 'try' is all I ever
want of you." That evening, I helped her pack the cake (Mort'll mail
it from town tomorrow). *There's* a particularly lovely "she taught
me." Some people always send birthday cakes to their beloveds
away from home. Of course, she's right about money. What a crappy
symbol—of the missing things in a person's background, childhood.
I thought that the big dough I earned with *Wasteland* had smashed
it for good. On the other hand, here's a maybe: isn't it worse, once
having had the money and now gone again?

B's birthday evening: we all talked to her. This family always phones its people on birthdays when one is out of town. Money or not. And for wedding anniversaries, New Year's Eve. Yes, me too—I'm also in the family that way. Nice!

Hilled roses for winter; got earth from back acres: fifteen bushels—glad I have that wheelbarrow. Wrote all afternoon—one more rewrite on story called "Little House"—seems to be quite a bit of interest at the *Journal*. The novel will wait; my soul can't: that's big slick dough if the miracle should happen and they take the story. A few mortgage payments on the house. Wonder if Mort *will* get a job—at his age? Jesus, so unfair!

Feeders up. Including the one on my stump. The new standing feeder Martin bought for his parents' wedding anniversary: front window area. I pushed it into the sod before the ice age could descend. Helen—who lies down to rest on the couch sometimes, or reads and listens to music there—will be able to see the bird action. And it's for Rags, too, that snoop of a loudmouth who loves to sit up and watch birds, but will bark them away if they come too close.

Eddie rough-plowed the farm for winter. But Helen-of-the-sad-eyes: no job yet, and how many springs are left to us in this house? Nevertheless, I bought a very big pumpkin (a dollar fifty). Came home and secretly put it, yellow as a sun, on the stone coping of the cleaned-up planting box, where the pansy pot had stood all summer. I can smell a new ritual being born. And this time, *I* have hope—for Helen and Mort. (So much easier to have hope for others than for me. Odd? But God damn it, I'm going to help my two friends.) Hollered into the window: "Hey, surprise." And got a wonderful smile from sad-eyes.

The pumpkin was a fat, sunny beacon out there—often with a hat of snow, and seeming quite rakish then, until the first hard freeze. Then it sagged, looked like a drunkard. When the drunk really passed out (a complete falling inward), I carried it back to the pile of bricks near the straw pile, cut it open so the seeds would dry. Somebody ate them—and a lot of the pulp, too.

Almost November. Heavy frost last night. Writing my novel: interesting memories. Sometimes I think childhood stays longest and clearest in the emotions. That gang—I can see all the faces—Negro, Dago, Yid—and the tough kid herself, the blond tousled hair and the scowl. Thirty-odd years later! So I drove in to visit V again, told her my young colored pal had sent me—out of a book. She enjoyed that. Brought her very gay swatch of varicolored Indian corn, tied it to her hospital window. She smiled, sick as she felt. Said in her casual way: "Don't look so sad, Ruth. I'm too black and bad and stubborn to die." Well, there's a poem, too!

Hey, Barbara's got a fellow—and it looks like the works. *Very* nice guy. Name of Diedrick: Dutch background, born there, about nineteen when he came here; they met at the international group, where Barb was doing her bit. His mother: widow, also nice, name of Rie—for Marie. They came for dinner. Barbie's really in love. Her eyes—what a beautiful sight. Her mother's eyes, too, watching her daughter in love.

Staked the fruit trees against winter storms. Then finished "Little House." Yes, it's a slick story, but with bits of real feeling for the land and the seasons. The trouble is, my nonslick self appears in most of these stories—and apparently ruins them for big magazine sales. Helen: "But slick or not, the you is honest. Some editors are going to like that. Some have—like ES." Me: "Send the *Journal* a telegram to that effect, agent." Laughter. Always good these days.

Warm—almost a summer day, in November. What an unexpected joy. Due at the Moody house for dinner. I love it there. Sarah J's definitely one of all my mothers. (Thanks, Arthur Miller, for the loan of *All My Sons*.) I've always had some older women (strong, warm) for friends—to respect, admire, do things for. V's mother was one, too. And I find myself writing about them a lot. Some day, I'll write a definitive book about the waif, motherless in her emotions, who's always looking for a substitute figure. Did Helen start out as one of those? I often wonder (though she's not that much older). After dinner, Pearl and Alice and I got to talking about WPA days. That's where we three met, and then Pearl dragged shy-me home to meet her mother. Instant falling in love for both Sarah J and me. When did Alice move in? Doesn't matter. All that does is the long, good friendship. And those WPA years—exciting, young-revolutionary, young-creative, FDR our god.

Brought the nine amaryllis in from the garage. I'd had them out all summer, sunk back of the narcissus bed; repotted them, then gave them the garage for an interim period before their dormant span in the cool, dark place that's supposed to make them bloom. The only such place I could find, after experimenting a lot, was the floor of the big linen closet in the back hall. Helen laughed her head off, but by God it worked. (We don't have a basement; and the storage space is too cold over the winter.)

Helen's mad about amaryllis, and had asked the Amish workers to build that wood plant ledge mainly for them; it's in front of the big south window that faces the porch. No direct sun, but exactly the right kind of light. It's her shelf; she cares for all the indoor plants. Plenty of other stuff there, too. Christmas cactus, grape ivy from Sarah J that I've trained up on garden tie, attached to the traverse rods (the bamboo drapes are never drawn at this window). There's wax ivy, two pots. Belonged to Helen's father (she always called him Bill). That ivy (and I've trained those up, too) never bloomed for Bill, and he'd worry about that; here, they always bloom at the right time, and when first that happened, Helen's eyes—one inherits all sorts of beautiful pain, I guess.

It's fun with the linen-closet amaryllis. I inspect the pots regularly. The flower bud appears first, way down on the still-short stalk, then eventually the leaves, as the stalk takes giant steps upward. When the first bud shows, I whisk out the pot secretly, put it on the shelf, start the copious watering, then holler: "Hey, kiddo, look what the elves did for you in the night," or some such silly crack. (My youthful drinking friends should hear me these days!)

At my desk by one. And did work. But God, I'm so tired of this sickening feeling of anxiety over a piece of writing. Got kind of drunk—evening—my room. Helen's expression very sad, when she came to say good night. She rarely mentions it—but her eyes ought to make me stay on the wagon for eternity. No excuse— none—I know it! It's just that this worry-depression kid has had her turnoff of head and fear-thinking habit for a long time. Though, since Helen, I don't drink anywhere near the way I used to.

Next day: At desk by ten in the morning. Still monkeying with end of outline. Not sure what that girl in the book should do. Shall I soften that scene? Or would that be dishonest? On the other hand, writing is *not* photography. And this kid isn't all me. All right, green-thumb it. What would a girl like that do in such a vicious corner? The blue and red streaks of jay and cardinal, to and from the feeders, keep flicking at my eyes. I'm surrounded by beautiful green and space, and writing in detail about a ghetto street of my youth. Fascinating. Wonder—I really do—how childhood can stay so vivid. Torment? Well, write it. Maybe you can un-torment a lot of kids to come. Or their parents—who'll know how to gentle the children—*if* I do this book right.

A Friday. Worked on book six hours plus; I think the ending is falling into place. Evening: I almost always go in to eat supper with Ma and Sadie and the family on Fridays. (Yes, it's still the Jewish Sabbath in my heart.) Still say "going home," still giving Ma the weekly dough—when I have it. Fannie comes, too. Money, too. Then I drive her to her nightclub job (or our niece Mildred sometimes does), and I spend the evening with my blood family.

Wonder if Fannie ever has my awful feeling: waiting with dread for the day Ma will die. But Fan's my dead opposite, thank God: gay, happy, so outgoing. I've rarely seen her even blue. I'm grateful: my depressions are enough for the whole family! But what makes siblings so different, I wonder.

Cut down the asparagus fern; they're brown and crumbly. The pumpkin still yellow as sun, though. To work, writer—the pumpkin'll blaze without you.

Afternoon: to V's (she's back from the hospital at last, thank God), to transplant her roses—an old promise. Brought her a small pumpkin—got one of her rare smiles. My poor friend—lots of heart pain—has to sleep in a chair. After I did the roses (three hours), we had a couple of drinks, and very good talk. She thinks the theme of "The Changelings" will be "forever"—Negroes moving into an area, and the whites running. "And even if your book's the great American novel, baby, it won't change that black-white garbage." But then she patted my cheek. "All right, honey, write your book. Just don't phony it up. Hear?"

Helen and I transplanted partridgeberry plants from behind the cemetery (lots of berries), and then she made three "friendship gardens"—that's what those Christmas bell-vases are called some-

times. One's for my room. What an artist she is. A few drops of
water, then she Scotch-taped the top down (can be opened easily
for more small drinks); big red ribbons in bows on all three. The
moss she found for the bottoms is particularly lovely.

Thanksgiving Day. One of my beloved rituals and roots. Yesterday we did a special shopping at Heinen's, the fine store she likes
so much. The food was expensive as hell, but this *is* her favorite
holiday. ("Oh, how full of thanks I am for our kind of life!") And
the whole family is together. Temperature in the thirties, lots of
snow. And the Western Sunset lily bulbs haven't arrived yet from
the nursery! But I mulched the area thick with straw, to keep the
earth unfrozen—bricks on top, to make sure the straw will stay.
House is full of laughter, talk, music, delicious cooking smells.

The day itself, morning: all slept late except Helen and Ruth.
I love this part of it. At the kitchen table, I hold the bird (always
has to be a hen turkey, and never frozen) while she stuffs it, then
sews. (In my parents' house, it was only the Jewish holidays that
were important.) Later, Barb'll bake apple pies, Martin will "do"
the fruit platter for dessert. Helen's already made her famous mince
pie (meat, brandy).

About four o'clock, drove in for Ma. That's turned ritual, too:
bless my friend, Helen. The first time my mother came to Thanksgiving dinner (on South Woodland), she was shy and nervous—
about the "fancy" table and the "high-class" people (reminded me
of her youngest child at that first lunch on Shannon!). But even my
mother could not stay uneasy with Helen for too long. Or with Mort
and the kids. Today, Ma had baked *challah* especially for the big
event. How she giggled at the fuss everybody made about her bread.
It's wonderful to see what a Helen can do to an old woman like
that. It's the warmth and genuine love, of course. That opens people like flowers. My little mother—who ever kissed her in Russia,
or in rotten Brooklyn, or all the years in Cleveland? Helen and the
kids are really kissers! And Ma kind of pushes at them, but she loves
it. Dinner was beautiful in all ways—to this child with the two
families.

Planted the lilies. Vivid memory of those Western Sunsets on
South Woodland, when Helen was convalescing from the sympathectomy and watching the hummingbirds at those flowers, to
forget her pain. A lovely poem—there to here. Lots of snow, and

cold, but the lily mulch had worked. Had to kick at the half-frozen
straw, but the ground underneath was soft. Came in with numb
fingers, hollering: "Planting's over for the season!" Helen warmed
my hands—that smile. "Wonderful. Now, are your hands warm
enough to hold a pencil?"

Hey, God, thanks. I've finished the (rewritten) outline. That
sample first chapter—no! But I think I know how to start the book
the right way now.

December 2: First *real* snow. Worked drowningly on book.
Good. Later, Helen: "Ruthie, look!" Four deer. At a point about
halfway to the river line—but all the trees are bare, so the view was
amazingly clear. We watched from the living room, then the porch.
They were jumping—gamboling, I suppose. They stayed a long time,
then—bang!—gone. We had coffee, and talked. Not about deer—
about life; but the deer pushed the button. It's so damn good to
talk to Helen. Always feel better afterward. Deer—my God. Well,
can't a book be, too?

December 5, 1953: *Started the actual writing.* Mess-me: began
chapter one three different ways. But the third time, I finally got
into it. When I *knew* what the next few pages were to be, I tore out
and mulched the berries and the row of artichokes. Helen (at front
door): "Ruthie, you come in here right now and put on a jacket."
I came in. She (my smiler): "You've gotten started." I hugged her,
called out a triumphant bellow that made Ragsy come running and
barking. The house was full of laughter and glad noise unto the Lord.

Sloppy but honest fact: in bed, I found myself saying "my
prayer" with passion—about my new book (and a job for Mort).
That thing I found in a library book and fell for, when I was extremely young and needy; and decided to say every night—just in
case God was listening or something. I've been saying it every night,
drunk or sober, quite a parcel of years. Why a strange sort of
sentimental-poem-prayer out of a book? Not sure. The Jewish God
and prayers (Orthodox) belonged to my father, to men and sons,
and neither Pa nor the Hebrew made strength for me—or warmth.
Only the music did—the chanting and singing I love to this day.
So I guess I had to find me my own prayer-meaning; and in a library
book, of course—they were so holy to that kid. Has nothing to do

with being Jewish or not; I've always been glad to be a Jew. That's one ghetto I didn't have to smash.

So I said my prayer in the dark, out loud:

Dear Lord, kind Lord, gracious Lord,
I pray Thou wilt look on all I love tenderly tonight.
Weed their hearts of weariness, scatter every care,
Down a wake of angel wings, winnowing the air.
And with all the needy, oh, divide, I pray,
This vast treasure of content that was mine today. Amen.

And felt—what?—more hopeful about everything, I guess.

Drove Helen to the library in town, for her annual "do" of Grace's Christmas carol card. Every year, she finds an old carol; copies music and words onto a large, especially beautiful card. Friend-Grace (sixty-eight this year) adores Christmas and carols— and Helen's frozen and canned Christmas gifts. *And* the May basket Helen always prepares for her (Grace being an old "labor gal" with bells on, and May Day all tied up with the labor struggle for her), and Mort delivers on the morning of the day. The basket: violets in all shades, marsh marigolds, meadow rue, fern wildlings of all kinds; Helen wanders all over our land in muddy boots to find choice specimens. Last year, for a "funny," a little skunk cabbage went into the basket—and how Grace laughed. I love and admire that one, too (she's one of my three dear friends to whom this new book is dedicated).

Helen found an old Basque carol this time. I caught up (while she made artist at the same table) with a lot of magazines I can't afford to subscribe to. We smiled at each other between stints.

Christmas Eve. My beautiful, meaningful holiday she gave me. Helen's discovered a greenhouse on Mayfield Road, about five miles away. Sunnybrook Nurseries—run by a terrific gal name of Jean and her pleasant husband, Pete. We pick the growing tree, tell Jean when we'll be back for it (they cut it the day you want it). Helen likes the tree a day or so before Christmas Eve trimming. Into the garage, in a big bucket of water—stays fresher, of course, and the needles don't drop as fast during the week. Then, the morning of the big evening: into the utility room—to "warm up"—so that Mort and she can shape the branches into perfection. We have a spruce this year—fragrant, tall, and what I call fat. I never get used to the wonder of this holiday, though I am a long road away from the little Jew who used to peer at Gentile trees through the windows of houses I passed. It isn't religion in this house; it's the universal of giving and music, the beauty of love.

This year, Diedrick and Rie are here, too. Come evening, I put on Helen's recording of *The Messiah,* turn up the sound—and I'm home! Naturally, there's a fire. I'd bought a lot of extra pine cones, in addition to the ones I use to trim the kitchen mantle—and they burn like lovely flowers or stars, sitting on the top log. Everybody helps trim the tree. Helen looks so happy. She loves Christmas, but tonight is special: she can see her daughter's future—marriage and fulfillment—and the new span of Christmas Eves to start in another generation. And Mort. . . Well, the whole house is utter love tonight.

Christmas Day. Another big fire, and Mort lights up the tree. D and Rie spent the night, so all is particularly festive. Rie brought Dutch holiday cakes she'd made, and Barb had baked a million cookies.

Now the gifts are opened. That's a Helen-invent: each of us picks, in turn—hands the package to its label-owner, who opens, exclaims, laughs, often kisses. The dogs running, barking, plunging into tissue paper. Oh, sure, there are gifts for Friedie and Ragsy, too: dog candies, a bell, a pull-rope toy. (And I remember that first time on Shannon. Ghetto kid to herself: Christmas presents for a *dog*? Jesus!)

Later, I wrote for almost three hours. Took all sorts of frozen and canned foods from Helen (beautifully labeled) to the Moodys; I'm always there for Christmas dinner. Driving in: the whole countryside so perfect-winter that my eyes smarted.

December 31: We're all home for New Year's Eve. Which this family prefers—including me. My God, when I think of the drunken, meaningless New Year's Eves I had for so many years—with people I didn't belong with—and always ending up lonelier! Drinks here, too, but so different. Wine for the kids (Diedrick came early). Cheese and cold meats. A big fire, lots of records, good talk. Diedrick has become a real friend. Going in for social psych, and he's a fascinating talker. What is a real joy is to listen to Helen and him in action—give and take: talk, brain, ideas. Barbie and he plan to be married next July 31—and then off to Ann Arbor. He'll finish getting that doctorate; the University of Michigan has offered him a teaching fellowship.

The kids and Mort play Scrabble for a while (Mort and Martin are fabulous). Helen and I—who don't go for games—read, change records, play with the dogs. At midnight, Helen and Mort kiss; then she kisses the rest of us. "Happy new year, my darlings!" Then coffee and B's cookies. Beautiful evening.

I'd written for a few hours during the day. Symbolically speaking, Miss Sinclair, you're as superstitious as Fannie is about spilled salt. Well, why not? A new year—a new novel started. Okay! Happy new year, writer. Work your tail off. This is what you were born for.

End of a very important year in the journal: first book (novel number three) started in my beloved countryside, but Mort lost his job. Not his fault—company went bankrupt. Come on, God!—surely this good man will get another job soon, and Helen won't be so worried about losing House. Please, dear Lord, kind Lord?

A wad of late comments clipped to last page of this year by the believer-writer-gardener:

Note (warning): Better get snow fence for sure. Helen thought we could get away without spending money for that. Bad mistake. What drifts on that driveway of ours! And Mort may not shovel, Martin'll be off to college one of these days. Leaving? Ruthie!

Question: When did Uncle Hugo buy us that secondhand gas-powered rotohoe? Can't remember. But how did I ever get along without it!

Note (money): Got to have a water softener in this part of the world. Or the hard water from the well stains everything, including your teeth and the toilets, with all those minerals. Mort does the softening himself, instead of paying for such a service; salt nuggets—and we can't use the water for over an hour while he does it. He's very good at stuff like that. New facts: soft water makes the coffee taste much better. And it's slippery on the skin; hard city water fights the bar of soap and the washcloth, and leaves a ring on the tub. But a bag of nuggets *costs;* that'll be a forever cost, here.

Helen's favorite dahlia; I love this angle: all my friends (to whom I've passed on extra tubers) call them mouse-ears too. As if a horticulturist had named the flower, for catalogs. Kind of a nuance of immortality?

Note (psych stuff): So many people change when accosted by the country-vicarious. Ma, in Yiddish as usual (when first I drove her out here, and back at night): "It's so dark! Why do you have to live out here with that crazy woman? Where are the streetlights? I'll bet there are wolves out here!" So she loved my new-to-her eggplant and butternut squash (which Helen taught Sadie and her how to cook). My potatoes widened her eyes. I brought in the seasonal flowers (Helen sent along gifts of some of the vases her cupboards are jammed with), and my mother's eyes turned bright at the dwarf marigolds. My sister Sadie looked at a mass of lily of the valley, sniffed at them. "Ruthie, I just love them!" For Fannie, narcissus on her birthday—a ritual I made: fifty or more poeticus (she puts them into that Swedish glass vase I spent some of my own hoarded money on—the first vase in her life). And her eyes, when I walk into her small city apartment with the fragrant poem-alive... I tell you, people have flowers in them all along. And never know it until somebody smashes in the door. Thanks again, dearest Helen.

Real heart item: Helen and Ma have become good friends. With a woman like my mother, that's a production. Ma forgets sometimes, and talks Yiddish to her. But my friend as good as understands every word—by watching eyes and listening for inflection of voice (and besides, she understands a little German). She takes Ma to the doctor sometimes, or to the hospital for deep heat when the arthritis flares. "Ruthie's writing her new book, Ma—and she's going to make a lot of money and be real famous again. So she hasn't got time. And Fannie and Mildred have to work. But I have lots of time. And anyway, I love you."

To me, it continues to be so amazing—what a human being is *capable* of accomplishing with people, via the heart and the brain. But mainly the heart. This is what I must learn best from her. That the heart has room enough, strength enough, desire enough, for so many people who need that heart's ways—and don't even know it. Amen.

Holding the $10,000 Harper prize check for Wasteland. *Cleveland, Ohio, 1946. Photograph by Herman Seid.*

With a copy of The Changelings *at the time of publication. Novelty, Ohio, 1955. Photograph by Herman Seid.*

Autographing Anna Teller.
Cleveland, Ohio, 1960.

*Summer, 1987. Jenkintown,
Pennsylvania.*

Winter, 1990. Jenkintown, Pennsylvania.

Autumn, 1990. Jenkintown, Pennsylvania.

Part II
The Journal of Death

In a Dying There
Is Much Living

*F*or garden lovers, when *would* the season of death start? In spring, of course. The Old Lady can be quite a cynic.

Do many people think, as I did, that it's forever because year after year the seasons come in their magic cycle? The roots, the rituals, the perennial always returning and the children growing up; the boy off to college and then a job; the girl marrying, and a son born. Forever, permanent.

Until a strange, new season comes in the shadow of spring. And how did it start? With planting, of course. And with the 1963 journal.

April 8 through 15: Planted (four kinds) annual poppies—wedding bed. Some parsley and dill. Three rows peas (Little Marvels—no stakes). One red potato (short row). New bed of fifty strawberry plants. There will be small but delicious berries this year in the old bed. The new giants won't be ready to pick until next year. More time for writing this year!

April 16 through 22: Two rows mixed lettuce (five kinds). Fourteen dahlias, including mouse-ears. One row beets. One row green and one of wax beans (early: the usual gamble that there won't be a freeze).

Note (for me, the writer): This new novel I'm writing is an odd one for me. Subject-wise. Story concerns a lot of Fannie's past life—the forties and fifties—and it could be so hackneyed that it took me forever to come up with a different technique angle in an attempt to freshen the story. Wonder if I overdid that—made it too slick.

April 27 and 28: The narcissus bed is loaded. Many opening.

Brought in first vase full, for kitchen table—to Helen's joy. Later, for therapy, left the book and planted a row of gropplers.

April 29: Radishes in (three kinds). Wrote for more than five hours—but more and more depressed. After all that work, I'm not even *sure* of the technique. Too deus ex machina? Keep wondering what Ed would possibly say about this book. Helen: "Just go on writing, dear!"

Note (for me, the person): Helen now has a "mild angina condition." I don't like that one bit. Though my automatic protector swears it isn't bad, that thousands of people take those nitro pills.

April 30: Nature went freak-nutty, dumped tons of snow on our area. The early farm stuff will be okay, and the berries—but my poeticus! "Jesus Christ, Helen, the narcissus bed is half in bloom." She: "But half are still in tight bud. Stop hollering. There'll be plenty for Fannie's birthday."

May 1: Sun, snow melting, it's in the sixties. Of course the green and wax bean seedlings are frozen black. Helen (at my snarling): "In ten minutes, you'll have new seed in. And there are plenty of birthday flowers coming. Look." Right. By the end of the day, lots of new narcissus and some dafs open. Fan's birthday is today, but I'm due in on her day off, Sunday. Phoned her "happy birthday" and talked about a dollar's worth on our damn long-distance phone. There's talk that Geauga County will be on regular dime calls soon. I hope so. Phone calls to Cleveland have been murder in cash, all these years. Just because we're three miles over the county line, damn it.

May 3: I'm on part two, chapter eight. The book will be too long, but why think of cutting and editing now, sap? Write, write! Worried about dough. Didn't tell Helen, but already owe Fan $810. What lousy echoes of my past life as the writer who borrows between books.

May 4: Replanted green and wax beans. It's a Saturday, and I'd planned to write all afternoon. So, at lunch (Mort's working), Helen: "Ruthie, let's do the marigold-zinnia bed. It's so lovely out." Me: "It's too early." Helen: "That was our last freeze—my bones

tell me. Let's! Then I'll really know that the season has started.''
Me: ''You nut.'' Laughed, moved the radio out on the porch. And
the marigold-zinnia bed went in. The music was marvelous, for
hours.

In the P.M.: Helen tired; Mort, too—off to bed. I went to work.
She left me a thermos of fresh coffee, and a sandwich in the refrig.
An old trick she started on Shannon, when I was working nights
so often. I ate at three in the morning—having written from nine.
Closed the swinging door, so she wouldn't hear anything. Porch
door open: peepers in full blast. I felt good, for a change: the writing had ''tasted'' tonight. Fed bits of cold meat to Ragsy, who'd
come out of her bed, half asleep. Inside stillness like this is so
lovely—so rare.

May 5: Perfect spring day. Planted her new seed: portulaca,
mixed colors. Under Martin's bedroom window. Helen types (original and carbon) the daily letter to her kids at his desk—so she'll have
a new kind of color when she looks out. Brought in a big mass of
pansies from her birthday bucket. Then worked until it was time
to pick Fan's narcissus and go in for her birthday celebration.

May 6 and 7: Wrote out the tall, wood labels for back acres.
Helen helped. Worked on book for hours. For therapy, lined up farm
rows and stuck in labels. Then back to the book. Writing a lot!

May 8: Out very early—back chores—-until Helen woke and
came to her bedroom window. That's still the real beginning of the
morning for me. Worked on book most of the day. We'll go to the
store tomorrow. She wants to try out that new butcher shop that
just opened in Chester. It does look like her kind of store.

May 9: Helen at the window rather late, but the usual, smiling:
''Good morning, darling.'' I told her over coffee what was new outside. Then—very quiet—she: ''Ruthie, please don't be frightened,
but I think I'd better tell you what happened. In the night—woke
me up.''
She described it: a prickling, all over her left side and face. Arm,
side, and leg felt rather numb. She woke Mort and told him: ''Just
in case.'' Me: ''In case of what!'' She shook her head—smiled. ''I
feel perfectly fine now. And pretty soon we're going to the store.''

I hollered no, she should rest—talk to the doctor. But she kept saying she was okay and would go herself if I didn't drive her. She wanted a beef roast. Mort had gone to Canton for the day—a hard, outdoors job—and she wanted a good dinner for him. And anyway, Dr. N wasn't in his office until one, usually one-thirty.

We went to the store. All was well; she'd picked out the roast and cold cuts, and it *was* a good store. Then, suddenly, she got terribly dizzy. I grabbed her, half carried her to the chair near the door. She kept smiling (but later, she told me that she'd felt numb and prickly, her eye "peppery" and her lips dead). I got her home, to the couch. The dizziness left. We ate lunch, and she seemed her usual self. Talked to the doctor: four o'clock appointment. Then she put through a call to Mort, gave him the latest info.

But by the time she dressed, she was very dizzy again. And her voice sounded oddly thick. God, I was scared. Had to help her into the car; then in to the doctor. Sat in the waiting room and smoked; couldn't read. It took an awfully long time. Then Dr. N called me in. Helen was sitting—smiling at me, of course. She: "Honey, I have to go into the hospital. To—sort of ward off something." I looked at him. He: "Incipient stroke. She's going in right away."

Turned out he couldn't get a room that fast at Mount Sinai (her hospital, and her family's, all their lives). There was a private room at Saint Vincent's (close to downtown: more than an hour's drive from home). Me: "Can't she even go home first—nightgown, toothbrush?" No. That frightened me more.

In the car, me (acting casual): "I'll bring your stuff tonight. Want the radio?" Helen: "That would be nice, dear—thanks." Me: "Still dizzy?" She: "A little—not bad. Saint Vincent's is a good hospital, you know. Virginia isn't easily pleased—and she liked it." After a while, softly: "Incipient. Know what that word means, writer? Please don't be frightened." Me: "I'm not! He must know what you need. He's good." She: "Yes. I trust him."

There was a wheelchair. A lot of nuns. I thought of V, all the times I'd visited her here, how she'd finally moved to Detroit, unable to work any more, and was living with her sister Suzanne. Upstairs, helped Helen get undressed; she was swaying a bit. Me (trying): "I'll come twice a day. Can't have you bored by anybody but me!" Then she was in bed, in one of those coarse hospital gowns. "God damn it," I muttered. Helen: "Go home and write me a book." I thought of the marigold-zinnia bed she'd been so insistent about. But she couldn't have known about this. More green-thumb stuff?

Helen (big smile): "Gardener dear, do me a favor? I'd like you to put in the cukes and pickles tomorrow morning. So plan on it—write today. And that'll give me a lovely picture in my head when I wake up. Promise?" I nodded. Some doctors came in, and Helen said: "Good-bye, dear," and held out her arms. As I leaned for her kiss, she whispered: "Please don't be scared."

"Put in the cukes and pickles." My car was full of that. And I remembered the first time I'd grown cukes—on Shannon.

I was farming next door on the empty lot, by then, our own yard not enough work-therapy for the explosive writer. I was finally writing that first novel. Helen (with Christmas-carol Grace's help) had gotten me a "grant" from a wealthy man they both knew: ten dollars a week, for one year; and I'd quit that boring typing job I found after WPA. Half the ten I gave to my mother every Friday, when I came home to eat Sabbath supper with the family. The other five seemed like a lot of money to me (naturally, Helen and Mort weren't charging for rent or food).

That spring, Helen said, "Want to try cucumbers, for a change?" Uncle Hugo had just bought that little shack near Chagrin Falls, so I'd seen what a cuke bed looked like. Fun.

Helen did research on how and when to plant, and I got the seed in. The summer began; the seedlings came up, and they grew—and so did my novel. Late July. The day before the joke, there were four cukes, about five inches long. I showed them off to the family—sure, proud.

The next day, after quite a lot of tense writing, I ran down to farm. The tomatoes and beans looked good. The half-dozen stalks of corn were up to my shoulders. For a while, I used the hoe, working off my explosiveness. Finally, I went to the cuke bed, full of yellow blossoms, and peered to see if there were any new baby fruits. The four "kids" were near the rear of the bed—where the sun hit most of the day. Eventually, I got to that area and leaned to see if they'd gotten much bigger over a hot night. All of a sudden, I saw a huge cucumber lying there; it looked almost a foot long. Dazed, I thought: Did we miss this one? Or is it a changeling? I picked it up; it seemed to break right off the vine, and I thought: That means it's dead ripe, according to that article Helen read me. Excitement gushed through me; it felt as if I'd written a beautiful poem.

I ran into the house, yelling: "Helen! Look at this cuke we missed even *seeing*!" The kids were with her. They'd all been at the window, watching, and all three had the loveliest smiles as I said jubilantly: "Hey, isn't this something?"

Then they burst into tender laughter, and the joke came out. My huge cucumber was really a zucchini squash. Uncle Hugo raised them, had brought some over late yesterday, while I was upstairs. In those days, I didn't know a thing about that vegetable. Early that morning, Helen had "planted" the zucchini.

She: "That's supposed to make you a gardener for life, *toi*. Nature and her miracles." And I thought: My God, it's like I never really laughed before.

I drove out of the hospital parking lot straight to the library, groped for a pencil and one of the pads of paper I always keep in my glove compartment. Sat down with the book the librarian had found for me, and wrote a lot of it out—the horror starting in me to go with the fear.

"A stroke is the result of damage to a part of the brain. This damage takes place if...a blood vessel (artery) in the brain breaks and blood escapes, or a clot of blood blocks an artery in the brain. These are the main causes of a stroke...Usually, the part of the brain that is damaged controls the muscles that move the arm, hand and the fingers, and the leg, foot and toes on one side of the body. After a stroke, the patient may not be able to move the fingers, arm, and parts of the leg on the other side of the body. Sometimes the part of the brain that controls the ability to speak is affected (aphasia)—and sometimes, as with any sick person, the patient may not be able to think clearly."

I felt sort of dizzy, as the word *paralysis* came rocketing up. Helen? Who loved moving among flowers, loved to walk the streets of New York, to run to her grandson? And—oh, no!—that brain, damaged?

Then—a crashing thought: When my eyes were first tabbed, the doctor called it "incipient glaucoma." But I got the real thing, anyway.

Driving home, I heard myself say it out loud, over and over: "Dear Lord kind Lord gracious Lord I pray Thou wilt look on all I love..."

She phoned. She sounded as ever—and laughing. Mort was

there; they'd phoned the children (that had always been a family promise created by Helen: any sickness, and the whole family was to know; and any journey—the itinerary). Told me she was full of something called an anticoagulant and feeling fine, and had eaten a good supper. So had Mort—in the hospital coffee shop. Had I? That was an order! And she was already bored—so would I bring in her two library books and the *New Yorker*, please? Mort was going to the Aunties—to break the news gently. Dr. N had been there, and was satisfied, and really really! she was feeling wonderful. No dizziness, even.

And she did look fine, when I got there. I set up the radio: a Vivaldi violin concerto. That music here—absolutely unreal. Helen: "Dear, when you come tomorrow, bring your work? Those clipboards are in Barb's room—second drawer." Me: "What's that anticoagulant?" She: "Just what it says. Keeps the blood from coagulating—making clots. Mine is called heparin." (In my head: ". . . or a clot of blood blocks an artery in the brain.") She: "I'll phone you every morning. The switchboard opens at eight. So you'll *know* I'm okay. It'll be cheaper if I phone you. Direct."

Eventually, I went home. So terribly unreal. Mort was asleep when I turned off the living-room table lamp. Rags was in her bed in the neat kitchen, near the fireplace—her tail stub going in welcome as I patted her. All in order.

But I lay in my bed, feeling how the heart of the house was gone out of it.

May 10: Mort doesn't seem worried. He plans to take his lunch (that I'd packed, the way she always has, the night before) to Helen's room, eat there—her idea. His job is only about fifteen minutes away. I forced myself to plant the cukes and pickles. Rags misses Helen—it's so obvious. I had her out with me, but she kept wandering back to the garage. Whined at the door. Damn.

The phone—twenty past eight. Helen sounded marvelous. "What time did you get my pickles in?" she demanded. Me: "The cukes are in, too." She: "Good. Now listen. It's Friday—you're going to eat dinner at Sadie's, as usual. Everything *is* usual! So bring a big piece of your work, and stay all afternoon. And dear, will you please drop Ragsy at the Aunties? Mort'll pick her up this evening. Take the leash and a can of dog food." Me: "Good idea. She's wandering around, looking for you." Helen: "Aren't you?" But I didn't laugh, the way she did. I went out and hung the wren houses. I suddenly longed to hear those torrents of song.

Hospital: she looked as always. Told me Dr. N says she's doing well. I'd brought in two jammed vases: narcissus and dafs. She loved them. After a while, I wrote out some more recipes for dinners, to her dictation. Later, she napped, and I worked. It wasn't as impossible as I thought it would be. Just unreal—like everything else.

Home by half past eleven from Sadie's. Did everything Helen used to: set table for Mort's breakfast, packed his lunch (he isn't working—Saturday—but plans to eat with her), poured his cocoa and cut a pat of butter and put the butter dish on the cocoa pan, top shelf of refrig (a Helen-invent, ever since she was ordered to sleep late). Rags came, and I gave her snippets of cold cuts. She sat up—and I wanted to bawl at that usual sight.

May 11: On the phone, she sounds good. Walking around; and she'd found a pay phone close by: bring me a lot of change, I'll use this phone to call home, and we won't run up a big bill; this way it'll hurt less. Mort and I laughed (I was on the extension): Helen was clicking in the brain, as ever.

Mort left, and I cooked that damn Thursday beef roast. Rushed out, got together a many-colors bunch of flowers—including the first of the bleeding heart. Toured the joint, so I could give her a full report.

At hospital by half past two. She looks rested—terrific. But she's worried: wash week's coming up, and she's very disturbed at my doing the whole house—on top of writing, gardening, and the long trips to and from the hospital. Me (honest and stern): ''And for how many years have you been doing my bed and all the rest of the junk—to save me time for writing? Cut that out.'' (Fortunately, our gal, Margaret, who comes every two weeks, is very good and fast at ironing, cleaning.)

May 12 and 13: She's good, good. I give her reports on garden and farm, we talk, she naps and I write. But thank God she phones me every morning!

May 14: (Written very late that night.) Morning, on the phone, she was fine. Me (agreeing with her suggestion): ''Okay, I'll come in the evening. I do have a lot to do.'' And tore into all of it. Had

Rags with me most of the time; she doesn't seem so terribly lonely. Left Mort's food in a low oven. He'll stop and see Helen on way from work: his weekly bridge game's at our house tonight (usually Monday, but one of the men was out of town yesterday).

Hospital by seven. Uh uh, she looked pretty tired—and was in bed. She'd been up, either in a chair, or meeting me in the hall, on other days. Finally, when I insisted, told me what had happened. And I learned a new word: *episode.* That morning, on her way from the pay phone, she stopped to talk to one of the nuns. Who had noticed that Helen's speech was a bit blurred; ordered her to bed. By the time the house doctor got there, Helen had had the first of a series of those brief episodes: prickly sensation—arm and leg, face; numbness, dizziness, eyes bad: that peppery feeling, and as if they were unfocused. Me: "Where's Dr. N!" Helen: "I spoke to him. So did Mort. He's coming tonight. He's talked to the doctor here— they gave me some new medication."

She seemed a little scared, so I put on my best acting costume, and gave her a blow-by-blow description of every seedling up, the violets starting, chippies out by the dozen. She (smiling): "And did you get a lot written?" Me: "Reams. All around the washer and dryer."

Dr. N got there close to eight. Examined her, said she seemed in good shape. Helen had a lot of questions to ask. He was very honest. Proceeded to tell what can happen sometimes in a stroke— what those episodes often are prelude to. "But you are in really good condition. So don't worry." Me, I got sick all through my stomach, listening.

Suddenly, out of the blue, Helen had some kind of an attack. It was the most terrible thing I've ever seen. She called out in a strangled voice, completely unlike hers—jerked all over her body. Then she couldn't talk at all. Her eyes stared, bulged. Then—my God!—her left leg started to jump up and down—the entire leg—as if it were having a convulsion of some kind.

The doctor lunged at her, shouting at me to turn off the light; and he had that instrument with a tiny light at her eyes instantly. I went to her, too, other side. Grabbed at her shoulder with one hand and my other hand went to that leaping, twitching leg. Tried to hold it down, but warned myself not to force it. Dr. N was talking to her, moving very fast as he examined her. I just held on, tried to reassure her with my hands. That continuing, involuntary jerking of her leg made me want to scream. (Much, much later, I asked him what in God's name that was. He: "The sensor in the brain wasn't working.")

After a while, he told me to turn on the light. Helen wasn't struggling so much. Then the leg stopped, thank God. Dr. N: "You're all right, Helen. Listen! I find nothing wrong. Please relax. Right now." She snapped back completely, as he talked. He called for a nurse, certain medication. When the nurse came, I went out to the hall and smoked. My heart was still a banging of fear, my legs shaking.

Dr. N came out. Me: "How is she?" He: "All right. I gave her a sedative. Good night."

Oh, no! I followed him to the elevator. Me: "What the hell *was* that?" (He's used to me. He's my doctor, too.) He: "Hysterical attack, I'd say. Probably brought on by our discussion of strokes." Me: "She's not the hysterical kind." He: "She's a very emotional woman. And that was frightening talk." Me: "God damn it, what was that horrible thing that grabbed her?" He: "Now, look! I examined her very thoroughly. There was no sign of stroke."

I was full of begging stuff: Help her—that was no phony! I didn't know how to say it.

The elevator came. I went back to her room. There was a night light; I could barely see her. Asleep? I sat down, near the door. After a while: "Ruthie?" I came to the chair next to the bed, took her hand. It was warm, quiet. "You okay now?" Helen: "Yes. I'm sorry, darling." We'd always talked over everything, but I could not say "hysterical" to her. I stayed a long time, and we didn't have to talk. Finally, she told me to go home; she'd sleep now.

When I told Mort (in his room, away from the men), he looked anxious but said at once: "Helen has the utmost trust in him. So do I." I nodded, went to my room. Thought, cold as ice all through me: That was not hysteria.

May 15: She phoned at exactly one minute past eight. "Ruthie, I'm fine! It's like a bad dream. We have to forget it." Mort had just left for work—having stopped in to check on her. Voice sounded certain, crisp, strong. Told me Dr. N had been there early, said she looked fine to the exam, but she'd told him she wanted a neurologist to check her. She: "I am *not* worried. I simply want a damn good research job. Stay home and plant. Write. Come in tonight. I really feel fine."

Got there in time to be company for Helen and her dinner tray. She does look good. Told me she was dizzy twice, but brief, when she went to the john. It's across the hall; she's in an old section of this hospital. She seemed fine all evening. I tried not to think.

Home by eleven. Had stopped at Emil and Liz's—guess I was lonely for old, old friends. He's still cold to me. Has been, ever since *Anna Teller*. Three years of punishing me for that book—Jesus. But Liz gave me a drink, was her usual sweet self. On the way home: my old friends made me feel even lonelier tonight.

May 16: Morning: she feels fine, fine. Stay home until dinner, said she. I'm going to be busy most of the day with tests, anyway. Write me a good book today, *toi!* So Rags and I gardened. Then, writing. And hey!—the stuff looks pretty good.

These days, I permit Rags into my room while I work. Helen had trained her to stay out, even when doors were open. She lies quietly behind me—head on her big front paws. Sighs once in a while, or whimpers softly, and I say something soothing. I guess we're both grateful for each other.

I'm sort of tired. A lot of it is this different kind of writing, I think (fighting to make time for it, working at odd hours and sometimes in Helen's room). The seasonal work, plus the housework. As for that trip to the hospital and back—it's kind of a killer. But when I skip the afternoon visit, I feel lonelier—and guilty: I know she needs me—my smile, my descriptions of house and land. And this: I've taken to acting most of the time; in case she *is* scared. That makes me very tired.

May 17: Food-shopped, while Margaret washed floors. Phoned Helen for only a dime from the store—always a money triumph. She feels okay. Neurologist due soon—and tests. "Love to Margaret. And you write!"

Got together a very different small vase for the visit: fritillaria— white and striped. They look like little lanterns. Ah, the portulaca is up—don't forget to tell her. A new flower for the writer of children-letters. One copy to Martin, now working in Chicago; the other to B and D in Northampton, where D teaches at Smith, and Eric Jan is growing like a high-class weed. He'll be three in November.

Margaret worked like lightning, so I got to the hospital early. Helen tired but so smiley. Like the neurologist. Special tests: brain

X ray, brain wave, plus many others. A spinal tap would have been very important—but impossible (her bad back, to begin with, and it's still very painful from other tests; the tap would have done a lot of damage). They hope to come up with the diagnostic works tomorrow. But (she said it twice): "I can't wait to see the portulaca!"

On the way home, my actor's costume in shreds, I thought: She doesn't seem scared when I'm there. But is that because she's protecting me? The way she always has? I've *got* to sell her a real bill of goods on how strong I am these days.

May 18: Very restless (that medical report). Mort and I left at the same time, two cars. When Helen told us the diagnosis, I felt dizzy. Dr. N had said: "The neurologist and I concur. Blood clot at back of head—where two arteries join. Could have stroke on either side, or both. Or—not at all. No operation."

Mort (a mutter): "Good Lord." Me (instantly): "Nuts! Not you, babe." Helen smiled, said, "I'm not worried—I feel too good." Eventually, she sent Mort home to cut grass, nap, relax. Said to me: "Isn't it screwy? I feel absolutely wonderful. With that diagnosis." I thought: Hysterical attack? My God. How can I believe any doctor, ever again?

My acting held, all day. She ate well (I brought up a sandwich and we sort of had dinner together—laughing). Fine talk about my book, our flowers, little Eric. There was a gorgeous Mozart quintet on FM. She seemed comfortable, genuinely okay in emotions and body, but my head kept clattering with the words of that diagnosis.

After visiting hours, I "went out" (she was very insistent about it). Liquor, music, sex—and when I got home I didn't have to think about "could have stroke on both sides." All of me was turned off.

May 19: Sunday, but up very early, all of me turned on instantly—though I told myself sternly to remember how terrific she'd been yesterday. By seven-fifteen, I was out touring the joint, with Rags. Then—finally—I planted my morning glories. Heavenly Blue seeds all across the planter, and at my feeder stump, and some at the downspouts near the porch.

The phone did not and did not ring. Mort: "Maybe she's sleeping late—she felt so well yesterday." My heart had started ramming, but I forced myself to wait. Then it was nine o'clock, and I shouted: "Damn it, get her!"

I was on the extension. And oh, my God. Awful—everything
nightmare-changed. She told us there'd been three episodes in the
night—bad ones. The nursing had been very lax. She sounded terrified. I talked a blue streak—trying to quiet her: the glories, Chippy, anything I could think of.

We went in Mort's car, dropped Rags at the Aunties. Hospital:
she looked lousy. I insisted on a night nurse, said quietly: "Don't
worry, dear, I'll get the dough from Aunt Amelia. All they ever need
is to be asked, remember?" Mort went down at once, hired a nurse.
We both stayed all day and evening. Mort had talked to Dr. N; said
he didn't seem too alarmed, that the episodes were part of the pattern, and he'd had reports from the doctors on duty. I didn't believe anything, anybody. Though Helen did seem better, more
relaxed, by the time we left. At home, I made myself write. Didn't
know what else to do for my fear.

May 20: The thing is, people don't *tell* you what's going on, what
to expect. She phoned, shortly after eight. Even then I didn't realize what had happened, what was happening that moment. I think
that damn bunch of episodes—always disappearing—blinded me.
The doctor always saying they were only the pattern.

I didn't even focus at that thickish voice, as she poured out the
story to me: she felt terribly sick, everything hurt, it had been awful
at night. The private duty nurse had helped, and a doctor had
come—but awful, awful! Convulsive heaving of her body—right side,
leg, arm. The nurse had gone off duty at seven, of course. A woman had brought the breakfast tray and just left it—Helen had had
to eat by herself, and could hardly move. An egg in the shell, and
she'd felt so rotten that she thought she'd better eat, in case it
helped. Awful!

I phoned Mort at work, sped to the hospital. She looked dreadful. Mort was smoothing her hair, trying to comfort her. And—I can't
understand it!—even then, I didn't realize that she'd had a stroke.
Even after she said, in that blurred voice: "Hand, arm, leg—gone."
My head just wasn't working. Or maybe everything in me refused it.

Dr. N came. Then other doctors. Her voice was thicker; I could
hardly understand her. Mort went out, his face stark pale. I stood
in a corner, listening to the doctors, to her voice petering off as they
gave her shots, ganged around her with instruments. All my insides had fallen out, but I stayed there. In case I had to rescue her

in some way. Or she called for me.

The doctors left; Dr. N talked to Mort in the hall, but I sat and held her hand, said: "Helen, I'm going to help you. It's all right, dear. We're here—Mort, me. To *help* you." She tried to open her eyes, to talk. She couldn't.

This fantastic muting of the most articulate person I'd ever known—such an impossible thing. Mort came back. He'd phoned the kids; they were flying in.

Suddenly those convulsions started—right leg. The arm, too, but the real violence was in the leg. Mort groaned softly. Me: "Go out—smoke, walk around. It doesn't bother me."

No—it just *killed* me, inside. Helen's eyes opened as I put my hands on that thrashing leg. I could feel its sort of demonic insistence. I looked into her eyes (how frightened, how wide with shock, despite the sedation), said with all my phony strength: "Hey, you dear one, it's all right. I'm going to fix everything. Do you hear me?"

Her eyes said she did—and closed. Finally, the leg quieted. She seemed to be sleeping, and I was grateful. But when I took her left hand, it was so inert that I felt utterly sick. Never to plant a seed, to touch a beloved's face? I found myself praying that the sedation had knocked her out completely. All of this would be full torment for a brain like hers. There was that word we had both discussed in the past, when we'd read of such cases: *vegetable*. The person who lies speechless, motionless, often with eyes open but not knowing anyone; and sometimes it went on for months, for years. Dead-alive.

Once she said to me: "Ruthie, if that ever happens to me, promise me you'll end it. Mort couldn't do a thing like that." I stared at her; she meant it, said: "I couldn't bear that. I might know it all—in my mind—and nobody would know if I could or couldn't hear—feel. Feel! Promise me, dear." I did. Then she was all right; it had tortured her even to visualize herself in that shape.

I smoothed that hand and arm, thought: How am I going to help *her*? (My paralysis was of the spirit, my blurred voice the heart.) Everything in me rushed toward that one thing: how to push back into her the strength she gave me so long ago.

Barbara and Diedrick came (a friend is taking care of Eric); an hour later, Martin. Helen's eyes opened. She knew they were there, kissing her, but she was almost voiceless. Got worse as the night went on. I kept trying to quiet the leg; it would start up suddenly. Nurse there—very good. Doctors. Awful, unreal, terrible.

I finally suggested the family go home and get some rest; said I was fine, I'd stay for a while. They were so tired with worry and grief that they let me send them home. Why wasn't I that tired? My tremendous need to help her. And fury. Christ, I was angry at the unfairness of this thing.

I stayed until past two in the morning. She knew I was there—knew in stretches—until the sedation took over for good. I drove toward the country, cursing—doctors, fate, nature. Tears came to my eyes; I was thinking of stubborn Helen eating that egg out of the shell, almost paralyzed already—phoning home the moment it was possible.

I hit the countryside, my headlights picking up the spring so night-beautiful in tree and grass and bush. For a second, I thought: Ma died in May. But I fought that. Pulled other kinds of memory into me.

Like: When I finished that first novel, she found an agent (a good one, but not too big). The grant-for-a-year had long since run out. I'd found that job with the Red Cross, finished the novel evenings and weekends. She thought it was an excellent job. I? Full of wonder that I'd written a book that Helen thought was good.

The agent wrote back: "Shows promise, some talent, but unfortunately not a very good novel. Interested in seeing the next one."

I wasn't surprised. Helen was furious. "What stupidity. This is a fine book. I'm about to send it in to the Harper Prize Award competition. There's very little time to make that deadline."

I really thought she'd gone crazy. "The top literary prize in the country? Come on! Anyway, you can't send in a carbon. That's just not done." Helen: "There's no time to wait for him to send back the original. And is that a Bible rule about carbons? If so, I'll take the blame with God! Damn it, what do you have to lose?"

So she sent it in. And I tried to forget all about it. Went to my job every day, gardened and wrote short stories, read my head off, and had a wonderful two-family life.

Then a letter—October 1, 1945:

> . . .and before I tell you the pleasant news, let me first apologize for keeping you in suspense so long. The trouble was that we had almost 700 manuscripts submitted in the Contest, and . . .

I am now very happy to tell you that your novel, "Wasteland," is one of those we have accepted for publication. This means that proofs of it will go to the judges in the Contest, and from among the novels similarly accepted they will select the prize winner...Your contract is now being drawn and it will be ready to send you within the next few days. All novels in the finals will be published by this Company, regardless of which wins the Prize.

Now let me tell you how greatly I myself was impressed by "Wasteland." It seems to me a really distinguished piece of work...It is a social document of genuine importance. And it amazed me as I read the manuscript to see how unfailingly you made the characters come alive and become wholly understandable. You ought to be proud of the book. Certainly Harper & Brothers will be proud to put their imprint on it.

And now you must write and tell me something about yourself. Is this really a first novel? I find no record of any other book you have had published, yet the competence of "Wasteland" makes it hard to believe that it can be a first...We ought to be sending the manuscript to the printer very soon.

Cordially yours,
Edward C. Aswell,
Editor-in-Chief

Helen (tears in her eyes): "I'm so happy for you, dear." Me (completely dazed): "Sure, you promised me. But my God, Helen!" I didn't believe any of it.

Now she was laughing. "Miss Sinclair, I notice that this Mr. Aswell did not disdain a carbon copy?" Me: "Helen, my book. Published." She: "That'll be the first book I ever had dedicated to me. I feel immortal, already...seven hundred manuscripts!...And you just wait." Me: "For Christ's sake, don't throw the *big* miracle stuff at me." Helen: "Oh, but darling, I believe in miracles."

Five hundred bucks—advance against royalties. To me, a fortune. I passed chunks of it around—cash, gifts. There was much laughter in both my families.

And then the big miracle did happen. And Helen cried: "Would I love to see that agent's face when this story hits the *New York Times*!" And that joyous laugh came, to make the letter real. January 4, 1946:

...and never in my editorial career, I think, has any event given me greater pleasure than your winning the Harper Prize Novel Contest with your first novel, "Wasteland." When I announced the news to you over the telephone, you said you couldn't believe it. Perhaps the enclosed check for $10,000 will at last convince you that...

About the book itself, you know how I feel. Let me add this: "Wasteland" is that rare thing, a first novel written with the technical competence of a master. The theme of it is the best possible doctrine for the time we live in, because, in addition to being a fascinating story, a brilliant delineation of characters, it is a plea for tolerance and understanding of minority groups everywhere—a plea for the abolition of a wasteland in all the areas of American life.

God bless you!

Helen: "God bless Edward C. Aswell. Ruthie, look at this review in *P.M.* Oh, dearest, be happy."

Jo Sinclair's "Wasteland" is a monumental psychological study in family relationships, and something of a masterpiece in its ability to evoke the emotional frustrations of Jewish life in America. Above all, it is a bitter, surging poem; but the bitterness has in it the courage and strength of life. The writer is a relentless but tender searcher after truth, and she makes the reader realize that the novel can be as valuable a tool in the revelation of human experience as science...Not since I read James Joyce's "The Dubliners" have I felt so intensely the throbbing frailty of human life depicted in modern prose. The book burns with sincerity and honesty. Personally I've known Jewish people for years and I've waited in vain to hear a voice speaking the truths that I've known and felt were in the Jewish home. Well, here at last is that voice, and it is like a cry tearing its way out of the throat.

Richard Wright

Me: "Helen, this was one of my library teachers in writing!"
She: "Then relax a little. And we haven't seen one bad review. On the contrary! By the way, dear, I've ordered *The Dubliners* for you. A very small celebration gift from this family." And my other family?

Ha! My father looked absolutely stunned. He said: ''Ten thousand dollars for *one* book? Je—sus.'' Helen (tenderly): ''All right. Now even he knows you're not a nut—all that money you earned. Too bad he can't read English and know what this letter of Wright's really stands for. But let him be impressed by the money. And Ma? She *is* happy, dearest. Feel good about that. This is a medal for her—in the eyes of the world. You've finally given her enough, Ruthie. Ma's Ruthie. Won't that dissolve a scar or two? But dear, *I* know what this letter means to you.''

Dear Miss Sinclair:

Ed Aswell (after all, I'm a Harper author, too) gave me the galleys of your book and asked for my reaction; that reaction has no doubt reached you, in my review in the newspaper, *P.M.* I meant what I said. I believe that you have written truly a fine book, honest, sincere, true, and in some respects a terrible book. I'm not one to write letters to other writers; usually, I never even feel the impulse to do so; but when I finished your ''Wasteland'' I thought that I ought to let you know that I think it great. Honesty such as you put into words is seldom seen. And the suffering you depict is rarely ever admitted. And the insight you possess is surely not common. These three things—honesty, suffering, knowledge—well, they constitute what I think is the highest level of personal culture possible in our time. You have said about the Jewish family what I've been trying to say about Negro families. And you said it well, poetically. I don't know what others will say to you about what you've written; maybe you'll get some of the hot blasts I've gotten and grown used to. But that does not matter. You are right, and the more truth that can be given the more ready the world will be in the mood for change. If you travel this road of telling the truth, you'll have to be ready to travel light and fast; the more truth you tell the smaller will grow the ring around you. But you must be ready to accept that. The kind of glory you are going to get will have in it the sting of bitterness. But keep on. What you are really doing is revealing to those who live about you what they feel and do not know that they feel. And not many people are of so hardy and emotional a digestion that they can take it. Again I say that I believe that you have really written yourself a book.

If you come to New York, I'll be happy and proud to meet you. And if there is any way in which I can be of service to you here in New York, I'd be more than glad to help. With admiration for what you have done, I am,

Yours sincerely,
Richard Wright.

Me: "Oh, Helen. When I read *Native Son*, I—am I awake?"
Helen: "You are! Ruthie, see how wonderful and generous people can be? And to meet him—I'm so glad for you. Did Ed say exactly when he wants you to get there for the party and interviews?"

• • •

I drove—kept pushing toward home—hanging on to her, memory and now. All the past promises merged with the biggest one she'd ever made to me. The one she *had* to keep.

May 21: My God, it's inconceivable! She's better. By late afternoon, a bit of movement in hand and leg. Whatever's in me—like fire—I feel as if I can do everything in my world, but Helen-first. The kids are helping enormously. We've borrowed cars from the Aunties; we'll split up Helen, the house, Rags; and Mort'll go to work at least part of the day—for *his* therapy.

That smile came the minute I walked in. I was there all day, doing what I could with talk. Left at quarter till eight; Barb there, reading aloud to her mother. Get home and do some writing, babe.

May 22: Helen phoned—herself! Sounds happy: "So tired, but better. Dr. N says I'm improved. I'm to move arm and leg as much as possible. Physiotherapy soon, if all goes well. I slept all night." Her voice thick, but that, too, better. A morning nurse started today. She *ordered* me to stay home and write. The kids are going in early. Went out as soon as they left—Rags with me—picked huge bunch of violets, all shades of blue, and some white. Ordinarily, I don't have the patience for that slow job of getting the longest stems possible. But, by God, I'm going to bring her samples of all her flowers.

Toured a quick one—for a report to her. Weeded a little, and threw clods to make Ragsy happy. Then wrote-wrote-wrote...

Martin phoned—excited. The supervisor of nurses told him Helen would be okay in two and a half to three weeks—may be home by then. Is that possible? Do I believe it? (Dear Lord kind Lord gracious Lord!) Went on writing. I have so far to go on this book before I get even a first draft. But don't think of that. She's better!

Got to the hospital fourish. All of me studied her while I showed her the violets and told her about the garden, Ragsy, anything wondrous I could think of. . . The paralysis is there, yes, but she showed me the slight movements possible to her. Her mind is completely unimpaired, thank God, and the doctor's told Mort that he expects her to be walking. . .I sent the kids home—to rest and eat. All will be back this evening. Brought the violets close, for her to smell. She (such a smile): "Woods—lovely." In that clogged voice.

Helped her move her poor fingers, helped her eat from her supper tray. Martin's due to be nurse tonight: eight-thirty until eleven. Early evening: she had heart pains. I called a doctor, fast: medication. Then I sat close and talked—good as a Barrymore—about my book. Finally got her full attention, *pulled* her away from the fear.

May 23: Phone: a bit better. I got there at two. Had written all morning, while B and D cooked and chored, and Martin was with Helen. The writing is the only thing that can make me forget the jerking leg, the paralysis. Sometimes.

She seems less exhausted. They've given her a johnny-chair, which means no more bed pans—she loathes them—and that she's going to be out of that bed for stretches.

Martin grabbed me in the hall, worried: "I have to go back Sunday. My job." I reassured him. Thought: Third nurse coming up? Well, hell, I'll just phone Aunt Amelia again. Helen and Mort can't ever beg but I can—for others. But why the hell can't people offer, without waiting to be asked? It makes such a difference!

May 24: *Very* much better (phone). First physiotherapy due today. I saw her at six in the evening. Tired, but a different kind. A little more movement in hand, arm, leg. Her eyes are badly impaired (God, what a rotten sickness this is), but we're all reading to her in short stretches. Brought in tulips and asparagus fern; what a smile.

Didn't tell her, but at home, earlier, Barb told me she's homesick for her little boy. D was working on class stuff. He's a bit upset about his job; but neither really wants to leave.

May 25: Phone: Helen good. Speech slow but not too thick. Today's our anniversary of meeting. I brought her a paperback of Rilke's *Duino Elegies*—new translation. And a vase of her own grape hyacinth, Star of Bethlehem, and fiddle fern. Handed her the book, said laughing: "Get guilty. Because naturally I expected you to jump up and shop for my present." She: "Oh, I'm so glad we met in life!" Me: "Amen to that." And read her a piece of one of the poems.

The physiotherapy department is open only a half day on Saturdays, so she had physio in bed—arm and leg. I watched intently: I'm supposed to exercise her evenings here. And at home (I hope!). Therapist: "Don't force, don't buck nature. Just her leg tonight. Practice while I'm here."

I felt pretty tense. Helen (casually): "Dear, just green-thumb it." I laughed, and was okay. I felt my way—learned from toe movement, leg push and pull, where to go and when to stop. Therapist: "Good. Want a job?"

May 26: She sounds wonderful, long distance. But, damn it, this is the night Martin's leaving. And she needs all her beloveds right now.

Rushed out to the garden. Hey, the lilacs are busting—so early. Some florets already open, including a few on the white lilac—usually later to bloom. But no point in cutting before they're full open; they just droop. B and D went in at three. Martin slept. Mort's working—a lousy special Sunday job. Ran Rags around the dam. Then wrote. Forgot everything. Thanks, whoever!

Hospital by five. Hand and leg stronger. My job—the bad leg: ten exercises every hour—toes, foot itself, then entire leg. When she's stronger, it'll be both legs (arms, too)—a matter of keeping the good ones from muscle waste. What a disease—phooey. I notice that when Helen is tired, her voice is slow and it's harder for her to articulate. Said good-bye to Martin: he's leaving directly from the hospital tonight, but he'll be back as soon as he possibly can.

May 27: Bless the phone: she's good, good! I flew out to embrace the Old Lady. Ah, the bitch was doing her bit with the lilacs. Even the white: five lovely blooms wide open.

Hospital by two. Helen: "Lilacs! Already? And even the white."

Me: "Special for you. Earth and heaven are rejoicing over your recovery. Come on home. I can't bring you the whole outdoors."

Tears in her eyes—but that's one of the by-products of the stroke, I've discovered. Patient cries at the drop of a hat, and I hate it. But she *is* improved. Bored with bed—good. Leg and arm movements much better. Says she's walking better in the physio department. Voice very good today, but jaw rather slack, and eyes still bad. I told her Barb was cooking up a storm. Her last day, as she and D are leaving tomorrow. I listed the million things she was making for me and the freezer against future quick dinners. And so I got Helen to feel better, stopped the tears.

Put on the FM: the Brahms intermezzos, of all things. It got us to reminiscing about how I'd used the Number 117 for *The Long Moment* at the Play House, and Barbie had played the piano for the tape Mort had made—to be used in the play. Wonderful talk—good for both of us.

May 28: Told me she's due for physio mid-morning—a longer stint. Kids leaving on the noon plane, from the hospital. Damn.

Farmed, wrote. She phoned at one-fifteen (an extra call always scares the hell out of me). Seems that, while eating lunch, a brief session of dizziness, and *right* side of face prickly and numb. Passed off, but left her very tired. And scared—that's why she phoned (doesn't want to disturb Mort at his crummy job). Talked my head off; know I reassured her. Why can't I do the same for me?

Mort has a bridge game tonight, so I asked him to eat at the Aunties. At hospital by six-thirty. So she was fine! I learn some more vocabulary: "CVA—cerebral vascular accident." If only somebody could tell me what's coming, what I can do!

I'd brought in mock orange (the double-flowering japonica I'd transplanted from Shannon to South Woodland to the country). Her eyes: years of memories—but a smile. Good. While I fixed the vase, she gave me the news. Dr. N had been in at five and found her very improved. Voice, especially. Then she (very casually): "He said I might be going home Sunday." Me: "Sunday! Honey, how wonderful! Really?" Jesus, how is that possible? But look how happy she is.

She's quite agile; I had her out of bed, and the exercises went well; her arm and leg seem much looser. But my head: Sunday! Would *somebody* please tell me the truth about this sickness?

Home after ten. Too tired and nervous to even think of writing. Sunday? No, no, toss out wheelchair, responsibility, me alone with my "patient." And the book—No, don't think!

May 29: Morning: she's fine, so excited about coming home that she's restless, bored—but full of laughter. Told her to get her mouth ready for asparagus; it's coming, asparagus-pig! *Big* laugh. Drove to Bloom's, bought twenty pounds of sunflower seeds for the Chippy play I'd written while I couldn't sleep. When I got home, put the carpenter bench in front of the porch, thumbtacked two aluminum pie plates to top, one on either side of the carrying slit. Filled the pans, heaping. It's Wednesday; takes about two days for our creatures and birds to get used to a new restaurant, so I started rehearsals today. Wrote for a nice chunk of time, then finished preparing the farm for Mrs. M's flats of stuff. Tomorrow's the big day. Everything's ready; even the rain barrels are full.

Helen phoned about one (scared me, sure), excited, to report the latest. Bought a cane, known as a walker—it's got four legs—from the physio department. Only four dollars—isn't that wonderful, *toi*? Dr. N and Mr. P (head therapist) both said she'd be walking on her own in a month or so. "And then, no wheelchair—be independent," said they. Me (dazed—to Me): It must be true. They wouldn't lie about a thing like this! Helen went on: Sunday definite. Please phone Sam-Beauty about coming in to cut her hair—as he'd promised to do at the right time. And Uncle Hugo had dropped in and left two hundred bucks.

God bless everybody. Including God. Phoned Sam: her hospital room—tomorrow?—shampoo and haircut. We've been "taking" from him for years—strictly haircuts, though it's a beauty shop. Swell guy. Loves to fish—and of course Helen invited him to come to our pond, any time, and he has been coming for years. Mort named him Sam-Beauty.

Hospital late afternoon (left Mort a load of dinner). Brought lily of the valley. And a corned beef sandwich and strips of pickle I'd bought at a delicatessen. Me: "I hear there's a patient here who's bored with hospital food." Helen: "Ruthie, you angel! Today, better than a poem." But I saw her eyes when she looked at the little bells of the flowers, said as casually as I could: "Better take a good whiff of that vase before the garlic happens to you."

Watched her eat with relish, and entertained her with a full

report on home—but kept the Chippy play a secret. Helped her a little (the left hand isn't much good for eating). She's talking a lot— very excited about leaving, and particularly about the shampoo and haircut: "I want to be clean and fresh for home!" (I know all about it: she wants a clean, fresh, whole body, is what.)
Home by ten. I'm getting up early to drive to Mrs. M's for the farm and flower flats. I *want* that ritual. It should make me feel good to think about it. But Helen? At home here, with only me—instead of nurses and doctors and therapists? I start writing, where I left the notebook. Thinking, like a kid: Lord, help me?

May 30: Fast fast day. Helen had her hair cut and washed—and a very early bath: phoned her from Mrs. M's house, got all the news. She wants terribly to be home watching me plant. Me: "Hey, don't be a pig." Good laughter.
Drove home and started at once to plant in the prepared earth, and to water each row to keep off as much transplant-shock wilt as possible. Both rain barrel levels went way down. Gorgeous day. Rags loves it. Still setting out Copenhagen cabbage—and a tiny grief called Sarah J goes into each of the six plants as I firm earth around them. And, of course, I put in three hot pepper plants for Emil, damn him. I love him and hate him at once.
Began to miss Helen fiercely. I phoned her twice—gave her reports on what was set out, what remained; not for her sake to-day, but for mine. I'd started missing her on the drive to Mrs. M's.
Got to hospital at six-fifteen—gay as a lark (very little of it act-ing, too). "Farm's in!" Music—talk—joy. But just before I left, He-len told me (so casually) that she had fallen today, trying to get out of bed. Insisted it was nothing—didn't even hurt.
On the way home: A pounding. Will she fall in the house? What if I'm outside, or in my room (*will* I have a chance to write)?

May 31: Up very early. Out the window: aha—the Chippy re-hearsals are now perfection; the bench is loaded with their inces-sant movement. And with blue jays, sparrows, cardinals, Tufty-Ts—when the mump-faces depart briefly to disgorge. Had coffee with an excited Mort. Today, he's pricing rental of wheel-chair and johnny-chair. Off he went. Out I went—with Rags. Watered everything. Not too much shock wilt. Some years they have what I call the grand wilts (on very hot planting days), and it takes quite a time for the seedlings to stagger up again. Set out the planter flowers: the fragrant white petunias and mixed-colors annual dahlias Helen loves. Should look lovely—especially after the blue of the glories starts. I've started training the glory seedlings up the short stakes, and a few have already made the garden ties.

In by ten past one. Got a real lesson—went to the physio department with Helen (she in a wheelchair), and Mr. P showed me how to exercise her shoulders and arms when she's home. Also gave me a manual, said it's full of important rehabilitation facts. Saw Helen walk—with that cane. She's pretty good, already.

At home, in bed, I read the manual. It has a title, like a novel: *Strike Back at Stroke.* Jesus! I read it as carefully as if it were Faulkner. Stomach rocking, after a while, at the definitive stuff on exercises, how to get the patient out of bed, helping her walk without a cane (right arm around her waist, other hand holding patient's left hand out for balancing). As background music, my head kept clamoring: Dear Lord kind Lord...

June 1: Filled the Chippy dishes. I do several times a day, and they're performing like stars. They'd better—this is dress rehearsal day. Rags and I watered everything (most of the wilt is gone). Phone: she's fine, so excited, can't wait for tomorrow. So I changed linens on all the beds, cleaned the house—fast but thorough.

I'll wait for flowers inside until tomorrow—they'll be at their freshest. Tore into town for food (the best), then to a Jewish bakery for the kind of rye bread and rolls she loves. Home, put foods away; and Mort came soon after with the wheelchair, johnny-chair (she hates the word *commode),* toilet bars for bathroom and lavatory, and three shower and bath bars. Odd: my stomach sinks at sight of them, when I should be happy they've been invented.

Rags and the wheelchair: sniffed, growled, circled it, barked. Finally, me (stern): "Now listen, Rags, you get used to this chair." I patted it: "Nice chair. Helen's friend. Get used to it!"

She didn't, so I rehearsed with her. Rode her around in it; then pushed it all over the house, talking "nice chair" to the tensed-up dog following me. Her third ride: she seemed a bit better. And she was no longer biting it. Oh, God, the *details* of this sickness!

Helped Mort fix her bed according to the manual: take off casters—blocks of wood of proper height under each leg—easier for helper to care for patient. "When patient is better, remove blocks—

bed low enough for patient to get out of it on her own. Board at foot: patient's feet rest against it so that the toes point straight up.''

Me: ''Phooey.'' Mort: ''At least, she won't have to go through that rolled-up towel business. Or some of these other things—she isn't that bad. Don't feel so terrible, Ruth. You know her.'' Yeah, I know her. So I went out and brought in a small vase of mixed violets and lily of the valley, set it (doily under vase) on the closed johnny-chair. Mort laughed so hard that Rags came barking. I felt better.

Helped Mort fix bars for both toilets. He'll wait for the tub bars. She loves showers—but it's a bit soon for even a Helen. She'd reminded him, so now he tied two luggage straps to foot of bed. A Helen-invent (her bad back) for people who have trouble getting themselves up from a prone position in bed. Arthritics and such can use same trick in getting themselves up from toilet. You take hold of the ends of the straps (they should be near you, always), and pull yourself up with far less pain and discomfort. She's taught a lot of people her strap-invent, and I've heard Grace bless her for it.

Eventually, quick dinner. Rags ate, too, but was still muttering growls at her new enemy-on-wheels. Mort left while I was cleaning up. At the sink, I thought suddenly: Why haven't I written a poem to welcome her home? Answer (phony?): You're *living* the poems now, kiddo.

Hospital at seven. Helen okay, but hot and restless; she wants home. Stayed until ten—it was obvious she didn't want to be alone (we'd sent tired Mort to bed).

June 2: Up at six. Rags smelled the excitement, followed me wherever I went. Brought in vases and vases of flowers—for every room and the porch, and my room, too. Got a lot of preliminary food stuff done, so I can be with Helen more later. The Rags plan (Helen's): we put her on the latched-shut porch when we leave for the hospital, lock both doors into the house from the porch. After Helen is inside, sitting firmly, we let Rags in.

Now, what else? On thinking of the chippies, I decided to save their opening-night performance for tomorrow. There'd be too much for Helen to see the first day home—the play might make her too tired. So I moved the bench around the east side, hidden from porch or windows.

By nine-fifteen, we had Helen down, into the car—a completely radiant woman. She insisted on stopping briefly at the Aunties; all three were waiting in the yard—and Uncle Hugo had a basket of zucchini and leaf lettuce ready as we drove in. Kisses, and then on the way—home, home!

Me? Peculiar sensation. I'd had her paralyzed for life, and now she was sitting between Mort and me, my arm supporting her. Mort drove slowly, and Helen tried to look at everything. When we hit the real country, she said: "Oh, my beautiful outdoors." The radiance never left her, though she was sweaty with fatigue; told us her face was still numb. When she saw the house itself, a little muffled cry came from her. Then we heard Rags barking. Helen laughed—big.

Got out, we helping—but she insisted on using the walker from car into garage into utility room; only then, the wheelchair. Very tired, but so triumphant about having walked into her house. Me, I was already uneasy as hell about Rags (that heavy plunge of love?): barking, flinging herself against the porch door as she heard Helen's voice.

In the kitchen, Helen (such beautiful love): "Ragsy, Ragsy, it's all right. I'm home." Me: "Be careful, for God's sake." Helen: "Mort, open the door, please. Oh, *toi*, what lovely flowers. *Open* the door—I want my dog."

Rags practically flew in. Her feet instantly up on the wheelchair; sobbing, licking Helen's face, making the most heartrending noises. It was a weeping. Helen: "Put her in my lap, please."

I watched Rags get embraced with one arm, kissed, comforted. And I thought: Oh, Christ, a dog—look at love. The poor kid quieted down, finally, just squeezed herself tight against her mistress. Mort wheeled them both onto the porch. Helen: "Oh, Ruthie—the garden. Dearest, so lovely."

I carried Rags to the glider, stuffed her gently into her favorite corner, and muttered my own brand of love at her. She just lay there, exhausted, watching Helen. Lord, Lord, a dog! Brought the coffee I had in the pitcher-thermos, cookies. Mort ate a lot of them and fed bits to Rags, smiling in a kind of dazed way at his wife from the glider. Helen kept looking at the beds of flowers, the large vase of mixed lilacs I had on the porch table. Her eyes luminous—so beautiful to see.

After a while, she wanted to walk on the porch—with the four-legger. Very, very slow. Rags growled, but Mort hung on to her.

Shrimp salad and hot rolls for lunch: big smile from Helen. So odd to see her at the table in that wheelchair. I kept thinking of Eric in the high chair, pulled up to the table because he insisted on being a member of the wedding at meals—young as he was.

After lunch, Helen and Mort went to nap. When she saw the vase of flowers on the johnny-chair, I got a wonderful laugh and a kiss. They slept for about three hours, door closed and Rags stretched out in the hallway in front of it. I went to my room and finally cried.

Very festive dinner. Later, after I'd done the dishes, I exercised her a little (on couch). We'll start on the whole series tomorrow—if she's less exhausted. All her kids phoned, and that added the last star for her to the homecoming. What a smile, when she talked to Eric.

By ten-thirty I felt so tired I was shaky (but she didn't know it). Helped her with all the steps of getting ready for bed. Mort was already asleep in the other bed, but he had rigged up the bell that rings in my room: safety-pinned the button part to the bed near her good hand, and she promised me that she'd press that button if she needed me.

I lay in my bed, smoking. Feeling Helen in the house again—the heart beating here again. I would sleep tonight—because of that "lifeline" of a bell. One light touch on the black button, and I would hear. That was one of the first things she had dreamed up when we moved here—because our bedrooms were at opposite ends of the house. She was worried about me, for nights. I have a similar set-up behind my bed, and it rings in their bedroom if I press the button. It's a heart line. Tonight, I really know that.

June 3: Early: Mort off to work. Told me Helen's still asleep. Woke only once in the night. Me: "Johnny-chair?" He shook his head, and we grinned. She'd walked to the bathroom, using him and the four-legger.

I rushed out and moved the bench to center stage; filled the pans heaping. Went back, peered in: still asleep; Rags on Mort's bed, sleeping, too. I fixed a pretty bed tray (folds out into legs): doily, a small-small of fresh violets. Listened for bell every second.

Ran very fast, gathered strawberries for a surprise. Peeked around at the bench. Fine—the curtain was up, the performance was on: plenty of chippies and birds. Peered into her bedroom window.

Would she ever be standing here again, mornings, calling out to me? (Oh, please, God.) Ah, she was awake. I called good morning to *her*, in her bed. And the day began—with Helen in it—as I ran into the house.

She started right in monkeying with a luggage strap. Me: "Hey, wait! You don't have to do everything the first day." Helen: "I *want* to." And she practically did. Helped her out of bed, to wash. She used the four-legger for that inch-by-inch walking into the kitchen and living room. I suggested the crying chair for exercises—it looked perfect to me. (It was.) I'd brought the FM and a big hand bell to the coffee table; planned to take them, and reading, wherever she wanted to go. Nice: we had Schubert trios for the legs and toes. She seemed better, but the walking, plus even the eating, not to mention the exercises, are solid exhausting—though she kept smiling.

This is an extremely gutsy, stubborn woman. The walking, any moving, is so hard, but she even tried to do the wheelchair by herself. The carpeting makes it impossible, and her left hand and arm aren't much good for anything yet, let alone that. Yet she *fights* to do for herself. She moved the chair a little in the kitchen (tile floor). What triumph! Made my heart ache, as I grinned at her.

Simple lunch—brought it to the coffee table. She still hasn't noticed my play. I made her rest—couch; Rags on floor, right next. She fell asleep, and I ran out to heap the Chippy plates.

When she woke, she wanted to go on to the porch, and I wheeled her out. Yep, my little actors were right on cue. I must say their opening-night performance was a masterpiece. Helen was enchanted as they came in clutches of threes and fours. Fighting on the bench, in the plates; eating until their faces turned into extraordinary cases of mumps; then running home to stash their loot. All the birds came, too.

Beautiful—her laughter. Beautiful—the mild, sunny day; the music. Then the wrens started; they always do seem to sing their hearts out when the radio is playing so close. Helen looked at me, her eyes utterly lit. "Ruthie, thank you."

Once (trying to say thanks for my new life), I wrote her:

Speaking of rain,
Emptying small handfuls of wind

At your feet,
Scenting each room in your house
With lilac.
Painting the floors with grass.

Speaking of moon,
Scattering great handfuls of stars
At your feet.
Filling the cracks in the walls
With night sky,
Painting the ceiling with dream.

She promised she was fine, so I went off to do some necessary
hilling of corn and Van Goghs. Checked on her often (would I hear
the bell back there?). She wasn't reading; just looking at the play
I'd created, plus the Old Lady's masterpiece of leaf, sky, flowers.
Later, I cooked dinner. Time went: washed dishes, et cetera.
She was exhausted by nine, and quite ready for bed. At one point,
I finally threw a fit of fireworks at Rags—who keeps getting in the
way of the wheelchair, biting it, barking. Helen soothed *me*. And
I felt a lot of shame. Gave Ragsy extra snippets when I packed Mort's
lunch, and loved her up a little when I took her out for the night.
No writing today.

June 4: Up very early. Wrote until the bell. I've decided to try
this morning work whenever possible. Hard: unaccustomed to writing first thing in the day. On the other hand, babe, if a human being can relearn moving and walking, you can relearn pattern of
writing.
Helen today: a little freer movements of arm and hand during
exercises. Then she put on her own socks and shoes! Slow, tough—
but she made it, after a fashion. Walked pretty well with the four-
legger, but her bad leg goes rubbery often. Tired, but she insisted
on lunch in the kitchen, not lying down. And then the porch: "I
want to be *me!*"
Got her set up out there. Put Rags on glider; she can't jump
up anymore, poor old lady. Then farmed a bit, reporting regularly.
Helen: "And don't think you can holler me out of making dill pickles!" I planted another short row of dill.
The gardening is sort of a way of touching her. And touching

stillness inside of me. I made her a small: forget-me-not, and one lovely graceful branch of bleeding heart (four hearts tapering down in size to a very tiny one at the end). The plant is so far from the porch that I know she can't see nuances.

Evening. Wish Mort would offer to clean up the kitchen after dinner sometimes. I finally asked him (wanted to help her to bed), and of course he was extremely willing. But the *offering* would've been nice.

June 5: Wrote almost three hours before morning bell. Good. Helen: also good. For a change (during exercise and trial walking), I gave her a record concert—some of her favorites. She (eyes wet): "You're such a darling." Me (acting casual): "I'm saving the Toscanini Ninth for the no-crying days." She: "They'll come!" Me: "Of course."

Afternoon on the porch: the chippies were particularly charming. Helen (suddenly grave): "I want you to work for a while. I'm fine here. *Please*, dear." So I did—though I listened. But worked for almost two hours!

After dinner, tore up to food-shop (two stores in Chester are open until nine). I don't want to leave her alone during the day. Then Helen had her first shower. Mort helped, of course. Used bath stool, sat in the tub. She had a marvelous time—her laughter, Lord, Lord. I soaped the washcloth for her, then washed her back and legs with another one. Got soaked myself from the shower fall of water; the three of us laughed like loonies. How little it takes to make a person happy.

June 6: Weak day; back to bed right after breakfast. I brought the radio. Asked her to dictate more recipes. Sometimes she's asleep when it's time to start dinner stuff going. Got her to laughing when I asked how long to boil potatoes, how much salt in the water. But I really didn't know.

June 7: Damn!—overslept. No writing. Helen weak—rubbery legs. So I put her back to bed. Ordered her to rest. She: "Don't holler. Dear, I just want so much to—." Suddenly from the west, a pheasant's call. We smiled. Me: "Rest. You've got time for all of it. *Believe* that. Now I'm going to write—make you happy."

I, telling her to believe? What a switch of roles! But I did write.

And, by noon, she was better. Sat in the crying chair and read the morning paper. Then I exercised her—to the New York Pro Musica. Me: "Do you realize that I had never heard of a countertenor before I met you?" Helen: "Do you realize that I had never heard of a bagel or a potato knish before you?" Wonderful laughter.

After Mort came home, I drove to Sadie's for Friday night. Helen had insisted. Late as it was, I found a nursery open, and picked up a potted bleeding heart—in bloom. At Sadie's: the whole family was very tender with me—about Helen. After Fan left for work (Mildred drove her because I was so tired), I went to Ma's bedroom, sat on the bed, and thought of her at the last—not knowing me. Why did I do that!

June 8: Up early, planted the new bleeding heart at the east side of the front window—where she'll be able to see every detail.

She seems improved this morning, though there are bad spots. For example: the walking very, very slow. I directed her casually to the front window, then said: "Look—surprise!" The hearts seemed as fresh and lovely in their shady spot as if I'd painted the plant to order. Yes, she was very pleased. So was Mort.

And hey—did the new plant pour its hearts into her? She's the type. Because, after a while, she wheeled the chair by herself in the kitchen. And then—by God—she peeled potatoes for dinner. And sorted clothes for wash day. That really galvanized me; I went and wrote my own heart out into bloom.

Later, I helped Mort install the bars for showering.

June 9: Helen feels swell! Used the four-legger all the way to kitchen for breakfast (too often, that early, it's the wheelchair). A gorgeous Sunday. She on porch—chippies cavorting like mad. I wrote for a big chunk of time, then ran Rags around the dam (scaring frogs—plunk—into the water). Stood there, and the Bach from the porch came across the pond—so very beautiful.

Rest of the day: good. Quite a few visitors, including my sisters and niece. She loved it. Though she was pretty tired after the last talker left. After supper (in bed), she insisted I go out and see some friends. "Please. It would make me so happy."

Home by midnight—went back to her, as she always wants me to. One light touch and she was awake. Trek to the john and back. I filled her in on my evening (it brings the world to her, I know).

Mort sleeps on, snoring, and we giggle at the racket.

June 10: She had a shower—standing! (Those bars are wonderful.) My tenseness left, as I watched her laugh at the old, familiar "home" of a shower. We were at the blood lab by two-thirty. There was a wheelchair at the medical building, and she rode smilingly—the four-legger in her lap. Through at the lab and up in Dr. N's office by three. She walked in—insisted—and even he looked pleased. I phoned Mr. P at Saint Vincent's, as I was supposed to. He was pleased with her progress; and to phone next week again—or phone any time I run into a snag on the rehabilitation.

Dr. N: "Get off the heparin until Thursday—level's too high. See me in a month—unless there's an emergency. But you must get tested at the lab every Monday on the anticoagulant level. I'll phone you on any change of dosage. You are doing *well*." Lord, thanks!

June 11: Wrote for almost two hours before bell. Helen woke weak and tearful. This up and down! Back to bed after breakfast. Sit-exercise, but no walking. In bed, she fell asleep to the radio music—Rags next to her.

And I? Went out and hoed—hard. And looked into her window regularly. Wondered about my book—thought of all the books and plays I hadn't written yet. Out here, away from her need, I can put aside the actor's costume and props for a while, and wonder—about a lot. Including Helen, depressed. She'd always been pure hope and joy—with enough to even help the real depressive. God, what a cruel disease.

But after lunch, she seemed better. Practiced with the four-legger: hard, but she did it stubbornly. She has a little bleeding in the mouth. Dr. N (on phone): Blood level still too high—nothing to be alarmed about. Tiredness may be result of yesterday's trip. Rest.

Me: "Rest, damn you. Rome wasn't built in a day." She: "I'm sorry. Go write me a book. Please." When I checked, later, she was asleep on the couch—Rags on the floor near her. I wrote, around prepping dinner and setting table.

Then—oh, Christ. The next time I checked, she was weeping—terribly. I ran to soothe and find out. These weren't stroke tears; this sound was so hopeless and sad that my heart turned sick.

Finally she was able to tell me. She'd had a dream: she was

well—her hand, her walking, her whole body. It was such a vivid, happy, beautiful dream that when she woke...

I talked, said a lot. But, roaring all through me: Oh, God, why do You allow such pain in people's souls?

At last, brought her some tea; and she did feel better. Smiled at me, thanked me. Later, on the porch, she wrote letters to the kids—pen and writing board, instead of the old way of typing. As I did the table and dinner, I wanted to punch all of rotten life. How sad that dream, that deep deep yearning to be whole again, her own self.

June 12: Morning: weak. But soon, much better and stronger. This insane teeter-totter of stroke reactions makes me feel so tired in my heart. It's a lot like the seesaw of me and depression.

Mid-morning: she asked so eagerly, really a begging, that I finally agreed. We drove to the Heinen store she likes so much. Slow, slow, but she walked in with the four-legger; sat on the window ledge. All came to the eager-eyed woman, and made a lovely fuss (store personnel she'd talked to so often). She looked so happy, and me, I just wanted to cry.

Yes, she was tired when we got home, but the depression seemed completely gone. To bed, after lunch. And I worked—wondering hard.

Afternoon. On getting up, she attempted a few steps without the cane. This nutty disease! But maybe that intensely painful dream she'd had? And the trip to the store, the world? She has that type of spirit, God knows. Those few steps on her own—she was so excited, so happy. And proceeded to go right on: fixed the ground meat for spaghetti, standing at sink and stove with no help from man or cane. After dinner, on and on: sat at kitchen table in wheelchair and hulled the new batch of berries I'd gathered. Talked, made wondrous plans for "tomorrow." All three of us laughed and laughed. God, I was grateful for her ease. However momentary. Sufficient unto the day?

June 13: Up early, but too lethargic or something to write-work. Went out to get some body movement. Planted some leftover seed, weeded—all very quiet stuff (let the patient sleep). Walked around the perennial bed way—and hey, the east groundhog is out! Made me feel so much better.

I was cutting asparagus, when—suddenly: "Good morning, gardener dear."

She was standing at the open bedroom window, smiling—and it was as if the bad dream had gone; and all the past years of this morning-window, this house, this land, were back. I shouted: "Good morning, good morning! And guess what? Johnny's up top."

I ran to her. "Babe, you made it! On your own." She: "*Told* you. Asparagus for dinner?"

In the bedroom, she was standing without the four-legger, arms out to balance herself. No wonder some people believe in God.

June 14: She threaded a needle, sewed two buttons on one of her dresses! I wrote for almost four hours. Went to Sadie's for Friday night, felt dazed with thanks-to-God all evening.

June 15 through June 18: She's good, good—every day! I wrote a lot, gardened almost at ease. Nothing was too hard or too much for me. And the swallows came. And the frog orchestra—especially hot evenings and nights—turned the world into a regular Mozart mass, lit by church candles of the fireflies. And I wrote and wrote.

Peas are coming out of our ears, and I've given away pecks, sternly forbidding freezing them. But *she* shelled. *She* frenched green beans. *She* cooked wax beans with dill and sour cream—the wonderful taste and smell of a thousand past seasons. My God.

June 19: She, calling as I wrote in my room: "Ruthie, Hummy's here!" And all his friends and relations. Because the bergamot was in full flower; and, in the perennial bed, the delphinium; and, around the corner, the honeysuckle was a mass of bloom. All Hummy food.

I stood behind her wheelchair for a long time, and we watched that miraculous little speedball—the almost blurring whir of wings as he fed. Once, two of them—and they tangled in the air, and the song was two—and loud, as if they were quarreling. Once, one of them just hung in the air, near the big wall of screen, and seemed to be staring in at us (they do that quite often, and sometimes at my desk window). Then off he darted—and Helen's laugh!

Mid-afternoon. When she was inside, resting, I planted a surprise for the fall: eight Van Gogh seeds, in the bare spaces among and in front of the bergamot. She couldn't really see the back-acre Van Goghs that well from her room. Here, she'd see the goldfinch come and eat, and they'd sing only inches from her wheelchair. Wonderful evening. We sat on the porch, watched the fireflies. I put on the Toscanini recording of the Beethoven Ninth, and we had fruit. Cherries are in season—Mort's favorite. Rags is mad for them, too. Helen gives her a bite of each one she eats. Rags, tonight, sat up next to the wheelchair, and the good hand fed her the usual bites—and for me, ritual and pattern came soaring in—pure beauty and meaning.

June 20: Damn that crazy disease. This morning, her voice not too good; tired most of the day. Slept a lot. I set up my writing on the living-room table—wrote in chopped-up fragments.

In the night, the bell. At last! I was in my robe and slippers—running instantly toward the light in their bedroom, automatically closing the swinging door on Rags. Helen was having chest pains—bad. The nitro pills hadn't worked. Mort phoned the doctor at three or so. Dr. N: Try Darvon—may be pleurisy. Bring her in tomorrow.

The Darvon worked. Mort fell asleep as I went to bring Helen some tea. She: ''Please don't worry.'' Me: ''I'm not!'' Dirty lie.

June 21 through June 25: It was pleurisy. Threw the diabetes out of wack, of course: she had to go back to insulin. I tried to get her to lay off the exercises and walking, but she was insistent—lousy as she felt. Spent a lot of time in bed; no porch.

No writing. Too much to do. Couldn't go to the blood lab Monday, but Dr. N (phone) said to cut down to half dose—she'd be okay.

June 26 through June 29: Not too bad; and the exercises weren't as hard for her, and she walked for longer stretches. Diabetes is straightening out; tests better. The needle is so hard for her (she uses her thighs for the injections), but she obstinately refuses to let me do it. The thing is, she's used to protecting me—in the psych channel, especially. And this is no time for the student to tell the teacher that she'd graduated. *Had* to.

When I finally went out, that last afternoon, there was the first pickle. About two inches long. I didn't even rub off the tiny warts, just brought it in, with its hat still clinging—and held it up. ''Hey, look what the Old Lady did for you.'' Wiped it off with a tissue, and she said: "Take half, dear—it's the first." Me: "Hell, no—too small for a pickle-pig like me." She ate it. "Oh, Ruthie!"

Rest of the day, and evening, she seemed better. The pickle? Yes, she's the type.

June 30: Better. I went out early, to Sunday-air my guts. And there were the east Johnny-babies. Four—plus Ma and Pa. Eventually, I got Helen out on the porch. I glanced over: the babies were being very cooperative, two of the fatties even sitting up. For a few minutes, I let Helen watch the chippies (she'd missed them). Then I turned the wheelchair. Wonderful! Those babies were a new play. Mort came to watch for a while, too, then went to cut grass way over west, not to disturb the show.

After a while, Helen: "Dear, it's almost your birthday. A big one." Me: "Fifty—my God. And only four lousy novels." Helen (laughing): "Pig. And a play? Those short stories, anthologies, translations? And let's not mention that prizewinning Fund for the Republic TV play. Or all the honors, citations. And the fifth novel coming up. Oh, *toi*, it's just the beginning." Me: "Okay, okay, as long as you're around to remind me." Helen (not laughing): "I'm around. With that same promise."

She stayed better all day, so I decided to go to Fannie's, after all. To celebrate my coming birthday—the old ritual. Picked a lot of flowers—enough to drop some off for Sadie and Mildred, too.

Nice! We phoned home, and Helen was fine, and Fan talked to her, too. Afterward, my sister blurted: "I've been putting a dime in the charity box every day since she had that stroke." (The same type of tin box Ma used to put pennies in—at moments of fear or gratitude—known to us children as a *pushke*.) I kissed her (something we do rarely—still). My birthday gift from my sister, my floater of novels, my believer in Jo Sinclair? Fifty bucks. Fan: "Don't holler. I've got it, you haven't. Why don't you buy something real special for Helen out of the money?" Jesus. I thanked her, but I couldn't tell her the *real* feeling in me. A book dedication is the only thing that can ever pay her back for the stuff she's given me all these years.

July 1: On the kitchen table, my gift from Helen and Mort— beautifully wrapped. She's always given birthday presents "first thing of the day." A Bach suite for unaccompanied cello: *Casals*.

Rushed out to explode some of the birthday depression out of me. I want to write more books, more plays! Unfinished work: is that why my birthday usually depresses me? That great book—oh, God.

Five Johnny-babies today. Well, that's a smile. Decided to work in the front ivy and garden plots: the weeds are bad. Then, suddenly, Helen: "Happy birthday, gardener dear." She'd walked out the front door—as of old, when I was working in the front. Stood leaning on her cane, smiling—the true sun. And I hadn't even heard the door.

Rags came bounding toward me, and I shouted: "My God, don't fall!" Jumped up from my knees and ran, sat her on the planting box coping. She: "Surprise. For an old lady of fifty." It was wonderful. All depression flew off into her birthday kiss, the cello recording (we played it right away), the look of her—better, better.

Between birthday phone calls and mail, I did quite a bit of symbolic writing. Seems more important this year than ever. At the blood lab by two-thirty. She *walked* into the building with the four-legger. Dr. N: he's satisfied, and the blood level's good.

Home: yes, better. Not even that awful tiredness after the trip. We'd picked up a boughten birthday cake, to her disgust and my laughter. Dinner was marvelous—she cooked it. And the day ended at my desk: me facing the Me. All right, try it again, this fiftieth year, writer.

July 2: Helen put on her own shoes, walked six steps without the four-legger!

July 3: Helen made a big chunk of the carpeted floor with her chair! And cleaned and cooked a batch of asparagus. Stood with no help at all—sink—and no rubbery leg for quite some time. My God, my God.

July 4: Helen dressed herself—every bit of her—then came out on her own (cane) to surprise us!

So I farmed, I wrote up a storm. And when I came out of my room, she was in the kitchen—having a marvelous time with little chores completely impossible not too long ago: a paring knife, cutting vegetables and leftover meat. "Miracle" seems so renewed.

. (The journal changed a bit. All the work outdoors—the old sorcerer's apprentice working over time, I suppose. And inside, helping her, watching her carefully—so that she did not overdo through sheer eagerness to be the "normal" woman again. Working my book around all of it. So the journal was written in spurts and jags—much of it undated, except for the month of the happening.)

July: Hot and dry, but a light year for Japanese beetles. Good. First tomato—red. As usual, Helen cut it in three—and Rags had a bite of her third. The first few are always so precious. Then the deluge; pick, pick—and start taking into town—instead of finishing chapter ten.

Martin in for the weekend—everybody, including Ragsy, happy. He tries to get here as often as he can. It's an eight-hour drive, but Helen still hates to have any of her beloveds in a plane. He's still all music (good salesman that he is by now), and what a pleasure of a guy. A wonderful eater, too! And I always fill his car with produce when he takes off—enough to last him two weeks or so, and get rid of some of that accursed harvest.

Oh, joy. She appears at the bedroom window every morning now. My heart absolutely soars over that one returned ritual. "Good morning, dear one!" And as I run, so often I'm reminded all over again that in my parents' house nobody ever said "Good morning." Not even in Yiddish.

The Johnny-babies have turned into teenagers. She hasn't walked outside yet—our terrain is too rough. So I brought her a blue egg shell—about a third of it gone. Saw her eyes turning wistful. Oh, yes, she'd been the one to find the shells in the past. And the snake skins shed, a particularly large wild daisy. Me (softly): "Helen?" She smiled. "All right, I won't be a pig. Thanks for reminding me."

July 31: (B and D wedding anniversary: we'll phone tonight.) And we *really* went shopping. She and the four-legger; in they walked, and continued walking—me behind with the cart.
Fruits and vegetables: she picked out the stuff, and handed it to me. Meats—she did it; and it meant walking, leaning, straightening up. Got as far as the dairy case (a longish way) before I finally turned uneasy. She handed me the carton of eggs, laughing

exultantly, but I said: "Helen, please. You said you wouldn't be a pig?"

The lovely brightness didn't leave her eyes as she let me walk her back. There are benches now; I helped her sit, and went to finish the grocery list she'd written out at home. When I checked, secretly, there were two kids with her, all three laughing as one boy tried out the four-legger. I watched for quite a long time.

Once, I wrote her:

I give you today
In the palm of your hand,
Like a very bright coin
I have spent.

I give you today
Very soft on both cheeks,
Like the gentlest of kisses
I had from you.

I give you today
For the deepest part of you,
Like an old, sweet song
I heard you sing.

August: She was the one who first called it the "wall of blue." At the open front door, looking up at the wonder of life as interpreted by Heavenly Blue morning glories. Like a garden growing in the air. There were dozens open wide against that background of green and redwood.

"A wall of blue," she said, and her voice... A woman in a wheelchair, looking at the complete opposite of paralysis and rehabilitation. The gardener smiles, but the poet-friend weeps inside—wants terribly to write the true words for those yearning eyes, that trapped body. Not I—minor poet that I am. Only music could, I think. Try "Break in Grief"—from the Saint Matthew's, for example.

The surprise Van Goghs at the bergamot are in bloom. All eight seeds did themselves proud. Artist Vincent, you should be here to paint these sunflowers, and this woman in the wheelchair as she looks at them—at me, in thanks. Then paint my hurting heart, friend.

The first yellow tomato. The first big pink. Now the flood. Now the ocean of cherry tomatoes; and, as usual, I keep one of our fine bowls filled with these washed cherries on the porch table. Rags sits up, next to the wheelchair, and Helen bites open the little tomato—so that Rags doesn't have to burst the skin and spatter seeds all over the floor. The season is in order.

Ah, the mouse-ears are starting. Helen was so thrilled when I brought in the first three. Worked three and a half hours!

Oh, Christ, here comes the sorcerer's apprentice bit. It's true, you can't turn off the crops, once they've started. Or keep them halted until you finish ten more pages. Helen: "Dear, *please* don't give all the pickles away. I am going to make dills." Me: "The hell you are. And I don't have time to."

Time to gropple. I bring in the first small Katahdins—dirt on them, so she can smell and touch. Helen: "Beautiful!"

Time to pull up a thousand and four onions. Sort them for rot, size them in piles for the storing—do all this in front of the porch, so that Helen can be a member of the wedding. With Chopin.

Mid-August: Hey, hey, the kids are here! For a big chunk of time. Laughers, lovers of people and House, land—and more eaters, hurrah.

Mort's home, too, of course: took his two weeks of vacation to match this visit. He and Helen radiate pure joy. It's a shame Martin can't make it a whole-family affair (too much travel work). Barbie cooks (she's planning lots of biscuits; Helen's a far journey from being able to make those). The house is full of talk, music, a child's high, excited calling, noise-noise (except when he naps or is being read to). Wonderful. But: in three, four days, will the writer be able to blot out some of it, in order to work? Ah, but it's so marvelous to be with them. A neurotic's conflict!

Eric Jan still calls his grandmother "Pooh." And Mort "Gramp." He calls Rie "Oma" and me "Missy." I call him EJ a lot.

And little old EJ has decided to help me farm (Rags with us)—mornings. For a minute or three, he held the basket as I harvested. Then, of course, he wanted to pick, too. I started him off with pickles: not too small, twist off the fruit instead of yanking and tearing the vine. It didn't take long; he's quite a little brain. We'll work up to tomatoes soon, and other stuff. Lots of fun, this proud little assistant. But, of course; everything takes twice as long. Well, write when he naps! Or evenings, damn it. Yes, but then it's so good to sit on the porch with articulate, knowing people, and talk. Helen's brain and voice right in there, pitching. D is teaching something called sensitivity training; it's fascinating to hear firsthand about T groups, the newest facets of behavioral therapy—stuff Helen and I have simply read about.

Eric Jan is a beautiful child: very blond, very blue of eye, stocky and sturdy. Curious about everything, daring (he's sitting in Mort's lap on the sitting mower, "helping"—can't wait to run the machine all by himself). Climbs trees like a monkey. Has fallen deeply in love with this house, this land—it's obvious. The noise and energy stop only when you get him engrossed. He's a *talker* (and a damn good one—what a vocabulary, already!). And how he loves books—to be read to, and to pore over pictures. Helen is so good at reading— and telling stories. But Mort's no slouch at bedtime reading, either: the grandparents take turns. Rie is here a lot—wonderfully cooperative with shucking and shelling, et cetera. And does *she* adore her grandson.

But oh, Helen. So happy. EJ is intensely interested in everything she does; watches; asks questions. Has tried out the four-legger, often. Has had rides in the wheelchair—with Helen, with Rags, and alone—works it like a little dynamo. I'm crazy about this vital kid, who is really beautiful as a little human being.

Swimming, every day—including EJ (held by his father, one hand under tummy). EJ in the inner tube provided by Gramp. EJ getting the giggles when a bass or bluegill nips. "The fish kissed me! Pooh *said* they would. Where's Pooh?"

Pooh's up on the porch—with one of us (whoever doesn't go swimming; me, usually). I have gone down, for an hour or so, twice, when Barb or EJ begged hard. Wonderful; one forgets. Sometimes, as I'm floating in an inner tube after a fast swim, thinking about my book or about Helen's progress, I hear music drifting down. A few times, it was Barbie playing the piano. Lovely.

Four days. Then I set the alarm for five, tiptoed out and made coffee, wrote for two and a half hours. Until EJ was out of bed and instantly all over the house in noise. That's how he wakes: fireworks, drums. But this time, I grinned.

*

Corn's ready. We have contests: who can eat the most? EJ wants to win so desperately that Mort and D let him—twice. What triumph, at the top of his voice. Helen eats only one or two ears these days (me, two). Rags eats her usual one, in her bed on thick sheets of paper. EJ laughs and laughs at the sight.

The time's flying. Most of the day: talk-talk, laugh-laugh; all of us—but especially mother and daughter (that *is* such a special love). Plans: they'll be back for Christmas—driving—arrive here on the twenty-third, stay through New Year's Day.

EJ's getting to be an expert harvester—except he often picks the pickles too small. Gets excited and just lunges. Same with tomatoes not quite ripe. Well, what the hell, there's plenty anyway.

D and Mort are painting the gutters. Barb and Helen cooking. And life's kind of terrific (even though I'm not getting enough writing done). The morning glory buds I brought in yesterday, for example—wide open, so blue, in the small Italian vase on the kitchen window sill. Mother and daughter both cried out in delight when they came into the room this morning and saw the way they had "grown" and opened there. Their eyes made me feel so happy.

That's one of my better ideas. I've done it with Pearl a few times, bringing buds to the Moody house; and she was enchanted the next day with the wide-open blue. She rarely has time to plant extras like glories. (Sarah J used to have Heavenly Blues every season.) And I've passed it on to others: Fannie and Mildred, my good friend Edna.

This afternoon: finally felt so restless that I went to my room, closed both doors and most of the windows, and wrote. Worked hours. The drowning happened—so rare these days.

When I finally snapped to, the house was mighty quiet. I rushed out to the kitchen. And there—ha! At the kitchen table, Barb was finishing up (packing the seventh wide-mouth mason jar) dill pickles. The peck of too-little-to-eat ones that her son had picked that morning. Helen was helping (she put the dill into the jars). When EJ spotted me, he screamed: "Missy, surprise!"

Me: "For crying out loud. And I didn't even smell the brine cooking?" Helen: "Writer at work—oblivious." I got a big hug from Barbie—very excited: "Are you pleased? My first dill pickles!" EJ:

"I picked, Missy! I'm the surprise, too!" Helen (tender-wry): "You can't holler about this. *I* didn't do it. And you love dill pickles."
I do. And the original maker of them. And her daughter. And the little boy who learned to pick them this season.

And what a brain he is. He came in from the orchard yesterday, and asked Helen when Johnny was going to eat the apples off the trees. He remembered—how is that even possible with a child this young! Last year, the kids had been here in October, and the early ripe apples had fallen from the five-in-one tree; and, of course, the chucks had eaten them—sitting up, twirling the apple in their front paws. Sometimes they pick apples—from low branches.

So I went up to the store on a secret mission for Helen. And this morning, I followed the next step of her plot: very early, I went out and placed five apples under the tree you can see so well from the porch. Hid the rest. Took about a day and a half for the groundhogs to discover the boughten crop. Then Helen called her grandson out to the porch. They talked a bit, then Helen looked east, said very casually: "Well, well, look." One of the chucks, on cue, was sitting up and eating an apple. Another was under the tree, inspecting the others. Smash hit. EJ: "Pooh, they did! You said—and they did!" Reminding me of me saying: "You promised—and you never break a promise." I, of course, am to put out apples every morning: a new kind of Old Lady Nature!

Item: Barb's trying to have another baby, but big trouble conceiving. She's so much like her mother—even this way. Helen had no trouble with her first child, but went through hell to have Martin—after a series of miscarriages, including twins. But she wanted a second child, and, by God, stubborn Helen got him—had to stay in bed for months, the last of the pregnancy. She's told me of how she used to dream about those twins: all born and whole and beautiful—boy and a girl, red hair.

Dream-into-life scene: Helen "went swimming" today. It hasn't rained in almost a month: everything is dry and hard. So she told Mort to drive her down to the dam—the east go-down. After all, why not?—the go-down and the dam are plenty wide enough for his small car. Never occurred to me—or anybody else. Nor that she must have yearned to be down there with her darlings. So down they drove—slow and careful. I brought the wheelchair, EJ the four-legger. And everybody went into the pond, with Helen on the dam—laughing and waving from her chair. And Mort did his usual cattail-pulling job, bigger grin than usual. And Ragsy went in eagerly, now that Helen was around.

I floated around in one of the tubes after a swim. Every time I looked up at the woman on the dam, I remembered how often we'd walked down here—looking for thistles, watching frog and snake, and sumac beginning to open out of tightness into flame.

Ragsy and EJ were in an inner tube, being pushed by D, when I came up on the dam, dripping, and wiped my hands so I could have a dry cigarette. Me (too casual): "You okay?" Helen: "Oh, *toi,* stop crying inside. I *told* you I'd make it down here."

September: Mort's back at work; the kids are gone; and the gardener's lost her assistant until Christmas (EJ plans to help me feed the birds and shovel snow). Definitely fall, and gorgeous. Helen seems quite good, and you're back on the book in big chunks of time. So what are you depressed about?

I think it's the role switch. I feel it more and more intensely—as I realize that I must not weep or groan to her—not even about my writing. It would be wrong. Everything in her must go into her own fight; ergo, I must always act strong. But I'm not sometimes. In my room, or in the gardens.

Uh uh, Rags is under the weather. When I came home last night, she didn't even lift her head as I patted her. Into Helen's room, as usual—and she's worried. Had talked to the vet, described Ragsy's symptoms and behavior (great lassitude; wouldn't eat much). Mort had driven to vet for medication, and we're to watch the poor kid, report tomorrow. Could be any number of things, he said.

By Saturday, Rags definitely very sick. Even the way she walks—a tired little old lady. Helen had her on the couch with her most of the morning. The vet says to bring her in tomorrow if she doesn't react to the second medication he'd prescribed. Helen sent me up to the store for kidneys and liver (Ragsy's loves), but she ate very little. Drinks a lot, shakes her head often, wants to stay in her bed. Damn. That character has crawled into my heart, so I know what Helen must be feeling. After our dinner (Rags wouldn't even come out of her bed), Helen phoned the vet again. I saw her face get gray. Then she said: "Yes, tomorrow morning." Hung up, started to cry. Mort and I ran to her. She: "He's almost sure Ragsy's had a cerebral hemorrhage."

I thought instantly: That's the other kind of stroke. Then—a terrible ripping through my head: Better Rags than Helen! And put my arms around the weeping woman. Did not tell her. I was ashamed, amazed at a superstitious side of me I didn't suspect I possessed.

Sunday: Helen insisted on going, holding her blanket-wrapped dog. After they left, I gardened—furiously. Didn't do any good. They came home with the little dead dog in a box. The way they'd come home after Friedie had been taken out of her pain. There wasn't much to say, except to tell Helen I'd find a beautiful place.

I finally picked a spot almost directly across the east go-down from Friedie's grave. This time of year, lots of sumac and daisies and ironweed, wild asters. In the spring, there would be violets, wild strawberries. And the pond is close, the dam she loved to run.

Helen looked awful, but I didn't fight her when she said she wanted to be close while Mort and I buried Rags. I brought out a chair: she couldn't come too far down because the slope is so steep there, but she stood and held on, and could see. As I dug—deep—and Mort brought down the box. Oh, God.

Martin came for a few days. He's so gentle and sweet with his mother. No, Helen did not want another dog (he offered). Yesterday, while Helen was napping, he knocked and came into my room. "How is she? Aside from Rags? Dad isn't sure." Me: "Much better. But Christ, it's so slow. I don't know how she stands it. Gutsy as she is." He: "Thanks, Ruth!" Tears in his eyes. When he left, very fast, I remembered suddenly that Rags had been his dog first.

A Saturday, mid-morning: She walked out the garage way with me. Propped the four-legger, went out on the grass—rough terrain and all—and walked a few steps. Her arms out, a kind of grotesque weaving and balancing that made my stomach rock. But I looked at her eager, happy eyes.

Afternoon: she wanted it—very badly—so we let her take a ride on the sitting mower. Mort turned the power way down, so that it would move very slowly. He and I walking along, close, he steering, I watching her look about so joyously. She wanted to see the back acres close up, not from just a window. I saw her eyes fill with the detail of leaf and fruit and fern right next to her, as she asked Mort to stop the mower every once in a while.

But the ride on the bumpy earth, and the heat, tired her badly. Got her on to the porch in the wheelchair. I brought iced coffee. Mort went to cut some grass. Helen: "Ruthie, that was so good. Like touching the growing." But she was looking off somewhere. Me: "What are you thinking about? So far away?" She: "Ragsy."

I was full of the old rage to punch the Old Lady. Helen (quietly): "Maybe Rags died instead of me." I blurted: "That's what I thought! Like a superstitious—but you?" She: "Sometimes it's very easy to think that way."

It's so odd without Rags—the barking, opening a can of dog food every day. Nights I've been in town, coming out of bed to greet me—stub of a tail going. When Friedie vanished, there was Rags. But Helen seems better in her emotions. And I'm writing a lot— some of the farming is petering out. On the porch, I avert my eyes from the tooth marks. Ditto at the living room window.

Note (to writer, about writer): I have, roughly, half a book. And that's only a first draft. Damn. I wonder what devil made me *have* to write? It's so hard for me—and often brings worry or depression. And now—so important!—I must not whine or curse about it to Helen. That used to help so much.

September 11: Outside work much less, writing more and more, two ducks on pond, Helen very good, the seasons in order. So let's start sort of dating the journal again. Stop running so fast.

September 12: This week, a noticeable improvement, especially in her walk: not so limpy. Arm and hand very good. There seems to be a wonderful gang-up. Off Darvon for four, five nights now (the newest painkiller in my vocabulary). Back on Seconal for sleep (in other words, she's not afraid of a stroke in the night and not being able to pull herself out of the effect of the pill). Scarcely uses wheelchair. Believe it all!

September 27: A Friday. All this past week: walking without the four-legger for long stretches. Hasn't touched the wheelchair in one hell of a long time. I went to Sadie's *before* Mort came home. Helen was so insistent about it that I thought it would be a good idea. Imagine me doing psych stuff with her!

September 28: Wheelchair went back today—on way to blood lab. Mort took her, and I wrote all afternoon. God, I'm happy. I hated that damn chair—turns out.

October 4: Helen did some of the wash today! Of course, I was there—but I didn't do too much. Sure wished Mort was home to see her. With the four-legger to help, she did amazingly well. Then she shook out a sheet and folded it (used the big worktable for support). Her eyes took on such a shining that I had secret tears in me as I applauded loudly. Oh, nature, you rotten beautiful bitch.

October 14: Helen baked a cake today! Barb's birthday—an angel food, of course. It'll take the cake four days or so to get to Northampton, so we'll freeze it, and Mort'll mail it tomorrow.

I helped, a little. With the heavy bowl, in which she beats the whites of eggs. And I cleaned up the kitchen. But, by God, she baked that cake. It was her usual—high and fluffy, perfect. Helen (her eyes beautiful): "Do you know how I feel about this cake?" I did, indeed. Talking of poems.

October 16: First radio freeze warning. Good. I can clean up, then really settle down and finish a book. This morning, I went out and found frozen garbage. Helen: "Oh, my poor wall of blue." Me: "Hideous, ain't it? Next year in Jerusalem, babe."

October 18: Hey, listen, somebody, cut it out!—she suddenly feels rocky. Flu? A virus? Dr. N seems to think it could be either (on the phone). Prescribed antibiotics.

October 22: She has fluctuated. Better, but then she gets clutched again. She's talked to Dr. N three times. I wish to God doctors came to the house, the way they used to.

To cheer her up, today, I put the Halloween pumpkin and turkey candles out on the hearth mantle. Early, sure, but they do gay up the kitchen. She smiled—big—when she came out for breakfast (she's insisted on that, but usually has to lie down for long chunks of the day). She loves candles and little creatures for holidays. Me, too. We've amassed quite a collection. Especially for a Christmas mantle.

October 24: My fear started. Even before the first shot of insulin, she became very dizzy when she reached up to the kitchen shelf for the alcohol. Threw up—a little. Had to lie down.

Lunch: had shot, ate, puttered around kitchen for about a half hour. Then she felt extremely dizzy—even lying down. Hot and cold. Suddenly threw up, violently. I talked to doctor. She's on medicated suppositories, as of tonight. Ate very light supper, fell asleep.

Me? No writing today. Not much sleep, either.

October 25 through October 28: Rotten. Wakes feeling shaky (and much earlier than usual). Insists on coming to kitchen for insulin and breakfast (the valiant!). But has to go back to bed. Sleeps—until a wave of intense dizziness wakes her up. Usually vomits, then—but I'm ready: basin, towels; then cold compresses (feels faint). Patterns: hot, cold, hot again; over and over, nausea. New: a buzz in right ear "like a tractor" (and my heart aches at garden versus this). At one point, loud noise in both ears—had difficulty hearing me.

Nurse scared, but doesn't show one bit of it. To doctor on phone, as patient sleeps: "How about for Christ sake coming out? She's sick as a dog." He: "She'll be all right. Have to give the insulin a chance. Diabetes out of kilter—acts worse than it is. This takes time."

About five that second day, real teeter-totter stuff: she woke feeling better. Ears clear. Ate good dinner. Felt fine. But later: went to look at TV—for a "change of pace," and screen immediately caused dizziness and faintness. To bed. Sickness passed off, but very tired. Five suppositories, so far. Fell asleep a little after ten. Nurse turns writer—has to!—works until one-thirty in the morning.

Saturday journal—a quick, staccato shorthand. (To go with my heartbeat, no doubt.) Medical god finally came out. Diagnosis: gastroenteritis. Threw diabetes out of whack. She's dehydrated. Test urine for acetone. Report by phone tomorrow. (Me, in my guts: You bastard. Took you long enough.)

Mort got testing stuff. Nurse: started pouring liquids into

patient, ordered lots of rest. Music good—that helped. Writer: worked about two hours. Gardener: late afternoon, hilled roses (thirty-two). Had to be done, tired or not. Friend: scared. Slept "on surface" all night, waiting for bell. It didn't.

Sunday shorthand: Acetone tests vary. One: negative. One: "trace." Turns out Doctor-god (on phone) is afraid of possible kidney failure. (What! Out of the blue? Why don't they *tell* us things before the last split second?) He: "If she doesn't clear up by tomorrow, want her in Mount Sinai for tests." (I'll kill him!)

Monday shorthand: Slight trace of acetone. Dizzy spell after breakfast. Noise in one ear (lasted almost half an hour). Doctor-god: "The hospital."
So I drove my disgusted friend to Mount Sinai: Two-bed room, but nobody there. Me (still acting my head off): "Nice view of the park, anyway." She (depressed): "Go home, dear. Write me a book."
Last journal shorthand shout, as I hit the house: Wish Ragsy were here!

October 31: Written close to midnight. I've been working on the book since seven-thirty. Helen's due home tomorrow. The few days of her hospital stay have been silent, packed. Writing, housework, tearing down to the hospital twice a day (thank God it's not all the way to Saint Vincent's). Very little gardening.
Not that the tests came up with anything conclusive. But at least they've practically straightened out the diabetes, so maybe she can get away from that needle soon. Afternoon visit: she was tired, still depressed. But still my Helen: insisted I stay home tonight. Doesn't like all the rushing around I've done.
Fannie sent me a check today. Sure—what else?—I'm running out of money again. Time to dash off a few stories for the slicks. Who, me? My soul contains this one book, this one dear sick friend.

November 1: She came home. Loved everything in the house all over again. Walking, working around the kitchen a little. But she's so tired that my heart pinches. Spent a lot of time with her today. Wrote after she went to bed. Yes, the work went badly.

November 7: EJ's birthday. We talked to an excited, happy three-year-old. Helen had sent away to the National Wildlife Association for a book (chucks, muskrats, possums, et cetera). He loves it, talked about our Johnny and the apples. She's ordered a matching record for him—for Christmas. I sent a (cheap) Pooh drawing book and a lot of crayons. EJ: "Missy, I love Pooh! I love you!"

Finally persuaded Helen to let me give her the insulin shots (then I *knew* how lousy she felt). I use her arms, and I know it's nowhere as painful as the thigh bit. Me: "See? Didn't faint me away with Freudian trauma." Even her smile is tired.

November 15: The thing is, she's "small-dizzy" a great part of the time, and then comes a wave of the real thing. This morning, one dragged her out of sleep at five. (To wake to that bell! The actuality of it, instead of the unheard music going on in my head so often.) Cold compresses—she snapped to, and shivered with cold. A cup of tea made her feel better. She fell asleep.

Miserable most of the day, every day. Has fluctuated—dizzy and better—nauseated and better; an unbearable teeter-totter. The doctor is sure it's the diabetes. I'm to try orange juice when she feels faint. Sometimes it works; more often, it just makes her more nauseated.

Horror note: that bell. I can't get over the amazing switch: she conceived this signal for me—my well-being. Now, complete reversal. Like that switch of roles between us. Now, that song of love and reassurance has turned into a sickness-pain music.

November 16: More of the same. I can't even bear to write it. What I'll write out is this: it has become difficult to work. Because I keep putting myself into her mind, spirit, body—thinking almost constantly of how frightened and miserable she must feel; and finding myself going to her very often as "rescue."

Loving a very dear friend is—I think—feeling what she must be going through. So you are not free. Free to drop her for work, for you. In her need, you are in a way trapped—bad word, but a close and good one here. It's a giving you don't plan; it's just there. And it pulls you, to try anything to help. You are in that person's emotions as if a kind of twin: feeling them, sharing them. Awful, beautiful, so painful.

November 17: Here we go again! No dizziness this morning.

Absolutely none. So—is she over the hump—as Dr. N said she would be? Do I trust it? It's Sunday—lots of Bach on the radio; how she smiled. Mort and I had to fight her not to bake a late cake for Martin's birthday. She helped make lunch. It tired her, but lifted her spirits even more. Now it's my heart that's on that teeter-totter.

November 18: Happy birthday, Martin. Helen's good again today. One very brief, not bad dizziness. Ate well. Out of bed for long stretches. Evening: wonderful birthday phone call. I felt a little hysterical with relief as we all talked and laughed.

November 19: She seems okay. Later: asleep when I got back from a quick food-shopping. So I went to work. This chapter I'm on is a heartbreaker. The old woman, of course (and I think of Ma, of Sarah J). The book really comes to life when she's onstage.

But Helen very, very tired all afternoon. Ate only part of her dinner. In bed and asleep by nine. God, this up and down: it'll drive me nuts. And what's it doing in *her* head?

Ten-thirty: the bell! I'm still writing. I run, to that dread-clanger. Mort's whole body's in the sound; his finger's still on the bell. Is this it?

Yes. In her sleep—the stroke woke her. What a fantasy of cruelty. Voice no good, as I leaned over her and put my hands on her face. Light convulsions—right leg. As I went into immediate soothe-talk, I thought with a real hatred of God: She was practically all better.

Mort picked up the phone as soon as I appeared. Helen (thick blur): "Leg." Her eyes: Ruthie, help me! My hand went to that jumping leg. She hates it so, it scares her so.

Mort was telling Dr. N what had happened; and that *she* had pressed the button—and kept pressing it. Jesus. I got the leg to somewhat stop—into a twitch, instead of the jerking. As I talked on, reassuringly, bitterness and fury burned in my head: to do this twice to a human being?

It all went very fast. Helen insisted—in that voice of blobbed spit—that she was going by car, not ambulance. Insisted on a robe, a coat, shoes. All the time, pieces of my head went on clicking: It's not like the first one (not yet, anyway!). She's staggering, not crumpling or half-fainting. Color's gray; exhausted, yes; but Helen's kind of stubbornness very much here.

We got her into the car—somehow. And I was in, next to her,

holding her. Cold, but no snow—driving would be easier. Me: "Helen, this one isn't too bad. You walked. The leg jumps weren't too bad, either. I don't think there's any paralysis." I had to be honest with her; I knew it was the moment for it, for the strength that could come from it. She (blur, but strong): "Yes!"

Hospital: wheelchair waiting—the rush to the elevator, into a bed. Nurses, a doctor. Then, shortly after: suddenly her voice cleared, the twitch-jerk much better. Rather miraculous stuff. She was smiling, talking to us a bit. I could see her relief. Dr. N arrived, examined her quickly: "She'll be all right."

Mort and I got home at three in the morning. I brought out my bottle, poured at the kitchen sink, straight shots. We clicked glasses. He was laughing: "She's okay!" I nodded, smiled, but thought: You poor sweet sap of an optimist. Okay, feel better. You might as well, while you can. He went to sleep. In my room, I had another drink—to chase all the demons. Thought of Ragsy, suddenly. Threw that out of me fast.

Finally in bed—but the lamp still on. Shivering, smoking one after another. Too many memories, on a night like this. For example: in August, when "it was all over," we were on the porch, watching Chippy. I'd taken a break from the writing, and she had been getting dinner started. Very abruptly, she: "There was one thing I couldn't stand thinking about. That my brain would go. That ghastly word—*vegetable*. Ruth, did you remember your promise? When I was lying there paralyzed, unable to speak like a human being?" What I couldn't stand, right then, was that a living creature should have to feel the fear of such an awful threat. She (insistent): "Did you?" Me: "That's impossible! Not your brain!" After a while, she (quiet): "You did remember. All right, go write me a book."

Write me a book. The promise of *that*.

I tried to sleep—but the memories are all of writing, rejection, more and more work, rejection again and more work. They scare me; all the rejections had Helen laughing and soothing and scolding—ordering them away.

God, God. Did you really think she'd turned you into an established writer—certain of her talent? Look at the past. She had to thrust the weapon of her belief into your hands over and over, and keep closing your fingers over it. That last novel? It never would have been published if she hadn't been around. With that brain of hers. And now? Second stroke: will she live or die? Fifth novel: will it live or die?

Books merge, and death memories, too (Ma, Sarah J, Virginia's mother). They make torment in a head like mine. And yet, maybe it all fashions different kinds of weapons. That last book of mine, especially. It *had* come to life. She'd say, right now: Believe!—in all sorts of miracles. In my promise, too.

And so I took out the weapons of my memories of that fourth novel, and the forever of her promise, and closed my own fingers over them. God, make them shining swords. So I can battle through this night of fear.

Memory swords: 1959.

March 14, a Saturday: At six-ten in the evening, I finished final typescript of "A Breaking of Prison." Oh, baby—871 pages. And it's already been cut deeply. This is the third time around.

The paper and carbon Helen stacked for today's typing are only half gone. I came out to the kitchen, looked at her. She: "Ah, that's good." Kissed me. Went and got my bottle, poured me a double shot (she who hates my drinking).

Helen (tenderly): "Sit down, *toi*. How are your poor typist hands?" Me: "Hurt." She: "I'll bet. Relax, dear. What you need is some outdoors. I'm so glad it's almost time for gardening." Me: "Helen, those guys in New York are going to hate this book." She: "Maybe. If so, there are other publishers." Me: "Why did Ed have to die? I trusted his opinion so much!"

If Ed had been around, would I have tried so hard (and at such length) to explain my Poem to the world? I could have had two books out of this one: there are definitely two different stories, completely different sets of people. And yet they merge—and make tremendous meaning tied this way. Helen agreed when she read the first draft. "Ruthie, cut by all means—but keep what *you* know must be there. You're the writer."

Easier said than done, friend-believer. And this book... When Ed Aswell left McGraw, I thought my world had ended. A lot I knew about endings. Okay, with much difficulty, I got out of the McGraw "we see your next book" clause. And when I sent Ed—at his next job—a ten-page outline of this new book, he wrote back at once to tell me it sounded as if it would make an exceedingly good, valuable novel. His postscript made me feel good: the first contract he was drawing up on his new job was with Richard Wright, still in Paris.

Endings. That November night—last year—when I turned to the obits in the *Times*, and saw the impossible news of his heart attack. . . . No, I didn't fall on my bell, to scream for Helen. It was long past midnight, and she hadn't been feeling too well. It was my habit to read the *Times* in bed, last thing of a busy day. There I was, alone with Ed's death. The next day, Helen gave me hell for not waking her up, to share my grief. But there were enough pieces for her to pick up even then.

A few weeks, and suddenly a letter from his publishing company; they'd gone through Ed's files, read my outline, and it sounded great. Could I come to New York to discuss it? Naturally, they'd pay for the trip. Helen: "Good! You'll settle the book, and then we'll stoke up on plays. I'll raise some money."

But she got sick—and the inevitable diabetic flare-up. So it was me alone. I flew, first time in my life. I wasn't going to sit in a train all those hours, and jitter. I insisted—promised to call her the minute I hit ground. I loved the flying, but that trip. . . Jesus, first time in New York without Helen. Four days. Not good.

Met my agent for the first time. Fine—I liked her a lot. My "new publishers" (lunch in a very classy French restaurant) were three sophisticated, very articulate men—and Ed's dead opposite. Oh, they were very nice. Wanted to see a piece of what I'd already written. Or, if I preferred, an advance on the strength of that outline.

I said no to both offers. Explained that I never showed a book until it was finished; my stuff was cumulative—it mounted, all through a piece of work; had to be seen in total. And that I never take an advance until a contract is offered. I did not tell them that I could not spend money unless it was certain. It had to be for the next book—and to pay back my sister for helping to finance the current one.

Kept seeing Ed's eyes—perceptive, gentle, so warm. And everything in me stayed near-panic until I got home. But she was better—and even out of bed, to hug me. The house was beautiful, peaceful. Miracle of Helen. Again. She: "Finish the book. That's first."

I finished it. We discussed the first draft. I trusted her judgment. And she always trusted me, too—my talent, my "gifts for the world." She thought this book was a gift. I went back to more hard work, cutting, editing, probing for truth and meaning.

Three drafts later, on that Saturday when I came away from "The End," she said calmly, "I'll separate the last batch for you after dinner. You can start proofing as soon as you want to.'' I always do the whole book myself—down to checking page numbers, boxing, and wrapping. She's along for the last step: mailing it.

Next morning: I told Helen I couldn't bear even looking at that typescript, let alone starting to proof. She (smiling): ''Nice to know you're normal. Let's do the seed order.''

After we'd done it (late because of the book, and she wouldn't dream of ordering seeds without me), Rags and I did some early gardening. Cleanup, mainly. It was a good turned-off day for my head. That evening, Helen and Mort took me to a movie, to celebrate finishing the book.

It was a good movie, but my soul stayed with the novel. The fear is in layers. Aside from the writer, and her intense worry about the possibly lousy job she's done, there's one more cross (yes, I can use that word). I've had it before; it's about using friends, or relatives, as the basis for some of your characters. This writer is always uneasy about people's reactions to being used. Especially if the picture is a violent one, or too bare-bones honest. And here's a writer who feels guilty, even though she knows that this is an integral part of her way of writing—and that the story can be valuable—a lesson, a finger of accusation, a song of sorrow—or hope.

I do believe it's hope here, though it will not seem so to my book's Emil—based strongly on a very dear friend (and his family), yet quite changed. This guy in my novel could give one hell of a lot of readers a beautiful gift of understanding. But I'm pretty scared—even this long before publication (and who knows if it'll even be published). My live Emil will be furious with me. He's the type. Probably order me out of his life—and the life of his family (twenty-five years and more of friendship)—and I will be so sad. I love him, and I love his wife and kids.

But I can't help it. I had to write that book. It grew in my guts for all those years—becoming a compulsion to write a very meaningful story. Other friends are in this book, too, but they are not Emil's kind of person. I believe they'll understand—and even respect. He won't. He'll suffer (but so will I). He'll want to kill me. And I will crawl. But I *had* to write this book. Some people call it betraying friendship and confidences. Not so. Writers don't betray. They use—and change, and build—and give to the world.

But let's be honest: I fear most of all the rejection of this book I worked so hard to get right.

Finished proofing; wrapped both copies—by ten. Then—only then—did I start drinking. (Helen's been in bed since nine.) Sat in my room, drank slowly—and thought. Of Ed, gone. Of my constant anxiety over writing, all these years—the same; and yet the same yearning to write something so really good that even I would recognize a fine book. Thinking: I have felt that kind of book inside me for so many years, and yet I can't get it out. The writer is the person. What's wrong with the person? What part of me is so broken that even a Helen couldn't show me how to mend it? On the other hand, is it that maimed part of me that makes me *need* to write?

And need to drink? No, don't think of Dylan Thomas, William Faulkner, Brendan Behan, F. Scott Fitzgerald. What's the point? This is you!

I keep drinking. What I want, as ever, is the blurring of pain. Yes, depression continues to be awful pain. One of the worst: the pain of despair. Before I die, I want to be able to describe it for the world. People should know about that. Thousands must feel this way—and yet how many of us can describe it?

Depression, despair: now I think of last Friday—at "home." It's still that to Fan and me, though Ma's been living with Sadie's family since Pa died in 1949. She seemed a little more agile when I gave her a bath. I've taken to doing that every Friday evening. Ma's afraid of falling in the tub, but won't let anyone there help her. When I insisted, that first time, she said the familiar, half-bitter Yiddish: "Are you a stone, Ruthie?" Yet she wanted me to take over, wash and dry her gently.

No, Ma, I'm not a stone. And—I know—it's not your fault that I'm this way. But why do I go on writing about strong, loving, helpful mothers?

Next day—March 24: Sent off the two copies of the book to my agent. Helen's birthday—a perfect day, symbolically, to ship out a new piece of work. When I walked out of the post office, Helen: "Oh, *toi*, I can't wait to read galleys." She meant: I promise you.

Two days later: bitch nature—thirty-two degrees. I pulled the birthday bucket of pansies into the garage—just in case they aren't as tough as the books say. They're blooming in there, and Helen laughed so hard when she went to pick that I had to laugh, too, for about a second; but then my stomach book-sank again. Pond:

five ducks. Very fancy swimmers, but they didn't last in my soul. Helen (at my continuing, dark silence): "For heaven's sake, darling, that's enough bleeding for nothing. I won't permit it! How about that next novel while you're waiting? It's too early for real garden therapy. Please? And when you look up—all those ducks to entertain you."

So I started delving into that mass of stuff I've collected for the next novel. Lousy sensation: How the hell can I write another book? Today, or ever? But I spent about three hours on it.

April 11: Yep! I knew they'd murder my book. Words, bullets:

> . . .face red on the Jo Sinclair novel. The outline did seem wonderful, and Miss Sinclair certainly can write, but. . . Three of us have now read it, and I am embarrassed to report that we didn't like it at all. . .Nine-tenths of the book is second-hand action. . .tedious. As you see, we really disliked the novel. . .and awfully sorry, because we did like Miss Sinclair.

The short, accompanying note from agent: She feels the novel is much too long, needs cutting badly, but is sending it on to a second publisher.

That feeling of death-inside at a rejection. But Helen doesn't permit death, in any form. She (honestly furious): "The fools. Why can't people see a beautiful thing? All right, that's show business! Now you listen to me. This book *will* be published. It's good." Me (to the anguished Me): See?—you can't write any more. Helen: "How about planting the early garden? That's an order from your doctor. Back soon—have to drive up to Chester. Come on—now, *toi!*"

I went out. With Rags. Yes, I wanted to die, but I planted five kinds of lettuce. Dill. Halfway through the rotohoeing for beans, Helen drove my car back in, came over to me—the sun painting her smile wonderful. In one hand, two packages of Spanish onion plants, in the other a pint of Scotch. She: "Publication isn't the only thing I celebrate. There's guts, too."

Oh, count the ways she kept me alive.

Early May: We did the marigold-zinnia bed. Yes, lovely music on the porch; but no further word from my agent, who'd written the book's in the hands of an editor she's known for years, and he's very anxious to read the manuscript. Helen (calmly): "Dear, where'll we put the new Navaho zinnias? Don't forget they're smalls."

Middle of May: My agent writes she's having lunch with the editor and his assistant—to discuss the novel. They seem interested. Next few days: I worked hours on preliminary stuff for the new novel.

A week later—my agent: "...But he doesn't see giving you a contract at the present time...long report on what he thinks should be done...and if you decide you see eye-to-eye with him..." Helen: "Dear, this sounds very hopeful. And you know you can work with anybody who makes sense to you." Me: "This damn, torturous waiting!" Helen: "Let's drive over to Jean's and buy some anniversary gifts. (Laugh) Even though we're both broke."

So we drove over to Sunnybrook Nurseries, talking about Contemporary Theater, our meeting place in life on a May 25, long ago. I bought her a white delphinium (fifty cents), and she bought me a bronze mum (seventy-five cents). At home, she talked about the excitement of my play, so well done at the Cleveland Play House, while I planted our renewed day of friendship.

May 27: Rejection number two. Almost three pages of more bullets. Including:

> ...regret genuine, because we recognize and respect the passionate honesty of this novel, the quality of some of the writing in it, and its occasional passages of real power, but...would virtually mean scrapping most of the present novel and rewriting from the beginning. So very little of the material has been given overtly dramatic form...endless passages of psychological maundering, self-pity...and sorry to have been so brutal, but obviously no editor would take the time to go on at such length about a rejected manuscript unless there was a great deal in it that had interested..."

Agent (among other things): Such a long, comprehensive report never done for a rejected book. Suggests thinking it over before submitting again. Thinks in some ways editor has been too hard on me.

Thinks that the book has an overall power—and he does me an injustice by not stating that more firmly.

I read it all in the crying chair. Passed it on to Helen. She read. Cursed—something she does only rarely, but when she does it's the works. And I? Cried. At last.

She held me, didn't talk. Let me cry it out; all of it—including the exhausting work, the months of waiting, the crushing of the dream, this harsh proof of the writing failures and lacks of an author of three novels, countless stories, a play.

Finally, I'd had it, blew my nose, muttered: "Oh, boy. And I'm supposed to be a writer?" Helen: "You are, damn it!" Me: "This is one of the top publishers in the country." She: "Screw them. That doesn't impress me. So they wrote you the longest report in literary history—so what! There are plenty of other publishers. Now you listen. Until we figure out what to do, you're going to put the farm in. Period."

I planted the farm. For three days, I worked from early morning to late afternoon, virtually in silence; worked so hard that my whole body ached by nighttime. I thought of Ed a lot—realized how badly I must need the fine editor he'd been. Dead. Was I?

The depression was unbearable, but my friend held me together, in all ways: food, sleeping pills; out on the farm with me often—handing me the hoe, part of a flat of vegetables. Evenings: she pulled me out to read with Mort and her, played a lot of records.

Then a letter from my agent: Any ideas about publishers?

Me: "What kind of ideas would I have!" Helen (so quietly): "I've got one. How about offering the book to ER?"

Through my numbed head—a slash, finally: Helen had sold some of my stories to this woman when she'd been a magazine fiction editor. She had married the head of a publishing firm I'd never heard of, written: "If Jo is ever free, and wants a new publisher—please!"

Helen: "What have you got to lose, dear? Won't you write your agent and at least get some information about this publisher?"

After a while, my agent—to this effect: It's an old, old firm now sincerely trying to build up their list. Recently hired new editor in chief: KJ. Very well thought of in the field. He'd be the first to read the book. E knows about the two rejections—wants very much to

see the book. She's associate editor.
Me: "Enter, the Pulitzer Prize!" Helen (crisply): "Shame on you.
As for this new editor—maybe? Ed came out of the blue. Remember?" She's always such a giver of hope. Why can't I make that a permanent part of me? I finally said as much. Helen: "Try harder?"
So I did. With the beginnings of a new book. With another season's flowers, food crops. With stubborn touch on both families, friends. With Helen my strongest bridge to all of it.

Mid-July. Agent: Reports on novel exceedingly good, according to E. She begs some grace in holding it a while longer.
Me: "Jesus. 'Exceedingly good'? Who's crazy?" Helen: "Nobody. That, dear one, is definitely show business. Try to sit tight."
But at my desk (stints on the new book), the trying's tough. For example, look at the writer's money status. Fan sent me two hundred bucks. My niece (her idea—good kid!) is carrying my fifty bucks a month that I give for Ma's expenses. But how am I ever going to pay people back?
Talking of insecure writers: I'm getting worse about Emil. Any time I visit there, I come away feeling sick. *Could* Hemingway or Fitzgerald possibly have felt this guilty about using people? I doubt it, from anything I've read.

Late July. Agent: E swore we'd settle a yes or no the first of next week. They're impressed with the book. This might be a take.
Helen: "Easy, dear. Go out and farm yourself into a sweat."

Early August. Agent—telegram:

They want it. KJ came to my office to tell me. Did not call me to his office. That never happens with an editor-in-chief exclamation point. K considers your book most important manuscript in any New York office. E enormously impressed also. K says quote any small difficulties with the novel can be ironed out by judicious cutting. Anna tremendous character. Every word readable, exciting and beautiful. Close quote.

Me (completely dazed): "That's impossible." Helen: "Nothing is! Don't you know that yet? (A kiss.) Congratulations, darling."
I began to cry. Not dead, after all? She put her arms around

me. "Yes, cry. That awful mountain climb is over."

August 6, 1959—editor to author:

My dear Jo Sinclair:
The one thing I could not do when I first read your manuscript was to cancel a trip to London which was already scheduled. That's where the last four weeks have gone and I'm sorry.
Let me say at once that I consider your manuscript the most important manuscript in America today. It is a midcentury novel of tremendous beauty, power, and truth. It is superb technically in the building and maintaining of narrative drive and a quality of suspense. It is versatile, moving, and convincing. I believe it is going to be a famous book and a bestseller. In the belief that I am the first to believe completely in the future of this novel I went to your agent's office, I did not summon her to mine. It is this same instinct that makes me want to come to you with my belief and enthusiasm. It seems to me that the things that remain to be done with the manuscript, and there are some, exist for only one reason. Perhaps out of loneliness and doubt and artistic insecurity (and I have written enough to know something of these devils) you have been tempted to write this novel almost as if it were the last one you'd ever write. In some cases you don't trust your own work far enough. One old saw quoted frequently by painting instructors is to the effect that it takes two people to paint a picture—one to paint it and one to tell him when to stop. I think this is the first of your great novels. Good as the others were, they did not approach this in scope or passion. You may not feel like a young novelist at this point but you are one and six months after this book is published you will know that I have told you the truth.
I'll call you when I can find out which day next week I can get down to see you.
My best regards and deep admiration.

Jesus. I even *like* this guy. And he knows about feeling that this is the last book you'll ever do. And not trusting yourself. "The most important manuscript. . ." He's probably a nut.

*

He wasn't. And when he came, I liked him even more. We had some damn good talk about the book—hours of it. *Very* sensitive guy. Then, contracts! Advance against royalties: three thousand bucks. (*I* asked for that much; Helen encouraging me.)

Late August: The check came: Paid off Fannie. Paid off Mildred (two hundred dollars by now, for Ma's support). My God, life sure can be screwy.

Last of August. Yep, I know what a tough job this rewrite is going to be. Hell on wheels. But K is quite an editor. He listens. He sees.

Early September: The Van Goghs are in seed, and the goldfinch are singing their heads off. Nice—when I manage to look up from this *thing* I'm hacking and sewing. Often sitting for four hours at a crack. Until Helen comes into my room: "Okay, writer darling, time for a break. It'll even be good for the book. Move that body before it freezes into a writing position and I have to send it to a museum."

Later that month: The joint is a mess; the gardener has turned into the writer-with-a-deadline. I'm spending most of the day, and often part of the night, on "Anna Teller." The new title: K won. He's right: it is more dramatic, easier to remember than the other. And it *is* Anna's book.

And my own mother? I know she's dying, God help me. Poor little Ma, so thin and old—can't eat much—so scared. But she does show a spark about the book, the money, the first publicity.

Early December: The rewrite was finished, shipped out. I could have croaked of pure exhaustion, but a first smile came with K's telegram: "God bless people who keep deadlines. All here and safe. Love."

The book is dedicated to Ed. I had dedicated it to Emil—but he refused it, with bitterness and fury. Ed would have understood—and smiled. My next big book would have gone to him, anyway. But Emil, Emil, I'm heartsick about your hatred. And that's the word.

Early May, 1960—editor to author:

Dear Jo:
Yesterday I sent off to you the first copy of *Anna Teller* that I saw. It looks fine to me and I hope it does to you. It is I firmly believe a great book and I trust it will sell like one. The rest of your author's copies will go to you shortly and of course I'm eager to hear the "local" response. Love and thanks.

Late August—editor to author (telegram):

This is one of the proudest publication days of my life. Advance sales now over 12,000. We might have a hit. Love and congratulations.

In the author's copy of *Anna* (to be put with the other three inscribed books I'd given them, and the paperbacks, the translations), I wrote:

Helen and Mort: Safe under the roof of your hearts, warmed and loved, the person and the writer—replenished all over again—tries to say: I thank you both.

Ruth-Jo

A book—the fourth novel. Started outline January 1, 1957. Published August 22, 1960. Oh, but Ma, Ma, rest in peace.

End of memory.

• • •

Swords sheathed. Dear Lord, kind Lord, gracious Lord. It's not the life of a book I'm praying for tonight; it's the life of a woman. A person who helps books get written and published. I'm praying with all of that heart she un-muted.

November 20: She's in a private room. Nurses. Dr. H, neurologist, has been called in. Lots of dizziness, vomiting. I sit and hold her hand, talk: strong, full of hope. The actress! All day, I try to push strength into her.

November 21: In by nine in the morning. Dizziness and nausea seem worse. "Ruthie—my ear. Like a *tractor*. I hate that." Speech quite blurred—as I think of the plowed spring garden under the other kind of tractor's blades. Her leg twitches. Occasionally, those convulsive heaves. Me: anger, pain, pity, but with enormous strength at the core. Her leg quiets. She: "Thanks, dear!"

Home by nine that night. Helen (just before I left): "Bring your work tomorrow? Please." Mort stayed on with her. At home, turned on the FM (no Ragsy; the house is so silent): the end of the Archduke Trio, one of our loves. I cursed—loud. Packed Mort's lunch. He's bringing that brown paper bag to the hospital on his lunch hour. She likes that—but to me, Mort eating sandwiches in her room again...

On the radio now: that tender Bach "Sheep May Safely Graze." How I long to believe. Feel faith in the fact that people can live in quiet meaning—safe from recurring, idiot blows.

November 22: Got there before nine. Oh, she's so sick. But she smiled to see me. Blurred voice: "Bring your work?" When she seemed to fall asleep, I set myself up in the chair near the window— where I could see her. The leg twitch woke her several times, but when I helped she went back to sleep. I wrote—God knows what.

Suddenly Mort arrived—shaking, very pale. "President Kennedy was just shot in Texas. He's still alive, but critical." Me: "Mort, don't—not now!" She's crazy about JFK. I was afraid of a heart attack—something awful.

But Helen wanted the details. He told us all he knew as he ate his lunch; and I remembered something, very abruptly. I was working at the Red Cross; it was April 12, 1945. The phone rang in my office—Helen, weeping: "Ruthie, Roosevelt is dead. I just heard it on the radio. I wanted you to hear it from me—not be shocked too suddenly." I'd worshipped FDR.

I went fast to Helen of the stunned eyes, held her hand—tight, strong as I could. "Try to be quiet. Please." Mort had to leave for work. Helen (deep sadness): "Oh, Ruthie, how wrong." Me (actually begging): "Please, dear, don't get sicker over this. For us. We all need you so much."

She tried. Even ate a little. Eventually, fell asleep. By then, he was dead. Later, Martin phoned—that was good. Promised to be here tomorrow, stay through Thanksgiving.

Driving home—my car radio: the world is reeling about the assassination. Yes, as if, finally, everybody feels the way I do about Helen's second stroke. Sheer horror that such a meaningless thing can happen.

November 23: At hospital by ten. Brought the FM—I knew she'd want all the news (would she be able to hear over the tractor noise?). It's Saturday—Mort'll come later. When I walked in: a smile, lousy as she felt. Told me Barbie and Diedrick had phoned last night, after I'd gone, about JFK—knowing how she must be feeling. They're coming for Thanksgiving—she's so happy about that.

This second stroke seems so different. Her left arm is weak, yes—but there's apparently no real paralysis. Other things: her memory is bad in spots. She has periods of being what she calls "absent." Deafness off and on—especially in the right ear. On occasion, her eyes are out of focus. And sometimes, she's told me, she has that sensation of a dead face. The nausea and dizziness and vomiting—recurring so often. My emotions list these things—flashcards of fear.

I'm in most of the day, along with Mort. (Martin arrived at dinnertime.) When she sleeps, I write. Try not to think. Or weep.

November 24: At home, TV; in the car, radio—the JFK affair is becoming more and more ghastly. All of it to go with Helen?

Because she was really sick when I got there. Totally deaf in her right ear. For a time, in both. Then her left ear cleared. Dr. N in. An ear specialist; the neurologist. Helen is frightened, though only her eyes say so. So is Martin, but hides it from her. Even Mort of the poker face finally "showed," mid-morning. Dr. N talked to us in the corridor, far from her closed door: "Helen's heart is bad. Another stroke may kill her. She's in very bad health." When he left, Mort half passed out—into his son's arms. Me: "Martin, take him out for air. Then get some food in him. Mort, God damn it, snap out of it! She *can't* die."

Waited until Martin supported his father to the elevator. Thought, exhausted: Somebody's got to pretend to be strong and hopeful. Helen can't do it, right now. That leaves you, babe.

Inside her room, I white-lied about Mort having tea, Martin being starved as usual. She wanted to talk about Kennedy. And I listened, tried my best to soothe her as she spoke with sorrow about the man, the wife and children.

I feel numb. But I know one thing: I refuse anything that doctor said in the corridor a while ago.

November 25: The nurse phoned at six in the morning. Helen had had a light stroke—right side—at five-ten. We left in two cars—in case of sudden driving need. Helen looked dreadfully ill. Dr. N ran in very fast, examined her. But then: "An episode. She'll be all right."

Martin read her to sleep with the *New Yorker*. I took off for home—ostensibly to wash some clothes and food-shop. But I had to leave; I was exploding with anger, bitterness, frustration. Way home: longed for it to be that other season—where I could rotohoe myself into tired stillness, pick her masses of flowers.

Changed bed linens, washed some clothes, rushed up to the corner for essentials, made up bed for B and D. I was folding sheets when Mort phoned: "Intravenous feeding and catheter."

When I walked into her room, I looked calmly—as my stomach rocked—at the inverted bottle hanging there, the tube taped to her hand (last time it was her arm). Me: "Ah, how to eat without chewing. And I hear you can pee with no effort, no flush."

She laughed. So did Martin. Her color was better. "Bring your work?" Her voice was quite clear. Screwy! But I said gaily: "Right here. Snap out of it, huh? So you can help me proof galley." She smiled—big.

My acting stayed good. I wrote for a while, and could see how pleased she was. Mort and Martin brought me coffee, sandwiches. We took turns reading to her. And I wrote—in between things. God knows what.

November 26: More of the same. She does seem a trifle better, however. That's all I'll write—plus *Amen*.

November 27: Big snow in the night. The world is beautiful—so white and fresh. Sometimes a sight like this, in the dead winter, is more creative in the guts than spring. A sense of the seasons coming and going as inexorably as anything this life contains. It *is* meaning, damn it. And it's got to include Helen.

She phoned—on her own! Very good night, said she. Feels halfway decent. Mort had stopped on way to work. I ran to wake Martin: "Kid, she's better!"

Got there by half past nine. There's a gift shop downstairs—

and flowers. Bought a pepper plant. It's real fun—with those little red pepper-shaped fruits all over a green background. In her room, first thing I noticed: no hanging bottle. She absolutely loved the plant. It *does* gay up the whole room.

Still deaf—right ear. But Dr. N had said: improved. And had had the catheter removed, too. The ear man: the deafness is inner ear difficulty, due to particular brain area that's starved for blood. Medication: we're working on it. Me (quick): "See? Temporary! Anyway, can you hear my soft, lovely voice with one ear?"

Big smile. Told her all about the snow, birds, top-hatted pumpkin. That I hadn't had to shovel; my good old snow tires. I wrote a little, to make her happy. Martin came, making her even happier. Later, she talked of B and D coming in this evening for the holiday. Of home—and it must be so lovely now—and do I have enough bird seed—and do you remember that winter when we were snowbound and ran out of feed, so you hiked over to Lil's and borrowed some of their cracked corn, and came home snow-wet to the waist?

Her nurses are good. When she slept, I wrote and Martin did business papers. And I thought: How I'd like to write a poem. About death thwarted again, and a snow-hatted pumpkin making a bridge toward Heavenly Blue morning glories.

November 28: Happy holiday, world. Phooey. But she's having a good morning: phone-talked to all of us. Barb came out with me when I fed the birds. "Ruth, I brought a lot of new pictures of Eric. Mother had me put them up on the window ledge—propped all around your plant." Me: "And the red peppers make him look blonder." She kissed me, hung on. Me: "Don't panic. Let's all go make festive."

In the room: the peppers did make that child look blonder. Me: "He's gorgeous." Helen: "Isn't he? And it's like he's here, too. All my darlings. On Thanksgiving Day!"

Dr. N (he'd already been there): Improved. Later, I persuaded the family to go down and eat holiday dinner together. I'd be with Helen. Reluctant, but they went. She: "Ruthie, thank you for that. Please go to Sadie's later. To make me happy?" So I did, but couldn't eat much.

November 29 through December 2: She's uncomfortable much of the time—and really exhausted by now. After the kids left town,

I spent more time with her every day—talking, reading aloud, writing when she slept. Her eyes are lonely, but everybody will be back for Christmas, and I told her that in every variation possible. Dr. N: Even more improved. Then why all that dizziness, buster? And why are her eyes badly out of focus so often, and memory still not too good—in spots?

December 3: Helen looks okay, sort of, but at five or so she got very dizzy. Just *lying* there, damn it. Nurse gave her anti-dizziness shot. How can I believe that doctor?

When the nurse went off on her dinner break, Helen said that Dr. N had told Mort the following (and of course Mort had told her—we've always done that, so everybody can know exactly what's what): that the two or three weeks of fainting and dizziness preceding her nine days of hospital tests were—"in light of further developments"—a stroke: number two. That means on November 19, at home, she had had stroke number three. And on November 26, right here (he'd tabbed it an episode then), stroke number four.

Me (at core-Me): Jesus. And she? A kind of helpless look I can't bear. Yes, we've always told one another everything in this family, but is it such a good idea at a time like this? Me (calmly): "So that's enough. For even a pig like you. You always did want more than ordinary people."

I got a smile. Then I told her about the first redheaded woodpecker at the suet feeder. Helen (yearning): "No deer?" Me: "No. Or even ugly old possum. Don't you know they're waiting for you?" She really laughed—ah, what a wonderful sound in this room. She: "Remember that fight you had with the possum trying to steal the suet? I think about that so often—helps me go to sleep."

December 4: Woke, thinking: Four strokes—my God, dear God, what're You doing?

It's my dear friend Liz's birthday. I phoned her, and we had some good, rather lovely talk. But I got to the hospital elevator crawling with spiritual tiredness about *four* strokes.

However, the play was written anew as I rode up; my entrance speech perfect. And she? Dizzy, absent. I sat close all afternoon. She couldn't eat much. I watched the nurse, the shots administered—studied all of it: a short story, novel? I could have written every motion, every nuance in that room.

At seven or so, Helen: "Ruthie, I'm too tired. Phone the doctor." (Mort had worked late, telephoned, gone home to eat.) Dr. N: "I'm not concerned—that's part of the condition. I expect Helen to go home soon." Me: "What? How could that be!"

I noticed Helen watching and listening intently; adjusted my slipping mask instantly: "If *you* say so—wonderful! Listen, I've been thinking—can I learn how to give her those shots for when she does go home?"

I winked at Helen, mouthed: "Home." Her eyes!

Dr. N: "Do you think you could? They're intramuscular—very painful if you aren't certain. A nurse should come out there—" I interrupted: "A nurse, my hat. Hell, I'm practically a *doctor* by now." He: "Try it. Every day—at the hospital. Make sure."

I hung up, grinned. "The tiredness is normal, says Doctor-god. But guess what, babe? You're going home soon! And he talks like an ice cube about a thing like Keats and Bach! Doctors give me a pain in my sensitivity area, not only my ass!" She: "Ruthie, it'll make you feel awful." Me (honest as hell): "No, it won't. I *want* to give you your shots. Aside from the money on nurses that'll worry you."

I made a laugh. "Hey, did this green thumb ever hurt a pickle or a rose? So how can I hurt a darling? And I have news for you: gardeners become very strong in soul and psyche, after a while." She laughed, too, cried: "Home. Oh, Ruthie!"

Got home, finally. Tried to write—couldn't. Or read. Or— eventually—sleep. Every time I closed my eyes, I had a picture of Helen here—dizzy, passing out. With just me around.

December 5: Phone: a good night. Had sat in a chair. Yes, a little dizzy, but felt good about the chair. And home soon! Got there by four. She sat in chair again, and I applauded gaily. But she's so tired. Eyes bad. On the other hand, this is a good doctor!

Gave her an insulin shot. Then, later, my first intramuscular shot. Nervous as hell, but she swore it didn't hurt. The nurse says I'm good. Well, okay, I'm in training now. (How do you train the emotions!) On the drive home, I suddenly wished for spring so harshly that my eyes got wet.

December 6: She sat in chair. Walked a bit. But dizziness continues. And that ear! But her eyes are more focused; she does look

better. Later, after the shot, Helen: ''You were much more at ease today.'' Me: ''You're a very smart psychiatrist, doc.''
Driving home, I felt the winter rushing by like a piece of Vivaldi. And thought, to that wonderful, sensed music: I *will* do it. (Ruthie, are you a stone? Yes, God damn it!)

December 7: Made up a basket of Indian corn and gourds; on way in, bought bittersweet. Helen (with joy): ''Home!'' Sat up— filed her nails (how that familiar, long-missing sight thrilled me.) But why does that damn dizziness continue?

December 8: Morning phone news: Dr. N has upped the insulin to fifteen units, twice a day. It's Sunday: Mort went in early; I got there at one or so. She's still dizzy. Ear better—but only sporadically. Me: ''Report from the winter gardener: three amaryllis in bud.'' A *good* laugh. All right!—inch by inch?
Mort took off for the Aunties—stocks and bonds business. Radio: all the Chopin preludes, and we smiled over the memory. She: ''The marigold-zinnia bed.'' Ah, no brain damage; that's when I'd first heard these, and raved. But her dizziness was pretty sustained— turning in bed, sitting up to eat, walking to a chair. Nevertheless, that stubborn one insisted on walking down the corridor: ''rehearsing for home.''

December 9: At seven, about three inches of snow already— and still coming down hard. Feeders choked, all with tremendous hats. Used whisk-broom, then filled. What a flurry of birds. Beautiful.
Phone: sounds good. Though she reports she's dizzy when she goes to bathroom, sits up, walks. But she did them all. The sporadic deafness continues, too. Like a sap, I permit myself to think of poor deaf Beethoven; and that day Helen heard for the first time, with high excitement, ''Transfigured Night.''
She reminded me of the clock, and threatened me. I'm due to Christmas-shop for her today—on way to the hospital. She'd insisted I get a clock; my alarm had conked out. I'd fought her on it: ''You and Mort are broke—who needs a present?'' Now she, laughing: ''If you don't buy it today, I'll send Mort. And he'll spend more than you would.'' She had me on that, and knew it.
I checked on the condition of her tummy. Fine, said she. Didn't

take any work; today was going to be pre-Christmas. Brought Eric's bird-woods record she'd ordered from National Wildlife. I was going to have a style show for her—and joy up the day for a gal who adores that holiday. Put, in same bag, the book I'd bought at her order for her to give Mort: *The Rise of the West: A History of the Human Community* by William H. McNeill. She'd seen a good review in my Sunday *Times*, and it's what she calls a good read-aloud book. By Mort, as she knits or rests on the couch. That was one of the first things I'd gawked at and adored in this family.

Got to the hospital with a crammed bag. She was in bed; not the chair, damn it. Deeply tired—I could see it. Ah, but that Helen: when I laid out the boughten corned beef sandwich and pickle, the thermos of our own coffee from home, she kissed me. "Just what I wanted!"

I turned on the FM, brought the bittersweet and draped it over her legs. We had a Beethoven quartet with her snack and my style show. She could eat only half the sandwich, but enjoyed it. I started the show with EJ's record. She was so amused that I'd brought it, even though it wasn't a new purchase, and she'd seen it when it had arrived. "Oh, green-thumbed Santa—bringing my *whole* Christmas!"

I showed her the gifts Mort and she were giving. When I got to the calendar towel for the Aunties and Uncle Hugo (I'd picked an herbs motif), she liked it so much that I laughed: "Me, too. So I bought one for our kitchen. I've missed them—since you got cheap and decided to save a buck or two. Hey, look at the dill."

She was really pleased. Christmas all over her bed. Then I showed her my clock. After she said how nice, and that she liked the lighted face for nighttime waking, I said: "Six bucks and tax." How she laughed at my triumphant frugality.

I finished by handing her the card from the *New Yorker*, announcing a Christmas gift "From your friend, Ruth." My traditional present to her—the card always saying the same thing. She: "Dearest." Me: "You'd be bored without it—so then you'd bore me. Right?"

Another laugh of pure pleasure, but I could see that she was dizzy again. I made her rest, said: "One more surprise. After your shot. A reward for good Poohs." Her eyes got wet. I patted her cheek, said firmly: "No tears. Or no surprise." God, that reversal of roles! She stopped crying.

My intra shot was perfect. She said so, and so did Mrs. C, the excellent nurse who has been training me. Then I handed Helen the "reward." Really, a gift for both of us. It was the Beethoven *Triple Concerto.* I'd first heard it on the radio, fallen in love with it. She's always loved it. She looked up—didn't say one scolding word. (In our eyes: that hot, lovely day on the porch when I'd just heard it; Ragsy and she on the glider; the bowl of cherry tomatoes; the wrens singing along.) Helen (soft): "Don't Christmas-wrap it. We'll play it as soon as I get home." Me: "That's a deal!"

Not too dizzy when she woke. And eager to talk about the rest of Christmas: what kind (and price) of tree to order. When she got home, she'd fix up two or three glass bells—so would I please pick up partridgeberries and odds and ends of moss and greens when I drove over early for the mantle greens and holly and mistletoe. Me (to inner-Me): See? Patterns! The seasons! Now, it's the tree. In February, the seed order. *Has* to be.

December 10: Mort and I up extra early: worried about the snow. It's stopped, but, oh boy, what it left behind. He'd backed into the garage the night before: a Ruth-invent for really rough weather. I hadn't wanted to take the chance—and maybe get stuck. Mort made the drive, in one big blurt; and the road's always well plowed.

I tanked up on coffee, then went out with the shovel. Oh, no, I wasn't about to get snowed in. Morning phone: pretty good—the night, and so far. Sporadic dizziness, but light. "Bring your work. I love to see you writing in my room."

At hospital by three. Driving lousy, and the parking was a particular headache. But Helen's smile, when I came in!

Why does she continue to be so tired? How can she come home? And she's scared—her eyes can't kid me. (God, she never used to be scared—about anything!) So I talked a blue streak—the snow, the birds, my book. Put on the FM. The music was lovely. Piano— Beethoven, including two of the sonatas Barbie used to practice at home; we nodded over that, and she slept with a smile.

I wrote—God knows what.

December 11: Phone: dizzy, yes, but she'd sat in a chair for breakfast. And she'd read the *New Yorker* with no blur or nausea! And walked! And Dr. N had said the diabetes was even better today. She sounded excited, unafraid, full of joy.

This completely nutty, seesaw disease. What to think? At hospital: Helen still good. I walked her (dizzy and all) in the corridor. All the way to the end—small rest—and back. Damn it, Ruth, believe!

December 12: When I got there, she was dizzy. Told me she feels "left over." Teeter-totter again? After dinner, while sitting in a chair, she had an "incident." Scared us all badly. The nurse ran for the house doctor, while Mort held Helen, and I talked my head off. The doctor: valvular insufficiency of blood to brain. Nothing to be alarmed about.

Nothing! My God.

December 13: Between writing stints, tore into town for much-needed haircut. Sam-Beauty said he'd be glad to come to the house to cut Helen's hair. Good. And then—what got into me? A "just in case." On way home, I stopped and bought a lot of good food. Friday: I had the grocery money with me, anyway.

Brought her a sandwich from home: thick ham slice on rye; heart of celery; our coffee. "Got to get you more and more adjusted to my gourmet cooking." She (laughing): "Yes! Dr. N left ten minutes ago. After telling me I'm going home Sunday." Me: "Marvelous!" But my heart began to clamor. Funny: nine-tenths of me was joy, but that one-tenth? Pure dread.

While she ate, she caught me up with her day. Been down to physio, walked a lot—even though dizzy. Dr. N had told her the diabetes is, at last, under control. "Home, Ruthie, home!"

I had a sudden, fervent wish: that Ragsy were there.

Later, Helen (tenderly): "You're so tense, *toi*. Go to Sadie's for Friday night. And dearest, when you get home, either write a poem or get a little drunk."

Laughter. When I got home, there wasn't a poem in me. So I got a little drunk—and changed the linens on her bed. One more drink, and I had guts enough to fasten the bell. Then I dusted and ran the Hoover, all over our carpeted house.

There's my poem for the night, oh Lord!

December 14: Mort went in early, to get the wheelchair before visiting Helen. He: "The toilet and tub bars are ready, anyway. And the walker." I was all ice inside at that remark—don't ask me why!

Decided to do the mantle—so she'd have her first whiff of Christmas when she came into her house tomorrow.

By the time Jean (so happy about Helen's progress) had picked out a lovely little tree, I was feeling better. It would be cut, and picked up, the Tuesday before Christmas. By one of us: the kids were due to drive in that day; and Martin, later sometime, from Chicago. I thought of EJ's glee, and kind of grinned.

I brought home masses of evergreen branches (four different kinds—some with berries, some with little cones), and holly, two big bunches of mistletoe, and about a dozen large pine cones, some for EJ to toss onto the logs, along with the wax "pies" of color. Also, I'd got together the ingredients for two glass Christmas bells.

She phoned, earlier; said she was okay. I kept my job a surprise, said I'd see her later: lots to do, because some babe I knew was leaving some hospital tomorrow, hurrah. Big laugh from her.

I put on "The Messiah," of course, turned up the volume full blast and proceeded. Decorated the mantle: masses of evergreens, holly, the Santas-with-brooms stuck into whorls of green. The big, partially burned Christmas candles and the new bayberry I'd bought. The merry elves and grotesques that we'd all loved for years. Airy, big evergreens inside this kitchen fireplace, instead of logs. Now fill the soup kettle with smaller greens; poise the little Swiss gnome with the funny beard on one rim of the kettle. A real Helen-thing.

Mistletoe in the center of the (swinging) doorway. People stand and lean there a lot—and get kissed. The other bunch of mistletoe: tie it, red ribbon, to EJ's bed. Last year—Helen: "At the foot. If it's at the head, he may reach up and grab it, eat some. The berries would make him sick." Me (gaily): "Sick, my eye. They would kill him, dear Grandma-Pooh. It's poisonous to man and beast." Helen:"Damn you." But she put two small freezer bags around the original cellophane bag before tying it to the foot of the bed.

I laughed: automatically, me too. Back I tore—the music vibrating through the whole house and me: "Wonderful, Counselor, the mighty God, the Everlasting Father, the Prince of Peace." Living room: I laid a fire. A damn good one.

Looked around to find some more Helen-stuff. On the narrow wood ledge of the south window (and the three amaryllis buds are *much* bigger), there's quite a clutch of little creatures that the children have given her over the years. I picked a chipmunk carved beautifully out of wood—including quite a plume of a tail. Put him on the trained-up part of Sarah J's grape ivy plant, fastened him there with a green garden tie. Yep, definitely a Helen-thing: he's climbing, it's spring.

Made the two Christmas vase-bells—pretty good job. The little one into their bedroom; the big one on the living-room table, between candles. The music poured God into me: "He that dwelleth in heaven shall laugh them to scorn. Behold, I tell you a mystery."

Oh, beautiful mystery. Life everlasting. I ran to finish up. Then got her. At her "Hello?" I held the phone up and toward the record player. Gave her about a two-minute concert, then: "Surprise! Merry Christmas-to-be!" She: "Oh, dearest, you've done the mantle." Me: "Right. And Jean sends her love. Wait'll you see the gorgeous tree. Only six bucks. How do you feel by now?" Helen: "Fine. Really! Mort ate lunch with me. Why don't you both eat dinner here?"

Okay! And to hell with money, at this point. Got cleaned up. And off we go—and it *is* a poem; the whole day of Christmas-preparing for her, her, her. Okay, live your poems, then maybe you can write them. My head sang all the way: "Wonderful! Counselor! The mighty God, the Everlasting..."

Hospital: quite dizzy most of the day. But smiles, all over her. Dr. N: Dizziness bound to go away. Yes, wheelchair for a while. Fifteen units of insulin three times a day—careful of food.

Evening: I said good-bye to Mrs. C, thanked her again for the shot-training. She gave me (for home use) a lot of free needles and disposable syringes. (Wish we could afford that kind.) Left Mort there. I'm going to have a short visit with Pearl and Alice; heaven knows when I'll be able to see them again, and besides I miss them. But how I wish Sarah J were there tonight. And—yearning but nice note—I wish Virginia were here tonight, to talk to, to say her cynical-loving: "Take it easy, baby—Helen's just as stubborn as I am, and I'm still around. Hear?"

Took home the pepper plant—well wrapped against the cold; and the radio, EJ's pictures. Stopped and bought a huge bunch of mums—bronze and yellow. Had them put double wrapping around; I'd stuck a mason jar full of water in the car. What's a homecoming without live flowers?

December 15: Both of us up very early. The second wheelchair in the utility room?—don't pay any attention. Fix the flowers, instead. Prettiest vases in the house: kitchen table and window sill, their bedroom. (The Christmas bell in there looks fresh and lovely.) The rest of the mums in a large vase on the coffee table near the couch, where she'll rest.

Mort: "Looks like summer." We laughed: outside the windows, tons of snow. I rushed out to heap seed, hang suet, so that a million birds would be in on the homecoming. Then off we went.

I helped her dress (while Mort did the last-minute office stuff). Yes, she was still dizzy; and had to rest often. She was smiley but quite gray. I kept my hands on her whenever she stood, because of the weaving. When we rode home, my arm was around her to help.

Home?—my heart had begun to knife at me even in the hospital room. The knife turned sharper on the trip: intensely uncomfortable for her; queasy with the car motion, ear roaring. She was tensed, badly—I could feel it in my arm, as I steadied her and talked a little about how she'd feel better as soon as we got home. When we hit the real country, she did relax a little.

Yes, home. She didn't say much. In the kitchen, sitting in the wheelchair, she saw all the things I'd done. Her eyes slowly turned peaceful. A cup of tea helped the nausea. Then Mort wheeled her into the living room. She noticed everything—her eyes told me. And when she saw Chippy climbing the grape ivy, she actually laughed. Outside the front window, all the birds had come, and she watched them for a while—colors, swoopings and flyings and perchings. In a murmur: "So lovely."

She rested on the couch while I got lunch going. No, she didn't want music (to Mort's question). Whenever I peered in, she was watching the birds. She looked happy, thank God. Mort and she talked: the children, Christmas. I saw her touch the mums near her.

And she ate all her lunch (wheelchair at the table), seemed to enjoy it. But shortly afterward, a very bad attack of dizziness. It passed off gradually, as she lay on the couch.

Our friend, Juley Weil, came. With a pot of chicken his wife had cooked for our dinner (Helen has done that so often, with them and others). Mrs. Weil (another Helen) was in bed with flu, but she phoned: "Oh, dear friend, welcome home!" Mort lit a fire. Helen told Juley to look at the three-birch, the Weil house present so long ago. Wasn't it huge and beautiful?

There was fine talk. Juley is director of a home for the aged;

his wife, the head social worker. He asked Helen's advice about a particularly complicated case of paranoid senility. She's advised the Weils often; they deeply respect her mind, her instincts, her knowledge of such things. Today's talk from Helen was wonderful, as ever.

But then—so terribly sudden—she said she felt very sick. I got a bucket there in time. Threw up violently. Looked dreadful. After a while, Juley went home, his eyes sad as they met mine. Rest of day and evening in bed. Rough. Couldn't eat. But when the kids phoned, she made a tremendous effort—talked to them, and even to EJ. Same when Martin phoned.

I gave Mort his dinner in the kitchen; sat near Helen and talked my hopeful best. She said she felt very tired. So dizzy. I washed her face and hands in bed. My heart ached for her, but I was insistent about some toast and milk because of the insulin.

When finally I got to bed, I lay there in the dark, and thought of how beautifully that brain had worked in the intricate talk with Juley—and then the sickness had sucked her into nothingness. Thought, even before I prayed: God, please—give me back meaning.

December 16: When Mort left for work, at seven-thirty, told me she'd slept most of the night. But when she woke (almost nine), it was with convulsions of the right leg. And her head!

My God—her *head* jerking up and down. Oh, Christ. At nine-fifteen (I continue to automatically note the time for everything—to tell the doctor, I guess), she threw up.

Couldn't get the doctor—left emergency message. Brief convulsions (the one leg) at one-forty-five. Then at two. Dr. N finally phoned: "Nothing to do. Take anti-dizzy pills every four hours. Be careful about the insulin—check urine for color. No other shots until further notice, but be very careful about the insulin."

Dizzy most of the day—just lying in bed. Numb hand, leg (left). Right leg feels very sore from convulsions (I rub, gently). Finally got some tea and toast down her. She slept. I'd brought breakfast and lunch trays, but she was too dizzy to even sit up. She ate a little dinner from the bed tray. And she smiled at Mort and me. The valiant.

December 17: Better. Good night. She ate some breakfast—in bed. But dizziness, all the time. Lunch: ate well, to start. Sat up in bed (I had a doily, a flower, on the bed tray). But she had to lie down, very abruptly, before the meal was anywhere near over—a wave of dizziness.

Suddenly, to my astonishment and horror, I hollered. At God, of course. At fate, nature. Then, in a few moments, stopped—just stared at her, anguished. Helen (very quiet): "I'm so sorry. About everything."

I apologized—staring at that tray I'd tried to make pretty and appetizing for a sick woman. I felt like a rotten pig, and so ashamed—and tried to tell her about it. She took my hand, pressed it to her cheek. "Don't, dear. You know I understand. Please work. That'll make us both feel better. Ruthie? Write me a book."

When I came back, after cleaning up, she was asleep. And I wished so hard for Rags—to be squeezed close and loving. Well, I did work—in the living room. It would be a pattern, I decided. Early in the morning, I'd set up my work-in-progress on this table. So I could hear any sound. Take care of patient, get house chores done; and the writing smeared all around it.

And so it started out. She rang the bell when she woke. I helped her wash, get back into bed. The insulin shot; breakfast (as much as she could), and I had more coffee as she ate. I caught her up with night, morning, my book, the season. Lunch: insulin, her tray, another tray for my sandwich and coffee. Dinner: Mort in kitchen (he's more comfortable at the table—as long as I'm with her for company), two trays for bedroom.

Thank God I'm fast and organized. As it was, the day and evening melted away; though I did manage to write some—at times. I'd put the hand bell on her bedside table, and I knew she'd use it—she promised.

Discovery: a person does not change. No matter how sick Helen felt, she always noticed the "pretty" I'd put on the bed tray; or the small things I thought would entertain her—and thanked me.

One more discovery: memory is bad *and* good. The wheelchair, the four-legger, the proper way to help her get out of bed, to "walk her"—with me instead of the cane; it all makes me remember too starkly that first stroke. And yet memory makes me an expert for this one. And makes me the best-rehearsed actor this side of hell.

December 18: Better. Gave her ten units of insulin in the morning; fifteen at noon. All seemed okay. Lunch: she was sitting up in bed, actually enjoying the food, smiling at me.

Then!—she saw two of me. And screamed in fear. (Told me all the details later.) Followed, a big seizure as I grabbed the tray away. She was intensely dizzy—faint. Couldn't swallow. A kind of snoring noise came from her as I knelt on the bed and held her tightly. But no convulsions.

It seemed to go on for a long time, as I held and talked—God knows what I was saying in that phony, reassuring voice.

Then she was all right—but so very tired. I wiped her face, brought tea. All afternoon: legs and arms alternately numb and okay. I sat with her—talking a little, getting her to describe all that had happened because I thought she'd feel less frightened if she verbalized it. Leaving for brief periods to get chores done, all the fast stuff. She did not sleep. Didn't tell me why, but I knew—again: she was afraid she'd have a stroke in her sleep. It must be possible for me to turn off my head to these things. Otherwise, wouldn't I go nuts at my friend's torture?

Tried Dr. N twice—but it's his day off. I wanted to kill him. He finally called, dinnertime. After I gave him a detailed description of all the new, awful stuff, and the time for all, he: "An incident. The little blood vessels in her head. That was the double vision, too. Expect her to be better."

I wanted to shame him with words describing pain and fear in a human being. But I didn't. Maybe I was afraid of angering the only one I knew who could help her.

Evening: Mort, in his own bed, read to her until she fell asleep. I gathered up my living-room work, took it to my desk. Didn't know what to do. I finally started to cry—just sitting in my chair. It was the fear for her; today's had been the worst. Plus watching her suffer. Plus my feeling of that terrible, helpless responsibility—just me there, most of the time, to rescue her. How could I, with just love? But always acting as if I could.

December 19: No incidents, but dizzy most of the day. And very depressed. That's still so incredible to me!

Mid-morning: snowing hard. I pulled open the drapes, so she could see the beauty. And the birds: I'd hung suet and a seed feeder on the west chestnut tree—so they'd come to her.

Read her bits of the morning paper, looked up occasionally and followed her gaze: lots of my pals were cooperating at the feeders.

Helen was smiling, though I could see how dizzy she was. Me: "Want me to read you your precious funnies?" Helen (chuckling): "Thanks, dear, but you don't have to put yourself through that." I kissed her cheek, muttered: "I'm sorry you feel so bad." She: "It'll go away. I would love it if you worked." So I did, for a while. God knows how. But she was so pleased.

Evening: about eight or so, couldn't swallow (for quite some time). Small kicks of her leg—briefly. That new double vision bit—several times. Eleven: bad! Held her thrashing leg as Mort phoned the doctor. Who said: "Go on with the anti-dizzy pills. Cut down on the insulin tomorrow morning. She'll feel better." I don't believe him.

Eventually, I went to bed, prayed—my usual way in stress: out loud, hands clasped tightly. Couldn't sleep. Got up, opened a drape—let in the light of the winter night. ("Oh, *toi*, silly, country nights are never dark. In any season.") Walked around, smoked, leaned on my desk and watched the never-dark night on my open notebook. ("Write me a book, Ruthie.")

And thought: Helen, Helen, if I could only write you a new body. Amen.

December 20: Felt a tiny bit better when she woke. Quite dizzy, but managed to eat enough breakfast. And dizzy, off and on, all day. A few times, especially when she sat up, big waves of it—but of brief duration. Walking to bathroom not good. We use me and the four-legger.

Evening: Fannie phoned. I took the call in my room; told her how bad—and she grieved with me. And I thought of my believing sister putting money into the *pushke* for Helen's recovery. And I thought of Ma, and her pennies for a bridge to God. Helen asleep early. I forced myself to work. And after a while, somehow, the drowning came. I forgot the awful cruelty being inflicted on a human being; forgot the bell. I wrote.

December 21: She's completely exhausted. It's Saturday; Dr. N is due here today. He's "done some reading and research."

He came late afternoon. Examined her. His report: Helen probably has occlusion in the lesser artery, not the carotid—blocking blood to brain. Must have an angiography. This is a very delicate and complicated test, tracing blood flow and stoppage. Dye is injected into the brain's arteries, and doctors are able to follow its path through the blood vessels. Dr. R will do it—*the* expert at Mount Sinai. As soon as a room is available. We have to find the exact spot or spots of blocking.

Then he told us that there is possible surgery for her condition. Dr. Michael de Bakey—in Houston, Texas—has performed hundreds of operations on the arteries—tying off, bypassing, et cetera. With dramatic success. But Helen would have to go to Houston. He operates only there, with his very special team.

Helen looked stunned. So did Mort. Me, instantly: "Good! We'll all three go. The Aunties will be glad to pay for such a thing of hope. If this man is so terrific—swell! Off we go." In my head: But why did it take him so long to come up with this answer? All that pain and fear—wasted, my God. Do I even trust—no, no, she was just too complicated a case for him. But why didn't he know that a long time ago? My book? Take it along, punk. It's her, not a book!

Dr. N: "The test first. I'll let you know as soon as a room is available."

As soon? Now, now! But I kept myself from shouting that. There were instructions about the medication to start tomorrow. Could I—still—those intramuscular shots? Yes, of course! I told him.

He got up to go. Me (to Mort): "Stay here. I want to talk to him." To Helen: "Sew up a few things."

In the utility room, I finally let go to Dr. N: "Get that room tomorrow, buddy. Monday, the latest. I know how sick she is. Don't you?" He (visibly annoyed): "I know the full story." Me: "Don't get sore at *me*. I've been here day and night. I'm a witness to her suffering. What the hell are you waiting for?"

He was flushed, but controlled. "I can't get a room out of the air." Me (cold-biting): "But when she has the actual stroke, you do. Doctor—Doctor!—does your patient have to *prove* she's in hell? Well, she is. And has been. I can prove it to God or you." He: "I'll do what I can. Will you please send Mort out here?"

Mort went to him; I sat on Helen's bed, took her hand. I wasn't acting any more. Me: "You listen to me, dear. We're finally getting real help. The three of us are going to Houston. You'll go into the hospital and have that test, then we're flying down. Helen, you're going to get help. You'll be better. Now I know. Now I want you to know. And stop being afraid."

She: "Ruthie, I am afraid." Me: "I know, dear. But we're go-

ing to help you through every bit of it. For the first time, there's
something definite to do. And it sounds *hopeful.*''
   ''Ruthie, I want to be here for Christmas.'' Me: ''That test is
important.'' She: ''Christmas is. So terribly important.'' I decided
a little acting was necessary: ''You'll be right here—I'm sure of that.
The test can't take that long. And Houston'll wait a little while
longer.''
   I made myself laugh—to paint away her expression. Thinking:
This poor little one is *Helen?* Who was never afraid in her life? Her
eyes are a frightened beggar's. God, what are You doing?
   Me: ''Hey! It's going to be all right. And anyway, aren't you
proud of me for blowing my stack at a big-shot doctor? Think how
good it was for my lousy psyche.''
   I got a little smile; said: ''Besides which, what the hell kind of
Christmas could anyone have around here without you?''
   Mort came back: ''He's angry.'' Me: ''Tough luck. Maybe he's
angry enough to get off his ass. And we're going to eat dinner soon.
Then we'll talk out the details of this whole thing. Mort, why don't
you read to Helen? Let's get her relaxed—so I can shovel in a little
food. Then, later, you'd better drive up and get the Vesprin.''
   The brisk, phony actress; I was scared to death, but somebody
had to pretend to be strong and full of confidence. In the kitchen,
cooking, I thought—very close to tears: Finally, finally. She's going
to get some real help. I couldn't anymore.
   No Vesprin in liquid form at the Chester drugstore; Mort
brought back the oral type. On the phone, Dr. N: ''Try one. But
have the liquid kind on hand for tomorrow's shot, in case this
doesn't work. Phone me when she wakes, and we'll see what the
dizziness is like.''
   Mort got the stuff in Cleveland—after doing a lot of driving
(Saturday night; few drugstores open). After he went to bed, dead
tired, I sat in my room and drank. Because I was one jangle, from
brain to heart to toes. The whiskey didn't knock me out—and I knew
it wouldn't; that I'd be ready for any emergency. I blurred slightly,
enough to think almost quietly: I won't be alone with it anymore.
Just wanting to die because I can't help.

December 22: Very early morning: she felt absolutely rotten.
Mort phoned Dr. N, who said: ''Start the Vesprin shots at once.
Tell Ruth: one cc at eight, one cc at four.'' So I gave her the first

intra shot. And noticed numbly that I was still the expert.

God, she was dizzy. Had been off and on, all night. She ate a little. That damn insulin—she has to eat, no matter how nauseated it makes her. When I think how she used to enjoy food!

Another shot at four. She: "Not a smidgen of pain. Thank you, dearest." By four-thirty, the dizziness was considerably lightened. But walking (she wanted so eagerly to try) was more difficult. Light supper—in bed.

She fell asleep at seven. Mort said he'd go to bed with a crossword puzzle, be right there—why didn't I go and relax? At nine, she was still asleep. Much too hard, a heavy deep thing that frightened me. I woke her; I had to. She seemed almost dazed. Mort and I got her to the bathroom. Bad—the walking, her every movement and expression. No urine—to test for the proper insulin dose. There'd been none at lunchtime, either.

I insisted on talking to Dr. N. He: "Cut down the Vesprin to one-half cc. I talked to Dr. R, and she's coming in very soon for the angiography." I thanked him, instead of begging: Help her now, now! Please!

Later. Brief leaps of both legs. She fell asleep. Mort (poor guy, he's so tired) said he'd sleep, too. I went to my room, automatically got ready for bed, started to read—in my chair: I was trying to turn off my head. Couldn't. I was afraid, terribly afraid. Tried to think of spring—of Ragsy, the dam, flowers. Of the kids coming tomorrow. Of Martin, EJ—Christmas. Fell asleep in my chair, still waiting for the buzz of the bell.

December 23: It came. My light was still on, the book in my lap. Quick look as I jumped up from the chair: one-thirty. I was running, shouting that I was coming.

Insane night. I got there—she was feeling better. Light convulsions—left leg. She, with Mort, had started for the bathroom: the wave of dizziness, the half-faint. Mort had left her to press the button. We got her back to bed. No, the bathroom urge was gone (I'd asked, as we lifted her from the floor). I smoothed the leg into stillness. After a while, she felt all right; I asked and asked, not wanting to leave her. She: "Yes—better. Go to sleep, dear ones."

It turned into a night of real horror.

The bell: two-twenty. Then, again, I went back to bed—she felt better. Then at four. Oftener?—because it happened over and over.

I'd get back into bed; a cigarette, shivering, start falling asleep—
and then the waves of buzz-sound, pulling at me. My heart kept
crashing with the running, the worry, the talking, that finding of
Mort and Helen in the bathroom and the half-fainted body too heavy
for him to manage; and the sagging face of her too heavy for my
heart to manage. And then, after a bit: "Oh, I feel better. Dear, dear,
both of you—go to sleep. I'm sorry, my darlings."

My notes say: one-thirty, two-twenty, and four; but it felt like
every half hour or so. It felt as if she were having waves of small
strokes—little ones sweeping her, and leaving her—and then everything turning inexorably, cumulatively, into the killer storm.

Yes—at four, that was it. As if I were reading it—a galley page
of solid dread-proof—as I looked down at her in the bed. My entire
guts fell, as I automatically put my hands on her and began talking.
My heart fell, as I stared into her face: one eye looked as if it had
exploded and popped.

The leg was thrashing, and of course I put my hand on it. She
couldn't talk. Could she hear me? Did she even know me? Well,
maybe she'd know my hands—my touch of rescue. ("Ruthie, help
me!") I hovered, talking steadily, as Mort ran to the living-room
phone.

He was back: Dr. N would meet us at Mount Sinai—we were
to take her to emergency. Me (very quietly): "Get that ambulance.
She put the number on the closet door near the window.
Remember?"

As he ran, I looked down at her dear face, thought: Why did
the Old Lady have to tamper with even the beautiful eyes? Thought:
The kids are coming today. I've got to—what? Nothing. Everything's
all set. Even the beds are made—and food here. And Barb has the
keys—they can let themselves in.

A moan. Me, instantly: "Don't be frightened, Helen. Dear, I'm
right here. It's Ruth. I'm going to help you. Mort's getting help for
you right now. Don't be frightened. It's Ruth, me, Ruth."

Could she hear me? What had happened to that marvelous brain
under this onslaught? But her leg was quiet, finally.

When Mort came back, to dress, I ran to pull some clothes on,
too. Lights on all over the house, and garage, outside spotlight. As
soon as I got back to her, Mort went to get his car out, prepare for
the ambulance. I went on talking, identifying myself at all times—
I felt that was important—promising her help; until the men came.

Two—very good, very gentle. The stretcher; then one went with Mort to push away some of the living-room furniture, and I stared at my friend on the stretcher under a blanket; my head still ripping it out, over and over: Dear Lord kind Lord gracious Lord.

Bitter out—snowing hard. Mort would drive his car; I'd ride with Helen. There was a pull-down seat, so I could sit right next to the strapped-down stretcher. I took her hand and held it tight, close to my face.

They didn't start the red blinking lights and the intermittent siren until we'd left the dark country roads and hit the first, ''city'' part of Mayfield. There was an amazing amount of traffic; the siren screamed—to clear our way. Whenever I looked away from Helen's face, I saw Mort's car hanging on.

That siren was horrible. I felt it on my skin, prickling; knifing all through me and my Dear-Lord-kind-Lord. The red blinkers, off and on, made the light-from-hell by which I could see her face. Terrible nuances—dim, glowing red and fading, blazing again. Those eyes. There were such un-Godlike things about this illness.

All the way to the hospital, she called out the same, blurred sound, over and over. I thought it was my name; I wanted it to be— though I couldn't be sure, because her voice was clotted with that awful thickness of disguise that a stroke can pull around language fast as lightning. I leaned, to hear any possible whisper. I held her hand, often smoothed her face (know that it's me!—know that I'm with you, helping!). I talked a lot, a pile-up of strong words, promises to help—hoping with all of me that at least the tone of my voice was getting through.

Her whisper, clotted with aphasia, went on and on—all the way in red lights and siren out of hell: I think it was ''Ruthie—Ruthie.'' I kept hoping it was; kept telling her I *was* Ruthie, and don't be afraid, everything's going to be all right. I thought of Ma a lot on that ride—her last days in this hospital toward which we were speed-ing. I thought of young poems I'd written in my mother's house. The poems, years later, to Helen, after my un-muting.

Once, I wrote her:

Build a house
And I will have you in it
Like a kitchen god some days,
Or mornings like the sun.

Build a day
And I will have you in it
Like a sound of fiddles,
Or the echo of a song I love.

Build a life
And I will have you in it
Like the bone of truth,
Or pulsing like a heart.

As we pulled into the hospital driveway, I pressed Helen's hand to my face again. "And I will have you in it"—please, dear, please! It was five-thirty-five. Up an elevator: she was in a bed, the stretcher and the two men gone.

Miracle—impossibility: in a few moments, her eyes opened. She called Mort's name, looked at me and said my name. And I said: "Sure. We're both here. Naturally."

Her voice was very soft, exceptionally high pitched. No blur to it, at all. A little smile. "Barbie?"

Me: "That's right! Barbie's coming in today—for Christmas. And little old EJ, Martin—" Suddenly, she looked in pain and asked for a bedpan—her voice urgent, and badly blurred. Then she threw up, and two nurses jumped into action. One said: "Better go out."

We leaned against the wall outside, smoking. Neither Mort nor I could talk. Dr. N came, half running. Time—I don't know how fast or slow; he came out. "She's in a coma. I'm going to try to get her into intensive care." He went off, very fast, to the big center desk of nurses and phones. Mort ran after him.

I went to Helen. Stood and looked down into her face, at her closed eyes, her locked-away Self. I said to her—in my head, to her head—with all of my strength: Helen, you promised.

Rest of day a sickening blank—hospital and home. Until the kids finally arrive, and House comes to life briefly. EJ helps a lot.

December 24: Mort and I there at eight. She's in Intensive Care—fourth floor. Told we can see her for twenty minutes every two hours. She's in a two-bed room, but nobody's in the second bed. Martin comes. The three of us watch her in silence. Eventually, Martin persuades Mort to go to work: "to try and forget." Good idea. Martin leaves me alone with Helen part of the third "visit."

Says he'll meet me down in the lobby.

I look at her—not one movement; not one sound ("Ruthie, help me!"). I take her hand, press it hard. Very hard: feel me, feel. Suddenly my numbness shatters; I say to her, out loud but softly: "Helen? Come back. You promised—remember? Helen, you listen to me. Me, Ruth. Come on back, now. I'm Ruth, and you *can't* break this promise you made to me."

The twenty minutes went (I watched everything, including the allotted time, carefully—in case anything at all would help her). I told her: "I'm Ruth, dear. I'll see you in two hours. I'll be here whenever it's permitted—always. Now listen—try to come back. Try, Helen."

Early—at home: Martin was going to pick up the Christmas tree, then meet us at the hospital. Barbie, weeping desperately, "can't see Mother this way!" Half of me understands completely, the other half is coldly resentful. EJ: "Where's Pooh?" I didn't stick around for the answer. Later, Martin told me that the kids had thought at once of taking Eric to Rie's apartment, but were uneasy about tears and "why?" Christmas for Eric had always been this house, this land. And they'd thought, too, that the little boy would comfort his grandfather here at home. I nodded. Made sense—I suppose.

Visited Helen at two, four, six. Despite my battle, I often end up crying. "Only a miracle"—but oddly, I keep waiting for it. Fighting for it: when I'm alone with her, I always take her hand and talk to her, identify myself over and over. Always call her back. Always end with: "Helen, you promised. Do you hear me?" But I don't know if she does or not.

At first, between visits, I tried the intensive care waiting room up there. No good; full of weeping people waiting for *their* miracles. So I started going down to the first floor—the lobby. Martin brings us newspapers to pretend to read. Coffee. We talk, sometimes—but not much. He hands me cigarettes. Me, finally: "Tomorrow, I'll bring my work—sit here and write between visits." He (gently): "That's a good idea, dear. And this seems like a fine corner. Private."

I guess he knows that the writing may give me relief. That I have to be with her now, whenever possible. He doesn't know that everything in me wants to save her; that the toughie turns out to be a believer in prayer to God, in touch of living hand on coma-still hand: Take my insistence—return my clasp, suddenly—open your eyes, suddenly.

Later, Mort insists in his quiet, grieving way that we go home; it's Christmas Eve—Eric will be sad, probably frightened. Intellectually, I know, and I nod. A small—to keep safe in his heart; she'd be the first to agree. But emotionally—Oh, Christ. Oh, Faulkner: *As I Lay Dying*. What a perfect title, fleshed out.

Martin drives me, in my car. After a while, says: "Ruth, I brought a bottle of Scotch from Chicago. We all know you don't want to monkey with the tree. We do understand, honey." Not only his mother's son, but a friend of mine.

It was snowing heavily, and so cold. I stared at the Christmas lights on houses, all the way home. My head ached with the violence of a thousand things like *The Messiah* and a child's chipped balls for the tree, kept so carefully—and that laughing face.

I went directly to my room—the garage door. Barbie came to embrace me, wordless. Diedrick came in for a moment, kissed my cheek, told me Mort was reading to Eric. Me: "That's good."

Martin brought me the bottle and a glass of ice water, took out my own shot glass. Kissed the top of my head, poured the first shot, left. A brave family. I'm the coward.

After a while, EJ stood in the kitchen doorway to my back hall and called, "Night, Missy!" And I told him good night; you get taught deep by a Helen. Later, the men came in and had a drink with me. Not much said, but it was a good closeness. Later still, Barbie brought me a plate: sandwich, celery hearts, and olives—parsley for pretty. "Please, darling. Or you'll feel awful tomorrow. And then how will you be able to go to the hospital?"

Her mother's child, too; yes, and a friend. So I ate some of it—medication. Then went on drinking. I had my patterns: blur the pain, otherwise you'll go nuts. And this time, it was the biggest pain I'd ever known.

But so odd; maybe I was already nuts. In the midst of all of it, I kept waiting to hear the phone. Helen on it: "I feel better! When are you coming?"

The levels were murderous. In bed, blurring off into sleep at last, my head was crammed with: Dear Lord kind Lord gracious Lord I pray Thou wilt look on all I love...

December 25: A morning of agony began for me. Why did I force myself to sit through that? For Helen, I suppose. I don't even know. (The family would go to Rie's later, share some kind of Christmas with her.)

The tree was a beautiful knife. And I found myself looking for her old, chipped balls. Oh, she was there: each of us picked in turn, from under the tree, handed the gift to the named person on the label. Yes, Eric has inherited that Helen-invent—with parents or grandfather or uncle reading labels for him. I had a sudden sense of grateful thanks: no dogs, at least. Then I discovered that I was waiting to hear that "Where's Pooh?" It didn't come, thank God.

Ruthie, are you a stone? No, just crazy—for doing this because of "she taught me." What other reason could there be? I saw, one by one—as gifts were opened—the things I'd brought her to examine at the hospital (Barbie had wrapped them). I had that picture of her and the laden bed, the draped bittersweet, as the little boy called and laughed with excitement.

Well, it was over, finally; Eric was sitting in Mort's lap, being read to out of a new gift book. As I was leaving the kitchen, Barb hugged me, whispered with tears in it: "Thank you, dearest." In my room, I felt an actual sensation of dizziness. But I'd made it.

I took my work. Crazy? Or simply automatic? Got to the hospital in time for the two o'clock visit. Watched a coma. It looks like an infinitely deep sleep. The pulse at the base of her neck is very obvious; a kind of small leap. Never, when she was well, was I aware of it. Her hand is warm (fever?). It's alive and not alive.

Every once in a while, her breathing changes for a moment: it's like a halt, a sigh, an uneven taking in of more breath (lack of oxygen?). It never fails to tense me. I stare at her face—waiting for her eyes to open. I do! It wouldn't surprise me!

I press her hand between both of mine. I try to curve her fingers around my hand. I put it to my face. I'm still saying it, often: "Helen, come back. It's Ruth—me. Come on—you promised."

And still timing the visit; went down to my back corner of the lobby. Hundreds of people, in and out the doors. I holed in, began to write. What was real, what unreal? I began to drown in the words. My personal miracle.

Later, my niece came and sat with me for a while. She and Fannie had been there a few times. I saw Helen at four, at six. Martin had come—and Mort, Diedrick. D (very gently): "We brought my mother home. Barb's cooking dinner. She says please eat with us this evening?" I nodded. When somebody else is in her room, I grasp at her through hand touch. Call to her silently, over and over: Helen, you promised.

December 26: Dr. N (on the phone): "Very little left. Just the vigil now." I see her at noon, at two. Mort and Martin come. Later, D. We talk—brief, low. They leave me alone when I'm working. But why the hell am I writing now? Well, maybe it's as simple as: "Ruthie, bring your work. I love to see you writing in my room."

A little before four, Martin came to me. He had talked to Dr. N, who'd said: "Forty-eight hours or so. Brain gone."

Put my hand to the gray, sweaty face of her son. He: "I'm taking Dad home. Dear, please come soon."

I went up, put my case of work down inside her room. The other bed had a very sick one in it, as of that morning. So I talked to Helen in my head, with my hands—on her hand, her face: You promised. Please don't go away. I'll take care of you. I promise I'll take the most tender, loving care. Helen, please let me. Let me, let me.

But then, after a while, I just sat and watched the deep-asleep face. I think that the child, now silent in me, went on with the belief in miracles; but at last the Me of today knew. Kissed her, said: Good-bye, Helen. Dearest friend. I know—you couldn't really promise that.

Promise. The air burned with that word. My promise to take care of her merged with hers; hers with mine. And then a hurting-loving memory swept me back to an old, old one I'd made to her. I glanced at my manuscript case—part of my fifth novel. That old promise had been kept with another book—my third.

I had to leave; I could scarcely breath in that searing air. But I couldn't go home. I drove, for hours, thinking of that promise I had been able to keep.

• • •

1954, 1955.

Mort is still without a job, and the money is going much too fast. Helen has started talking about selling the house and buying a little, less expensive one. This evening, the three of us had a meeting in the living room, to discuss this more. I walked out without a word. Sometimes I hate the way she always plans ahead so "sensibly"—scientifically—yes, beautifully! But it's my house and land and roots, too. Catch *me* being intellectual about it.

When she came into my room to say good night, I scowled. She (softly): "Dear, people must plan ahead. Maybe it won't happen—

but we have to be prepared for any eventuality. You know me.''
Me: "But maybe you don't know me! I *promised* you I'd get enough
money to save this house. I know it's almost a year since my
promise, but give me a chance to make good, damn it. I depend
on *your* promise—always will. Then how can you think I won't keep
mine?'' Helen (kissing me): "I'm sorry. (Very, very gently.) But
that's one hell of an expensive promise for a poet to make. And dear,
I'll take the poet any day—to any mere house.''

After she left, I went to my desk in a fury, thinking: Damn you,
Ed, dear Ed, how long do you have to keep that son-of-a-bitching
novel before you say yes or no? I've got a promise to keep. Come on!

And it was my fury that blurted out the words—a bellow of some
kind. Because I wanted to pull down the skies and distribute the
clouds and rainbows of eternal spring to these people huddled in
today's twenty-degree winter of the year and the spirit:

> Hey, God, I'm going to be strong and cruel and knowing.
> Watch me! They say You see and know everything. Direct the
> light from a star so that it shines full on me. I'm going to walk
> out into things with a harsh, free stride—and I want to see my-
> self. I want You to see me. Listen! There are people in tears,
> who need rescue. Shine down that spotlight-star, God; I've
> got tears to dry, bread to find and give. Oh God, my God,
> keep watching—keep knowing. So You won't have to weep
> if I trample down little blue flowers on my have-to leap into
> succor. Having been saved myself—having learned how to
> plant all the small blue flowers.

Next day, I shoved the paper of blurting at Helen, said: "Hey,
lady, let's do the seed order early. My soul pines for a faint, sweet
intimation of spring '55. If you'll forgive the hack writer a small
amount of seasonal vomiting!'' (She kept that blurt as if it were
Keats.)

And then. Oh, then! February 7, 1955—editor to author:

> ...and over the weekend, I read your new novel and
> hasten to tell you that, in my judgment, it is your best book
> so far. I recognize in it a complete rewriting of an earlier
> manuscript you showed me some years ago. At that time, if
> I remember correctly, I had the difficult assignment of trying

to persuade you that you were not yet ready to do that novel. I remember that earlier version as being more of a sociological treatise than a work of fiction. But now, dear Jo, I think you have really pulled it off. The characters are true and real, and what happens to them matters enormously to the reader. And the thesis itself emerges not as a thesis but as a real issue of tremendous importance in their lives. And, incidentally, the problem has become a more urgent part of the American scene today than it was when you first tried to tackle it.

It follows, then, that we do most certainly want to publish "The Changelings." We should like to publish it next fall. I am dictating this letter before leaving... no time at present, therefore, to go into details about possible revisions. I do not see that as a major problem anyhow...

Meanwhile, in order that we may be prepared to sign a contract with you as soon as possible, please write and let me know what advance you want. We advanced $1,500 on "Sing at My Wake." What would you think of $2,000 on this...

I'd read it on the way in from the mailbox. Me (screaming through the house): "Helen, Helen, he wants the book!" Stuffed the letter into her hands, chased Ragsy all around the living room (as Friedie watched with bright eyes from her spot near Helen's feet), throwing the couch pillows at her, until she was one white, barking frenzy of delight.

Then I sat in the crying chair—and laughed. "I'm going to ask for an advance of twenty-five hundred. We need it more than McGraw-Hill, babe." Helen: "And a copyright in your name. Just as the Authors Guild advises. Oh, Ruthie, I'm so happy for you."

Phoned everybody—families in town, out of town; friends. Flew around like a nut—outside, with snow; in the house, with broom and Hoover (Helen and Mort laughing with me any time I bumped into them). Finally ran down inside and sat in my room, thought very quietly: Thanks. I promise I won't trample down any little blue flowers. Just plant them. In every bare spot around.

Mort in good spirits—the book helped. Ed said okay on the $2,500 and the copyright in my (real) name. Turns out you can't use a pseudonym in such matters. And the revisions *are* minor. His letter ending: "Once again, bless you, dear Jo!" I love that man. Contracts came. Jesus Christ, it's true!

Check came. Paid back Fannie what I owe her. On way home from depositing the check, I noticed that the crocuses are up—those spears of green that no further snow or ice can damage. Oh, beloved seasons—always on time, in order, like forever.

Then, in my room, wrote a check to Mort for $1,500, and a small note: "For House, which I love and need just as much as you and Helen do—and all your children—and all your grandchildren to come. Amen. From—yes—The Gardener."

Helen: tears and laughter. Mort: *wonderful* laughter. Helen insisted on writing out an IOU. Mort took the envelope with my name on it up to that box they rent at the Chester bank for their important papers—and I tried to shrug. But I couldn't. That night, I wrote her a personal poem (next morning, put it under her breakfast coffee cup, then went to work):

When gifts are given on this day,
You shall have music
subtly wrought as silence;
you shall have pictures
patterned in oils of "promise,"
or etched with the magic acid
old tears trace upon the heart.

When gifts are given on this day,
you shall have poems
writ on nothing more than water,
but as ever-fresh and never-dead
—as ever promised by these seasons
you gave first without one plea
from all my silent beggar Self.

Oh, when gifts are given on this day,
you must have the joyous lot!
—each ribboned, living clock
in morning-blue and evening-soft;
and, sweet between your tired palms,
possess the "promised" peace of night.

Later, she came into my room and said, very very quietly: "Ruth, thank you for the poem. I'll cherish it, always. As I cherish you—and our friendship.'' She didn't even kiss me. She didn't have to. And I?—went out and kissed Old Lady Nature.

March 1: On definitive revision and typing. Mort still jobless, but looks a lot better.

Mid-March. Ed: ''Your revised pages do the job perfectly. Just keep on grinning. You have richly earned the right, bless you.''

April 25: First galley proof (twenty-two pages)—special delivery, as usual. Helen: ''Oh, dearest, how I love this part of it!'' Me, too.
Several days later: Jesus!—Mort got a phone call about that job possibility we were afraid to think about. More than a year of unemployment! No, not a fortune in salary, but his field: inorganic chemistry.
Me (stunned): ''My God. Just like that. Out of the blue.'' Helen (so quietly): ''No. It's a part of that promise you made, Ruthie. The money was only some of it.'' Me: ''You nut!'' Mort (beaming): ''You know she's always right. Especially about promises. Thanks again, kid!''

• • •

Back into today, December 26: In the car, still driving aimlessly and fast away from the hospital where Helen lay dying, I groaned. Oh, Christ, promises.

December 27: At eleven-forty-five in the morning, the phone. I heard it, tensed, but went on writing that insane-escape novel. Mort knocked. ''That was the doctor. He says the terminal stage is approaching.''
Got there at three-thirty; couldn't stay away. Alone. I'd told Mort that's what I wanted—alone, for a while. The men would come later. Went directly up. When I walked into her room, and looked— yes, the change was there, finally. She was almost dead—but alive. I sat on the bed, close, watched her. Took her hand, put it to my face and kept it there. A warm hand, still—incredible. The pulse in her throat—still there, but a lie. I longed terribly to see the blue and Self of those eyes, but I knew they would stay closed. Yes, all my knowledge, all my realization; yet my mind cried once more:

Helen, don't go. Helen, you did promise me.

I stayed about a half hour, looking at my friend for the last time. Maybe I thought she would die with me there—holding her hand, helping in some way. But then, abruptly, I kissed her and left. I would not have her dead with me watching!

Started driving. Snowing again. Winter, but I was drowning in all the other seasons I'd shared with her—the springs and summers and autumns; all the seasons of laughter and poems; all the beautiful seasons of nature's promises eternally kept.

I drove; but it wasn't aimless, after all: I arrived in front of the Shannon Road house. I was just there, suddenly, parked in front, staring at it and through it down the years.

This is where it had begun. Where I had begun ("in my beginning is my end").* How small the house looked today; to the young waif, it had seemed a palace. Strangers had ripped all the ivy from the side, and the two white lilacs were gone from the front door area. The empty lot next door—there was a house on it. I thought of the zucchini she had sneaked into the cuke bed; but I couldn't hear her laughter.

Where it had all begun: a first novel, a first falling in love with flowers and birds, with the real Bach. The ripped and aching roots tenderly-sternly sewed together, planted in new, rich earth.

I drove away—to the South Woodland place. I had to. Parked there—in front of that second house of my new life, my real life. And I thought of the second novel she had helped me un-mute, even though she had been so sick.

I stared at the Norway maple I'd planted on the side lawn. I thought of the tile she's had in the kitchen for years, propped against the wall behind the cutting-board cupboard: "He who plants a tree loves others besides himself." A tree is a promise, too?—to future generations? Not from me. All my trees were planted for her.

Pulled away, very fast. Found myself on the way home. But I stopped at River Road—about five miles from our house. Turned left—off Fairmount, our road—and parked on the cut-off, where she'd taken me so often before the house was built: to "introduce you to the country." We'd sat on the grass here and watched the Chagrin River, and eaten the lunches she'd packed. And she'd told

---

* This and other excerpts from "East Coker" are from T. S. Eliot, *Four Quartets* (New York: Harcourt Brace Jovanovich, 1968).

me that she'd picniked here, as a child, with her beloved Bill.

That little girl, walking and eating with her father: I thought of her, starting to move into the world. I'd seen pictures—the girl, the young woman with the luminous, eager eyes. Her eyes had always been the real heart of Helen.

It was very quiet in the cut-off, and the thick-falling snow made a deeper silence. From the road, all the car sounds came like a faint whoosh, one after another, as people drove home from work; life was definitely going on. Incredible.

I stared out, and had the wonderful picture of her walking within this countryside she'd loved so: erect, smiling, those free steps, the way she'd glanced about at all the seasonal things. "Look! Ruthie, look at that elm!" But then, all I could think was: Helen, please—how will I ever finish my book?

In this countryside, in the third and forever home she had offered me for roots: book three, book four. But now, where? Home had been Helen so long that I knew no other; Helen and a piece of work.

She died at ten minutes of ten that night. Mort phoned to tell Barbara and me. It's odd: only then did my heart believe it.

Later, in my room, the door shut on all the others' grief, I didn't know what to do. Stood at my desk and looked down at all that spread-out manuscript. The Eliot kept going through my head like an idiot tune: "In my beginning is my end—in my end is my beginning." Over and over, until I wanted to scream. For Helen. Who had always come instantly to rescue me.

When I went to bed and started, automatically, to say "Dear Lord kind Lord gracious Lord," the words choked into a silence and despair so awful that I said out loud: "Damn you, God. Damn you, rotten phony of a God."

Part III
The Journal of a Soul

Yesterday—Not Long Ago

"Afterward" should be told in poetry. All of it with a spiritual color: black. With physical sensations: the constantly sunken feeling, the pain in the chest and head—as of bruise. No numbness, ever, until enough liquor, or a sleeping pill—then the brief cotton-batting.

Nobody around to write the poems. They all stayed unheard melodies. But not Keats's "sweeter than the heard"—oh, no!

Poem, heard, unheard, unwritten, but there: the cleanup afterward. Glasses, insulin and needles, medication—for Juley and Helen Weil's old ones. Clothes—to Margaret, our day worker (who'd really been crazy about her employer). The four-legger and toilet bars—to the Aunties. Keep the shower and tub bars; Mort: "They're handy for anybody."

Poem—unfair, sure: I never went back to Dr. N. Couldn't. Mort stayed with him. Why not?—he wasn't crazed with anger.

Sympathy cards and letters. What a poem that would have made. "It's better this way—she suffered so much—at least you have the solace of knowing she's at peace—et cetera, et cetera." And screaming through me, again and again: It's a lie. There's no *meaning* to her death.

The only letter that made sense was K's. He'd left his editor's job, and was writing again—far from the world that had brought us together for *Anna Teller*.

. . . never anything to say. I saw a line, credited to GBS (I think) to the effect that you don't lose a great person through his or her death—only through your own. I know how deeply you must have felt about Helen because I know how much

223

the few hours I spent with her meant to me. Perhaps the best way for us to mark her passing is to always celebrate her living. I hope you can get back to the novel soon, you know how important it is to yourself, your readers, to say nothing of your publisher.

I suspect that his letter was the real shove back into the book. I had been trying to write it while the kids and Mort took care of things. (EJ stayed at Rie's.) Pieces of writing: but even so, it was the only time my head turned off briefly without liquor or pills. New-old cliche: escape.

Here's a poem I never wrote: when the kids cleaned Christmas out of the house, I thought like ice: I'll always hate this holiday. And I smashed the Beethoven *Triple Concerto,* burned the herbs towel-calendar. There must be a kind of insanity . . .

Mort went back to his job. Silence permeated the entire house— as if it came seeping into the rooms from the bitter winter, from me. I wrote my book. When I wasn't doing chores.

But the neatness my soul insisted on, the order, seemed to make a deeper, emptier silence—an unlived-in place. The woman was gone out of everything. There'd always been a book, an open magazine, knitting, a pair of reading glasses, a plate with grape seeds or plum pits on it. Gone. And no music; she'd played that FM so much of the day. Once, I thought: My God, it's like a tomb. But smashed that like a record.

I wrote my book. When I wasn't crying—at anything that reared at me with Helen's smile or eyes in it. I wrote—like taking medicine. And I fed the birds every morning. Why?—I didn't care about them, or get anything from color or flight but tears. But I fed them, as automatically as I cleaned, and changed bed linens, and cooked.

Here's another poem I never wrote: maybe my inner Me did think it was God's fault; I could not, absolutely could not, say my prayer anymore. And somehow, the choked-off words I could never get back into my heart made an added emptiness.

Things kept happening. One day, there was the *New Yorker* in the mailbox, her name on the cover. Awful—the plunge inside of me. I put the magazine out for Mort, every time it arrived; I never opened it. Her name kept coming in the mail. Ads, all the organizations to which she had given a dollar here, a dollar there: civil liberties, the blind, Negro causes. And the garden catalogs. A ghost name in the world, as if she were still living somewhere. Quite a poem.

But instead of writing it, I ran to my book. Very brief escapes. One day, while I was feeding the birds, I remembered my promise to her: if ever she became a vegetable I was to kill her. Would I have done it? What an unheard melody *that* one was.

And weeping—my God. I hadn't cried much during her sicknesses. Was it the helplessness, now? There was no longer any way of fighting, helping her live—the things that had kept me from crying. If I were half the writer she said I was, I would describe with perfect words the cry-things in this mourner's life. Can't. I can only list them.

The title of the poem-list? *After Her Death*. Her drawer of organized spools, the pincushion with the three needles threaded with different colors, the thimble, the orderly boxes of buttons on the shelf beneath the sewing machine. Stabs of pain, then the helpless crying. Watering the plants. Pots, dishes. The list is everywhere, everything; it's one unwritten poem with a thousand stanzas.

Music? Christ, what a stanza. I could not listen. Sometimes, after a week or so, I'd try again—snap on her radio, still on the kitchen hearth (in the past—her idea—from that spot, I could hear it in my room, she in the rest of the house). Five minutes, ten, and I was crying. And it was music that made the crying go on longest.

The bedroom. I stripped her bed, finally; covered it with a light Indian-cloth bedspread I'd always loved—my teeth gritted all through the I-must-do-this. Every time, after that, when I went into the room to clean it, to strip Mort's bed for wash day... After a long, long time, I didn't cry in there any more. I just got a bad headache.

That poem with a thousand stanzas? Let's amend the title, make it two: *After Her Death: Winter* and *After Her Death: Spring*. My mourning was seasons, too. Though (like spring flowers still there when the summer flowers begin, and some of the summer bloom still gorgeous when the fall flowers begin) much of it merged.

Still winter. The stanza on the kind of drinking I did. The classic term is "slow suicide," I suppose. All I knew, nonclassic, was that the liquor blurred pain first, then made it disappear for a while by turning off my head completely. But I never drank until I'd stopped writing for the day. Must have been a matter of not tampering with the only weapon you have left.

Another stanza: the way reading changed—for such a long time. I'd find myself reading the same line, the same paragraph, over and over—and not know what I'd read. Fighting, I'd plow through again, forcing myself to make slow sense of a phrase, a few lines.

A recurring stanza: the way I couldn't touch back to my prayer. I used to try every once in a while. But the words always got stuck. I don't think it had been religion for me—yet that prayer had been a focal point in almost my whole life of nights. The cut-off kept making an ugly hole.

One more piece of the winter-afterward poem: pictures. She'd hated to be photographed, said laughingly that she was too homely and fat; so there were only very few around when I finally came up for air and wanted frantically to see her face. Diedrick made blow-ups of a snapshot he'd taken of Helen holding Eric as an infant, Barbie sitting next to her on our love seat. It's very good of her. She's smiling at her grandson, and the look is the love of Helen in hands, eyes, lean of body. Mort has a copy of that picture on the living-room table. I have one in my room. Plus five or six child-Helen pictures I found in an old album: all under the long glass of my record cabinet, along with Ma, Fannie, EJ and Ragsy, a few friends.

The stanza that was never written about night, in bed? Other kinds of pictures. They came as I tried to sleep—or when I woke suddenly at two or three: the convulsed leg, and I trying to still it. Walking her, exercising her, the friend in a wheelchair, using the four-legger. Or her coma face painted itself perfect as a Kollwitz. This is a double stanza; the end concerns me trying desperately to grab for my Helen: erect, fast walking, smiling, head always up. Awful. I couldn't even remember that woman.

The unwritten winter poem goes on and on. Like: at times, I'd force myself to drive into town—to my sisters, to a few friends. Rotten stanza. Everybody tiptoed—and I couldn't bear anything. Didn't talk much, almost always drank too much. Sometimes, the crying would start and I would leave abruptly. Or the crying would wait until I was in my car, on the way home, and I would drive half-blinded, choking with sobs I could not control. This is another double stanza: people seemed so dull. Her quick brain, her beautiful awareness, her wide interests and articulate way of discussing them; nobody else talked that way, green-thumbed that way. (When she was alive, and I'd had it all, I'd never noticed that about other people.)

A vicious stanza coming up. February: seed-ordering time. I dreaded it, wasn't going to, had to, wept over it. The new seed she always had to try?—of course. Picked a new, medal-winning marigold (as my heart sank out of me at the picture of Ruth planting the Helen-Ruth bed by herself). Without talking about it, Mort wrote out the check and I sent in the order, filed the carbon with all the others.

Friends urged me to visit them: Detroit, Los Angeles. The kids wanted me to come to Northampton. I said I would, to all of them; but I waited. For what? It must have been for that poem I should have written and didn't, titled *After Her Death: Spring*. Maybe I thought: Survival time for gardeners has always been spring. If the gardener-mourner lives through the winter of despair...

All phony. Though you don't know it for several years. Creative death takes that long to shape its terrifying question. But you've waited, using every weapon you could grab—the book first and last. Then it comes; you walk out into it. She isn't here, but her dearest season is. Will it be the same, in a tiny sense?

I was pretty good, going inch by inch, holding my breath, until her birthday. Then it all exploded in my guts, as I put back the bucket unfilled, unplanted, and ran into the house crying. Giant Swiss—all colors: my room filled with the ghost pictures of all the years of pansies until I drank my way out of the beautiful, grief-crowded art gallery of them.

Completely incredible: it went on—a spring without her. Everything was alive, everything starting on time. In twelve years, every perennial that stirs anew is familiar as my hand, and I know each spot where the pulse and throb of seedling will come green. I planted all of it, as she and I planned it; they are the shared years of gardening. Is that the poem, too? How this year, alone and without Helen, your eyes go right on naming each bulb and leaf and flower. But your soul goes blank as a broken camera to that push of life coming so insistently. Yes, spring tears in her beginning gardens are even worse than the winter tears inside her house.

And the pain is especially intolerable for the birds and creatures. They appear like flowers, at exactly the right moment. Chippy, the wren and goldfinch and Downy, Hairy, the swallow. The groundhogs—then the Johnny-babies. Sometimes, after I ran sobbing into the house, I could not go out again the rest of the day.

Oh, Christ, that spring. So often (crazy?), I really expected to see her—when I looked up from cultivating; or came round the corner from the back. Most of the rituals went on, though beloved ghosts always lurked in their shadows. When Mort fixed up the porch for the summer, I saw the woman in the wheelchair—shelling peas and feeding a few to Rags. When I sat on the glider, resting from the hard hoeing, and looked at the rainspout (where I'd planted morning glory like a fool), my eyes picked up the marks of Ragsy's teeth; I heard the ferocious, guarding bark.

And I ran. I ran from so much.

But sooner or later, I forced myself back into the old, familiar steps of a new season. Was that the poem, too? When you can't write the stanzas, maybe you try to do them? I started to gather some flowers for a few vases. I planted Iceland poppies—then the others—shouted at myself: Get the whole garden in, coward. Finish that book. Go out and see people—talk. Remember her courage?

Sometimes it worked—for a while. The seeds got in, little by little. Slowly, most of the other rituals and patterns were followed. But obviously, two of them had been smashed; no matter how often I tried, they still lay in splinters. I'd turn on the FM: twenty minutes at the most—then I'd be running to snap off the pain. And in bed, sometimes I'd start saying that child-I-used-to-be's prayer. Try with all my child-adult's heart to believe that it was a touch on something bigger and stronger than this lonely coward. Invariably, the words choked off in my head. And I would think, exhausted: Who turned away?—me from a kind of God, or He from me?

Then, oh then. The tree arrived. The hole had already been dug, and I'd added fertilizer. Is that what I'd been waiting for? Like a good gardener, I soaked the bare roots in a bucket of deep water; that evening, told Mort crisply that the tree had come, that I would plant it the next day.

Early morning, a beautiful day—sun, a little wind. I was alone. Mort had gone to work, and I did not phone anyone to come. I did not get drunk before, during, or after the planting. But I cried, from the first to the last step: tamping down the earth, watering, putting screening around the trunk against rabbits nibbling delicate bark. I was still crying in my room, when I leaned on my desk and looked out at the newest horizon in my life.

Two days later, I ran. Took a piece of the book with me—the current notebook, notes, piece of outline, and a writing board. The rest of the manuscript I stored in my steel file. Fire, any disaster?—

if something happened to all that writing, I'd be done for.

I drove to Virginia's house, in Detroit. It was good. Lasted five days, before I wanted to come home. We talked endlessly, caught up with the years, ourselves, the world, black-white—and Helen. Evenings, Suzanne joined us in more talk (she taught a long day of school). At night, in bed, I wrote for two or three hours before I slept. V had some powerful sleeping pills.

I got home a little refreshed, I guess. Because I was strong enough to touch the tree, and make my small peace with the label I had affixed to it in my heart. And now (the life of the emotions is so strange!), the tree was a part of the land here, part of the seasons. I looked for it when I lifted my eyes from the piece of writing. I went to it when I toured the joint. And it was while I was standing near the tree, one day, watching the coming of leaf growth, that finally I was able to remember my Helen—erect, walking, smiling at all the new season.

After that wonderful surge of feeling, I thought: Now, yes! The marigold-zinnia bed. But no music, babe. Don't take any chances.

What a stanza that could have made. Ten minutes or so—as I went through the familiar steps of the planting we'd always done together. Then I found my teeth gritting, my stomach starting to rock. Fifteen minutes, twenty? Suddenly, the weeping burst out. I ran very fast, to my room. Grabbed for a drink, choked it down— whiskey and tears. In the kitchen, with that second shot I'd poured, the crying over, I was shivering as I leaned on the cupboard, staring at her tile: ''—plants a tree loves others besides—''.

I finished that second shot slowly, thinking very tiredly of brave people and cowards. After a while I went out, did the entire bed, step by step. Crying all through it—but quietly. The wrens were singing from three different directions; and, back of the narcissus bed: ''bob *white*! bob *white*!''

The next day, I made preparations; the day after, I fled to Northampton.

That was the spring and summer after her death. Not one poem, but a series of unwritten ones—each with a hundred stanzas: turning my head off by trip or by liquor, sleeping pills. Writing my book wherever I was, whenever I was able, then the returning—a survivor again.

You really don't know that those survivals are phony. Each feels genuine for a while. The three weeks with Barb and D and EJ had been wondrous rescue. The Smith College campus and gardens, the intellectual stimulus of their friends, the special meals and home-baked bread, the side trip to New York (we saw *After the Fall* and *Dylan* and a Bergman movie—and I met with agent and publisher): I definitely felt like a survivor that time.

Back home, I started the small farm I'd planned—the back acres. The old main farm, in front, was green and lovely in cut rye grass. And all went well: gardening, writing, house chores, dinner for Mort and me (and occasionally a close friend like Edna). Evenings: I could read the old way again, or I'd see family, friends—calmly. Very little drinking; pattern and ritual full steam ahead. (Except that those two important ones remained in splinters. I'd try once in a while. But then I'd think: wait. Music and God?—that would take a lot of time.)

Enough vegetables for us and family and friends, lots of mouse-ears, lots of Van Goghs and Russians. But no wall of blue; I knew better. Rituals held. The perennials had started with fife and drum, the vegetable seedlings were up; I was out early every morning to tour the joint and garden, before going to my desk.

Phony, phony. One morning, when I sat on the carpenter's bench for a rest, very suddenly, I found myself looking at Helen's bedroom window. Had to. My head simply turned, and I was staring.

I suppose emotions often go their secret way with wily guerrilla tactics. Only in retrospect do you see the triggering of the attack: the new berry bed, that morning, was spotted with ripening strawberries; the asparagus bed was starting to shoot up the thick, good stalks. Yes, my stomach had rocked a bit as I'd looked down, but I had gone on briskly to the tomatoes, tied some, pinched out the suckers. Taken the raffia back to the wheelbarrow, where the tool basket sat—with my pads: pages which had stayed blank all this time.

It was about nine-thirty when I sat down, my eyes on those pads (no poem, not one note for a new book). She was usually awake between nine and nine-thirty. Yes, I was looking for the face, the smile. And I'd listened, probably, for the faint sound that window sometimes made on a still morning, when she cranked it wider. And I was listening, now, for the: "Good morning, gardener dear!"

I sat there for a long time, staring at Helen. Her birds singing everywhere—the mourning dove, cardinals, quail, all the wrens, occasionally the grosbeak and oriole. I sat there, watching, until every-thing blurred: quiet, quiet tears. By a very phony survivor.

And from then on, every morning, sooner or later, I encoun-tered my loving ghost at the window. I was somewhat like a pup-pet being manipulated. I tried to stay away from that side of the house; I tried to keep weeding, cultivating, my head down. Noth-ing worked; every morning, I looked for her at the window.

I don't know how, but I was able to go on gardening, go on writing. Why didn't I run? What was I waiting for, suffering this way? The plane ticket to Los Angeles my friends had insisted on sending was ready for any day I chose. The book would be taken with me. What the hell was I waiting for!

Then Martin was able to come, and I had my answer. The hole was dug—close to the base of the tree; the box of ashes was buried. Barb's family couldn't be there: EJ was sick, D in the midst of an important tutorial program for deprived Negro kids.

Me? No. Couldn't. But by the time I came home that evening, from the library in town, I had Helen buried at last. In her own earth.

For the next few days, I cultivated deeply, mulched a lot of things—left instructions: anybody who wanted food or flowers, come and pick. Or Mort would bring them in, if he had the time. Then I went to Los Angeles.

An amazing trip, almost from the beginning; for, on the plane, I was at once interested: the leap up, the clouds and sun; later, the Grand Canyon so far below. And I thought, suddenly, for the first time: Is it the house, the gardens? Must I leave there to really sur-vive? Very brief asking; almost at once, I shook my head, hard. Leave your roots, the room and desk made for you?—the tree?

At one point or another, I opened my briefcase, did about forty minutes of symbolic writing—and laughed at myself for being a sen-timental slob. And thought: But Helen would understand. (Yes, but would she understand that question of my having to leave the house?)

The amazing stillness, the interest in everything new, continued after I arrived and was welcomed by my old friend, Fritz, and her husband, Steve. My head stayed turned off, and I was so grateful that I didn't even question any of it.

I did everything they wanted me to: drove for hours with them to many read-about cities, swam and walked with them. Fell in love all over again, with ocean and mountain. Listened to the West Coast type of intellectual, and discussed the whole gamut from art and theater to politics and books. Went to plays and art exhibits. During the day, when both my friends worked, I wrote my book. And letters to family and friends. Drank very little—and always with them.

And, after a while, I felt like a complete survivor. I lasted three months—so I knew it must be real this time. A big chunk of my book got written, I put on weight—and thought: Babe, you've made it!

October. In the midst of the smog-suffused sunshine of L.A., I was suddenly so homesick that I could feel the frosty mornings and warming days; see the sumac, the beauty of the turning of the leaves on all our trees.

I went home.

Wonderful. Everything looked familiar. Nothing ached me, or made me want to cry. When I went out to tear up the frozen, blackened vines, Helen's window was just a window. Her tree: so very lovely. And I thought: Leave here? Are you crazy?

Several weeks. Then the smug survivor tried music. In a half hour or so, I found myself tense, jaw clenched. All right, just give it time. When did I try out my prayer again? Don't remember. But it still stuck like a bone. All right, all right, I thought; it's bound to come. And anyway, the book. I'm still safe!

The hell I am.

Late fall and early winter: silence closes in, and writing turns—so suddenly—difficult again. The anxiety is back: isn't this book lousy?—why is it taking forever?

And, oh yes, Helen is back. But the wrong way.

The phony survivor—again. In the winter silence, I rush upstairs, start monkeying with the Boston morgue. I read journals and poems I've been afraid to touch. It's ambivalent-me, fighting my death-part as I feel myself coming close to my grave again. Downstairs, I fight, too, as I try to end that novel.

When did I start drinking again? Probably on her death day.

Note: I know it more every day now. People are so different—in writing, in loving—in mourning. If the wise men have said, for thousands of years, "that which the earth covers over *must* be forgotten," at least one person questions them. I have seen too often that the earth heaves, the burial erupts out of peace, under the bomb of a survivor's recurring need.

As for this teetering survivor, the years and the seasons and the rejections merge. A kind of fantasy: everything in the writer seems to have turned into a nightmare garden. You plant at the desk, work with all your strength and skills—but nothing gets harvested. Everything you touch in writing insists on dying, eventually. Over and over. And yet you continue to replant. Why? One flower, Lord!—to make me feel a little like the gardener of the past?

Scene for merging: 1967, spring.

I was putting in the marigold-zinnia bed. Music had come back to me at last, and I had the FM on the porch. I was thinking of Helen, of course, as I did this deeply shared flower bed. The newest re-write of the novel was spread over my desk. I was thinking of that book, too, as I finished tamping down the earth on the second seeded pie. Straus's *Death and Transfiguration* had started on the radio. I've always liked it, hadn't heard it for a long time. Listening intently, I thought: Look what this man can do with music, to fill you with the *feeling* of transfiguration. A good writer should be able to do that with words. I went on working, thought of the dictionary *transfigure* (I'd looked it up often): "To change the figure, form, or outward appearance of; transform; to transform so as to exalt or glorify."

That last is the one I'm looking for, no doubt. And then, all of a sudden, I thought: "The Seasons: Death and Transfiguration." There's the title of Helen's book!

I stopped, full of some golden, excited mass of movement all through me. And a sensation of happiness I hadn't felt in a long, long time. Shaky, I went to the bench, dragged out my cigarettes as I looked at the blank paper in my tool basket.

My head went on pounding it out: That's it! The beauty here—person and land and belief. The physical seasons, that strengthen body and heart, that replenish love and the meaning of life, just the way she did. Yes, and the strokes: the seasons of the spirit—her courage, her fighting. People should know about such things. It could help them.

And me? I went on with it: a small picture, too, of what this woman did for one person. Couldn't that heal a few other people? Shouldn't the world know about a woman who could make a young stranger-punk like me open her heart enough to really want to live?

I began a book—on one of the tool-basket pads. Then I went to the tree for a while with my happiness.

Note: April 1968. Royalty check: *Anna*—$40.90. An old book is still alive. Thanks, whoever.

Stanza, a beautiful one, for the unwritten afterward poem: Northampton—ten days later. B and D had insisted I come—and paid for the trip, of course.

Merging, merging. There's a piece of work—a play—on my desk in the guest room (D's study, ordinarily), on the third floor. So I'm safe that way, too—not only the family-held way. Helen's daughter's home—putting in the garden for her, and cleaning up the tremendous areas of flower beds; getting fed food and talk and love.

At odd times, upstairs, I make notes; as if I were writing a new, small Journal of Life: "Extremely good visit. I really am starting to feel quite new. Bike riding with EJ on the Smith campus (resting at the Baskin bronze owl I love). Walking with Barbie and Muffy past Paradise Pond, to the magnificent college gardens and greenhouses. D showing me the fascinating psych labs and equipment he uses in his courses, in the social sciences building."

The family life of Barbara and Diedrick and Eric and Martha Ellen is beautiful. (Yes, there's a second child. EJ has a kid sister by now.) It stills me. Evenings are filled: often with intelligent, articulate, world-caring people. Including a new-to-me kind of Negro student, mixing naturally with white ones—young, certain of self, exciting implementers of this new American era. Fascinating. How I wished Virginia could be with me. No weary cynic now—want to bet? What poems she would write for us old activists, black *and* white, replenished by these stunningly brand-new ways of the sixties!

All very good for the country kid of silence, in her lousy ivory tower, who simply reads about the world these people move in and work in and for. There is tremendous life here, especially of the mind and spirit.

As for Martha Ellen—called Muffy by everybody in her world—Lord, Lord. Three years old (Eric's age at Helen's death); a very feminine, very loved and loving little girl. Brown dancey eyes; not beautiful in the traditional sense, but radiating the real beauty of the eagerness and excitement of a child full of gifts. Helen has a granddaughter she never had a chance to see and know. How she would have loved this little girl.

I'm intensely interested in Muffy. She's far ahead of herself in the brain (doctor's checkups). I think it's natural for me to look for Helen in this child. That brain? And do I see a little physical resemblance—nose, mouth? Not sure. She has great warmth, is deeply emotional—like mother, but also like grandmother.

One morning, she was helping me garden. We were weeding one of the large tulip beds. This is a college house, and the man who rented before B and D was a real gardener. Tremendous yard—crammed with fascinating flowers and shrubs new to me, and dwarf apple trees, dogwood, herb garden. The tulips were all red, tall, some wide open in the sun, some still tight; and Muffy was following my instructions with a small weeder.

Bright sun; the elfin child was in profile, and I suddenly thought of the picture I have in my room of Helen at two or three. There *was* a resemblance. I felt a light gash of hurt. Oddly, it was not torment-hurt. I simply thought of how Helen and this girl would have loved one another. Could see them together, smiling, talking.

In the Northampton yard, the weed came up abruptly, splattering bits of earth into the delighted little face; came up exactly as I'd taught (and taught her mother and her Uncle Martin, years ago). Muffy: "Missy, Missy, I did it right? Didn't I? Missy, look!"

I clapped my hands in loud applause, and she came hurtling over to me, hugging, kissing. So—here we go, in another yard, in another city: the generations and the years and the seasons merging. Was that what K had meant?—when he wrote: "...the way to mark her passing is to always celebrate her living."

Stanza—ugly—for the unwritten afterward poem: September 1968. The play was turned down—on the telephone. Not person to person, sensitively, with good discussion. A very callous rejection.

I was, immediately, a mess. That safe-I'm-writing factor: Christ, how important it must be! With each year, I know it more; depend on it more. It must be the wrong weapon, but that steel has been sharpened for years, shaped to my soul. Mine, mine. I know no other!

I was flung back in a second to all the other rejections since her death. Depressed—badly. Drinking too much. The familiar feeling: will I really have to die? (But hearing—so often—her sad-stern-loving voice: "Did I do such a lousy job on you, *toi?*")

Interesting footnotes to that brutal stanza: eventually, in the midst of the continuing despair and feeling of worthlessness, I felt disgust for myself. It had to do with Helen; with the fact that I was on my knees again, despite everything she had tried to teach me.

I knew it was not the teacher; I'd made my education an extremely shallow one—my feeling of disgust was still more proof of that. She was back again—but not the right way. Her death was back, not the strength and warmth of her life; the promise and belief she had tried to give me.

I stayed away from the tree; cultivated everything in sight. Hours, days. Felt my body get tired enough, but I couldn't turn off my head. I even tried "dear-Lord-kind-Lord." It wouldn't. Kept choking off, night after night.

Sleepless, long after that choke-off, I would think so often: I've *got* to stop looking for transfiguration in a piece of published work, or a play produced. I must feel home inside permanently—not earthquake-shattered any time a piece of my writing dies before it's seen by the world. And Helen dead all over again. God, how do I do it?

No answer. I remained in the trap of a major depression. It went on and on, as if the season had turned into a fantasy with no horizons, no boundaries; and stretched endlessly over a country of dying poems, memories, desires to work or love or make a flower bloom, or the need to touch the dreams of others in their books or plays or films.

I forced myself out every day. Battled my senses into flowers, weeding, picking food; into birdsong and the autumn turning of colors, the wildflowers around the dam. Into the heat of the days, the mist and coolness of mornings, the nights flaring with constant pinpoints of fireflies. Into the turtle, frog, fish, snake, toad; into the heavy heads of seed on the sunflowers, and the corn ripening, the crops bearing heavily week after week.

Mort, aware of my awful, silent struggle, left me alone most of the time. He was patient, gentle, no matter how drunk I got, no matter how erratically I acted.

And in the end, Helen's gift of life, not her death, won. Almost three weeks of gardening, farming; then, one evening, I pulled out that fourth rewrite of the novel. I hadn't touched it for almost a year. (The play had kept me safe.) I began to read—with a pencil, a pad of paper at hand. The depression didn't help; but it didn't tie me, either. I think I was able to read like a studying. I don't know at what point it happened, but I suddenly thought: Damn it, I still feel that this book has something to say.

That's when I began to swim up. The next day, I wrote to New York. On the way back up the drive from the mailbox, I saw how beautiful on all sides: Indian paintbrush mixed with wild daisies and Queen Anne's lace in the uncut parts of the rye grass, reddening sumac, yellowing leaves of tulip tree, green burrs on the chestnut, the blue morning glory on my feeder stump; the delicacy of the annual poppies in the wedding bed.

It felt as if I had been very, very sick, with high fever, but I was out of it now. So tired, but everything looked quite alive. I went to the tree. I rarely actually talk to it; my head is more apt to cry out: Helen, please.

It did now. I meant: Help me keep this hope. Help me not to waste it. And me.

It was early October. My agent wrote that she liked everything I'd said about revising the novel. And enclosed the latest royalty check for *Anna*: $24.34.

I thought harshly: See?—still alive. A book that was rejected by several publishers—called every variation of lousy. Get in there and work!

And one more stanza in the unwritten poem—a quiet one, full of family, new generations. Christmas 1968.

I'm typing the book. All the kids are here. Including Martin's wife, Judy. (Yes, Helen missed that, too.) Judy has brought her little dog, Eric his big one (and Helen's two little dogs come as tenderly haunting as she does during these few days of holiday).

I'm smiling a lot, getting acquainted with Martin's choice; got to know her a little on one visit here, and in Chicago—at the wedding. Judy's a very nice gal—a teacher of little ones. But my heart is perilously still: will this Christmas kill me in the soul again?

We had the ritual decking and beautifying on Christmas Eve. New to Judy, who comes of a Jewish background that would never include a tree. But maybe Martin can introduce her to the beauty and joy of the whole thing, not necessarily to my old friend, Jesus Christ. Get her close to guys like Bach and Handel, too (she doesn't seem to know them). We had the big fire, and color-pies for EJ and Muffy, and big cones that burned like stars. We had talk and food and laughter. I did not play *The Messiah*.

On December 27, about nine-thirty in the evening of family and talk and games, I excused myself and went to my room. At my desk, took a fresh notebook and wrote on the first page: "The Seasons: Death and Transfiguration." Three lines down: "by Jo Sinclair." That was at ten minutes to ten; and my picture of Helen was not the coma face, but my smiling, eager Helen—so happy about a new book, always. Sat for a while and stared out into the winter night, visualized her tree. Another good picture.

I looked at the finished-so-far final typescript of a fifth novel rewrite, piled backward yet. All right, friend—I'll finish it in this year coming up. Then, your book.

Later, in bed, I looked at my room in the dim light. I was thinking of that title page in a blank notebook. This room Helen had made for me with such love and belief?—it would have at least one more book written in it. And amen to that.

Today—And Tomorrow

*J*anuary 1, 1969: Happy new year, any Boston or Greek gods skulking around, to listen. What happens this year?

I'm finishing that final typescript of version number five. Every day—hours. I stack paper and carbon for the three copies, type through, disgorge, stack again. Helen, I think of you—close, warm—as I do your invent.

Mid-January: I'm reading proof on the typescript. My God. Stubborn, or have I stayed insane? Or do I really believe?

February 4: I felt sort of numb when I took the book to the post office. But at home, automatically cleaned my quarters—old ritual: get ready for the next piece of work. Couldn't help it: thought of Helen's excitement at the shipping out of a book. Coffee, talk, laughter. No torment—just a gentle yearning today.

February 21: Letter from agent: She finds herself "stale" on the book; and I still don't know how to cut a scene; but she thinks it's improved. Eager to send it out. Today.

Stale. Wonderful word. But I even understand. However, the cardinals have been *singing* for a week or two. The winter noise of Tufty-T has changed, too. And bulbs are pushing up. Come on—somebody—it's time my season changed, too.

February 23: First snowdrop. Well, good, the heart still lifts at certain things. Took it in; put with it two red flowers from the Christmas cactus. Lovely—a true small.

I'm trying to read my garden journal—for Helen's book: professionally. Not easy! Touring the joint—note to the Me (who hollers so loud and silent in the guts): Write a poem soon. However lousy. You must.

March 3: Wonder who's reading my old book? Before going to work on the new one, hung out two sacks of mixed nuts (cheap, at the discount store in Chester). Noon: Looked up from my notes—hey, Chippy's up and back! Wonderful to see him. It's spring if he's out for the day—no matter how much more snow we get.

March 5: Did I spot a groundhog? Or was it a large cat? Must see if doors are sharpened. Heard the mourning dove, first time. Beautiful grief—always. At desk: notes on "The Seasons" slow, but coming. Tentative shape for outline. *Must* show Helen's joy and life-life-life—before that death journal.

March 6: Woke depressed. Is it because the novel's in the marketplace again, and no word? Christ, I'm so sick of these depressions. You feel your own *extinction*.

Out I tore, for rescue. Wheelbarrow full of tool baskets, plus my pads and pencils. First time this season. Weather not bad. Cleaned up leaves and winter-sodden junk. Yep, the east Johnny doors are sharpened. Good. I try to organize myself: put up rain barrels soon, bring down dahlias—they must be sprouting right in their Sunday *Times* bags. So what? Well, then, touch the tree. Maybe the little sharp haw thorns can tear a depression into shreds.

Walk. Think hope. Think: you're going to a concert tonight. Free ticket. Cello stuff, among others. And maybe tonight the cello will make a poem happen in me?

I go in, to do more spade-work on a new book. Then the mail: *Who's Who in the Midwest*. "Please correct and add to, for the coming edition." Add what? No book since 1960. Only thing: "First recipient of JCC Playwriting Grant, Cleveland, Ohio, 1968." *Don't* add: But only half a recipient; fell on my face for actual production.

The last *good* credit was 1961: the Cleveland Arts Award in Literature (newly established—five hundred bucks and a citation, which Helen had framed, and Mort hung in my back hall, near the other two citations). Long time between credits. But what about that Jewish anthology in 1967? Yeah, all right!

The other creative stuff that happened in the long hiatus? You don't put that into a *Who's Who*. Like, in 1961, the Hallmark international TV contest; two scripts made the last twenty, out of fifteen thousand entries. That same year, *Wasteland* out in paperback—at last. So what?

These days, I find it highly ironical to be in reference books. The creative life versus creative death—a lot of proof in these books; but proof of which? There's quite a list: *Who's Who in America; The Midwest; American Women; World Jewry*. British: *The Authors and Writers Who's Who; Burke's Peerage, Ltd.; Directory of British and American Writers; Contemporary Novelists; Two Thousand Women of Achievement*. Plus things called: *The Israel Honorarium; Contemporary Authors; Honorarium Americana; Foremost Women in Communications*.

(Helen—after a while—laughing: "Well, *toi*, you're doing pretty well for a girl who groans that she should have gone to college and there's a big hole in her because she didn't.")

More than irony; I find the former prizes and awards listed in today's copy a painful laugh. But I always edit the copy. It seems to be important. To me, or to Helen the history-and-archives kid?

The concert very nice—but the cello did not make anything resembling a poem. Got home late, but Mort was waiting up for me. Absolutely delighted: Martin had phoned to disclose a secret—Judy was pregnant, and the doctor said twins. In seven weeks or so. Though the doctor told Martin that twins are often early. Mort added: Judy'd had trouble conceiving, for some time now, so Martin had waited until all was set before telling us.

Me: "My God, that's wonderful!" (My head smashing: Oh, Helen, Helen.) Mort: "Interesting, isn't it? No history of twins in our family—and Martin said none in Judy's." Quietly, I reminded him of that miscarriage (so long before I'd hit this family)—the little redheaded twins Helen used to dream about. He: "Lord, I'd forgotten that. On the other hand, Judy's been taking all sorts of fertility medication. Martin said that often multiple births are a result."

No. It's Helen—and her little, beloved dream-twins. Now, a poem should be written! Do you hear?

March 7 and 8: The twins make a difference. I find myself smiling as I think of them, of Martin as a father. Naturally, the writing's going well.

March 9, Sunday: Martin phoned at three in the afternoon—a wreck, dazed but so happy. The twins born this morning, seven weeks premature. The boy—four pounds two; girl—four pounds six. Mort and I on phone extensions; Martin: "Gee, those kids are beautiful! I'm in tennis shoes, and I need a shave—we went in the middle of the night. They're wonderful!" Judy's fine. The kids are okay—incubators, of course.

Beautiful, beautiful. But then, in a few minutes, I began to feel so strange. The house filled tight and full and sad-happy with Helen. I saw her eyes, her smile. I thought of the lovely dreaminess with which she had talked so often about her little lost twins. To miss these twins—as she had missed Muffy. But twins, especially. Like losing her own twice? Crazy thought—but look at *that* poem. No, don't!

March 10: Woke with all of me dark. A fresh snow over night— the world glistening with utter beauty, winter and spring birds mixing on the feeders, and under them. But the twins had dragged Helen back—the wrong way. Damn it, I shouldn't permit that. I should think only of the joy she would have felt; the new generation of her immortality. Not shouting inside of me this way—again: Unfair, unfair!

Brief tour of the joint, watched the tree for a minute—had to leave. Bitter. At my desk: but how can I write?

Then a pileated woodpecker zoomed in on the suet in the ash. That spectacular red against the fresh snow. Imagine—those twins have not yet seen a woodpecker, a chipmunk. All right! And so, with those better thoughts, I started the day's work on the Helen-book. Easter music is beginning on the hearth radio. Within an hour or so, a gift to me: the Saint Matthew's—a beautiful new recording. Thank God I can bear this music again.

March 11: Oh, no! Martin phoned: both children desperately sick. Especially the little boy. Though the girl is on the critical list, too. And they've been named: Andrew and Ellen.

Mort and I met in the living room, from our extensions. He looked stricken. Deliberately, I said: "Hey, easy, kid. It's *got* to be all right. Helen will take care of them." It comforted him, just as I knew it would. But me? Don't make me laugh. I know all about the Old Lady's rotten sense of humor.

He went to bed with a Seconal, poor fellow. But I didn't want a pill. I wanted to do something for those babies—not drug myself out of worry. Stay awake, alert, in case I was needed. Strange sensation: some mimic-bell buzzing in the night: wake up, Ruthie, come help me! But what could I possibly do for those infants, Helen's newest smalls? Couldn't hold them, soothe, talk phony comfort and strength, bring a flower in a small of a vase to fit their size.

Much later, in bed, lights out but completely sleepless; I kept thinking of Helen, shaking out that sheet, baking that cake, laughing. Suddenly I was saying—out loud—my hands clenched on my chest: "Dear Lord, kind Lord, gracious Lord, I pray Thou wilt look..." The whole thing, with all my begging heart.

Before I really knew what was happening. I knew only after it was over, after the amen.

I turned on my bedside lamp and lit a cigarette. Discovered my hands were shaking. Thought: First time since she died. How the devil do you like that?

March 12: Evening: Martin phoned. Little Andrew: touch and go. Ellen may make it—she's the stronger child. "Girls often are, they told me," he said in a choked voice.

Later: and still I say my "Dear-Lord-kind-Lord." As if I've made some strange kind of peace with—who? Me—or Him?

March 14: Food-shopped for the week (still do it early Friday morning, the way Helen and I did). Worked on book. After a quick lunch, walked the dam after examining her tree and thinking hard about twin-Andrew. No more Friday nights at home these days: Ma and Sadie both dead. (My cynical friend-enemy, the Old Lady: Sadie had a stroke, too, lay in a coma for two weeks; same hospital; I came every day, my guts shaking with too much memory.) Still on the dam: strange how I go on missing so sharply that night with the family. My other roots? So I phoned Fannie—for a touch— when I got into the house. I'm not surprised: she's putting money in the *pushke* every day for the little sick kids.

Evening: Martin phoned. Andrew is a little better, but his chances are only thirty–seventy. However, looks like Ellen might be out of the woods. Martin sounds exhausted, but try-hopeful. I did my best to talk further hope. Afterward, hunching in my chair, I thought bleakly: Is this going to be another Journal of Death?

March 17: Let's go, let's go. To a new book. The only thing for me, at this moment. (And where the hell's the old one, I wonder?) Dug into the Journal of Life again, pushing notes into right areas of the outline. Hours and hours—good.

Evening. Hey, hey, twin-Andrew is off the critical list! Grandpa comes beaming from his extension phone. Must phone Fannie to put a flower on her *pushke.*

March 18: I feel better. Live, twins. Live, Helen's touch on life. It's sixty-five degrees, and two ducks are having a ball in the pond. And it's gardening time again, thank God.

Planted, in Sarah J's bucket, this season's new seeds: pansies (and they're cheaper than plants) and viola; plus a few annual poppies and BBs Variation on an old ritual—okay, that won't hurt. Planted some Van Goghs near my desk window, so I can see them and the goldfinch close up. The ducks hung around all day.

And my head *is* opening to a new book. This one is strange in all ways. Not only the nonfiction angle, a first for me—but like this: here's a book that's in the rain barrels I just rolled over from the far trees (and opened Helen's spigot-invent to fill them), in the snowdrops—dozens in bloom today. Very odd feeling!

March 19: The bleeding heart at the front window is up—tiny flecks of red at ground level. My heart (how long will that go on?), but at least I don't look at the window for the wheelchair woman.

Some of JD's catnip is greening at the ground. Third year. Planted for Pearl, who was having trouble getting fresh catnip. Who loves her cat even more these days because she's entirely alone: Alice is dead, too. It was Alice who named this beautiful cat Juvenile Delinquent—what a wild, bad kitten that one was. And yes, I still miss Ragsy. So I raise plenty of catnip for JD—and give some to my friend Edna for her two cats.

Back at my desk—many hours. Then went out again and hoed to get myself unknotted. Helen's window—no ghost smile any more. "That which the earth covers..." No. It's just a tapering off. Sometimes. But then I took a pad out of my tool basket, made some very good notes for the book as I listened to the cardinals' pure sweetness.

Evening. Reading Viktor E. Frankl's *Man's Search for Meaning.** Fascinating book. As if the guy wrote it for me. I find myself

---

* (New York: Washington Square Press, 1968.) All quotations are from this edition.

longing, so often, to discuss this psychiatrist and his kind of therapy with Helen. That word I love, *meaning*—he puts such life into
it. This man is helping me—in spurts.

March 21: Worked on the outline most of the day (looking out
occasionally at the tree). Really got into it. Much past—plus the worry
about no money or promise of any soon. And here I am in the same
bind. Amazing, how life's patterns repeat—even though the nuances
are different.

By five or so, I was sunk deeply into too many memories. Tied
up the writing, as usual, before I began drinking. Wine. That factor
is new and different. Never cared much for wine, in the past. Started
drinking some at Edna's; to my surprise, got drunk there one night.
It's a cheaper, and far less drastic way of blurring, though it takes
more to get to the right point. And: hard liquor has become a real
menace, by now. Let's face that. Those blackouts, for example; I
couldn't remember afterward, or the next morning, quite a few hours
of what had happened while I was that drunk. Yep, sounds very
much as if I've made the big label: alcoholic. Jesus. And always
depressed the next day, disgusted, guilty. Of course. One really
lousy shading: shame on you for spending Fannie's hard-earned
money she lends you—on such a thing.

Mort got his dinner. He always does, whether I'm drunk or
sober. Dinner's always in the oven or well started before I begin.
Helen, or just automatic-Ruth? He's a nice guy; never mentions my
drinking.

I went to bed on the early side. Not drunk, just quite blurred.
Had an awful nightmare: I was paralyzed, couldn't move my arms.
Terrified, screamed—that silent bellowing in the head my dreams
are crammed with: Help me!—move my left arm! Fannie, Fannie,
help me!

I woke at that point, a mess. My arms were under me; I'd been
nightmaring on my stomach. When I could turn on the lamp, I lit
a cigarette. Thinking: Christ, what a classic case history this must
be. Helen was paralyzed on the left side. But why my sister? In any
past nightmare I'd always screamed for Ma.

This book. Will I be able to write it?

I thought with heartbreak of the hours of terror—real, no dream
to wake out of—Helen must have had—alone in the hospital; here
at home. Wrote some notes for the book. Then read more in the

Frankl book. The words make quite a combination of comfort and question in me. This doctor is a graduate of concentration camps. Tonight, I think: Haven't I created a kind of concentration camp within the Self?

In Frankl's book, some people survived only because they had something waiting for them out in the world. Something important to finish. That's how he did it. Well, haven't I something to finish? I read on, came to a paragraph that hurt. He quotes Dostoyevski: "There is only one thing that I dread: not to be worthy of my sufferings." The truth, now, babe: are *you*? No.

And this piece of the book—a punch inside me: He's writing about a woman imprisoned in the same camp. She can see a branch of a tree from the window of her hut. She tells Frankl that she talks to the tree often. And does the tree talk to her? he asks, thinking anxiously: Is she having hallucinations? She: "Yes. It said to me: 'I am here—I am here—I am life, eternal life.' "

I think of my tree. And I have a card she sent me once for a birthday: " 'If I keep a green bough in my heart, the singing bird will come.'—Old Chinese Proverb."

Ruth, remember right, read right. Snap out of it!

And so I read on, clutching hard: "But not only creativeness and enjoyment are meaningful. If there is a meaning in life at all, then there must be a meaning in suffering. Suffering is an ineradicable part of life, even as fate and death. Without suffering and death, human life cannot be complete. The way a man accepts his fate and all the suffering it entails, the way in which he takes up his cross, gives him ample opportunity to add a deeper meaning to his life. It may remain brave, dignified, and unselfish. Or..."

Yes, "or." Damn you, hang on to this!

March 24: Many happy returns of the day, dear Helen. I miss you, friend. I always will.

I waited in my room until Mort left for work. I can't say her name—except to me. It's raining lightly. On the pond, two ducks. Worked on the book until eleven or so. It stopped raining.

Then (trying to take pieces of the Frankl book along, in my guts) I planted for Helen, on her birthday. Mouse-ears, lots. The three kinds of annual poppies she loved. In May, I'll make the wall of blue. "You're never dead until the last person who loves you and remembers you dies." Then a tree continues? Maybe a book?

And I did work on the book all afternoon. Cooked dinner, even ate some of it with Mort. Had a small vase of philodendron on the table. And, of course, the children phoned; my sister, my close friends. Her name was called out, by people who'd loved her. Her twin grandchildren are fine, said her son.

Mort went to his Monday bridge game. I cleaned up and did the usual evening chores. But when I got into my room, I suddenly began to cry. Stunned: I'd thought everything was okay.

March 27: First rejection on the fifth rewrite. Yeah, write a poem containing that brief, smashing quote, kid—I dare you: "Terribly sentimental and old-fashioned." And no, he ain't enthusiastic enough to want it, even though there's probably still a market for such books.

Agent: Will send the book right out again.

Me (to inner Me): Easy! Go write that new book. (But it was better when she said: "Write me a book, Ruthie.") I was scared of the coming evening.

But I didn't get drunk. I read Frankl, tried to blur that way: "The meaning of life always changes, but it never ceases to be. We can discover this meaning in three different ways: 1) by doing a deed. 2) by experiencing a value (such as a work of nature or culture); and also by experiencing someone, i.e., by love. 3) by suffering."

But how can I take this into me for keeps?

March 30: Snow, twenty-four degrees. Okay, write—spring'll wait. So I worked most of the day. Evening (Mort's asleep, his door shut against the sound): I watched an original play on TV. Excellent script: story of heart transplants. First impression: this is the kind of TV you should be writing—then maybe the top agents could sell you. The play over, my head went on. How you've hated doctors. But *know* that they saved her grandchildren.

Suddenly felt a little dazed. The first time since her death that I wasn't feeling that awful bitterness about doctors and hospitals. The seasons. By God, they do change!

April 7: Warming nicely. First male goldfinch, yellow as bright sun; and Chippy—eating up a storm. At work by nine-thirty.

I've tackled the Journal of Death for the outline. Not easy— already. I find my entire self clenching. Finally ran away—out to the gardens. After a while, felt better.

The poeticus green up nicely. Looked at the "holes" back of the narcissus bed—where I used to take the amaryllis out and sink them for the summer. Glad they all died—too much her. I've filled the holes with early double dafs that needed transplanting. They're already showing color—glints of sunlight. Thus all old graves should be filled.

April 8: Wonder what's happening to my old book? Worked on the new one all morning. So peculiar: what's real—here, or the stuff in the book? These levels of the soul!

Afternoon: drove up to Chester for dime phone calls, gas, cigarettes. Talked to Fannie, to two friends, but everybody seemed unreal. Reminds me of therapy; when I'd come up from the Shannon Road recreation room, the upstairs world was the unreal one. The past I'd just lived in, down there, for almost an hour—that was the sharp reality.

This book is going to be torture, I know.

April 9: Seventy degrees. The clematis is coming. Single, white—gift from my gardener friend, Aunt Amelia, now so old and sick. Everything's too beautiful. Ran in to write, very soon. The only thing to do.

Afternoon: put up wren houses. Including the one EJ sent me. Made it at the Northampton Y. The hole is big enough for a blue jay, and the frail thing will probably dissolve in a heavy rain. I love it. Over that hole, he's printed a crooked WELCOME WRENS. I stuck it high in the small three-birch near the back acres—see it often, I will, and smile. Sort of a Pooh thing.

April 10: Cold and wet. Worked at desk for long stretches. In Sarah J's bucket: pansy and viola seed sprouting. I brought in eight blooming cemetery dafs—sun in my room. But as I worked, the rest of the day, no sun. My mouth dry with memory of the death beginning in this book without my having known it that year, that month.

April 12: Agent mail. Two down: "... too long and at the same time, curiously dated in conception and detail. I just don't think we can publish it successfully." And my agent has enclosed the current royalty check for *Anna:* $4.27 net.

Why did that seem to exaggerate the slap of the rejection? Oh, sure, it's still a slap; so how neurotic can a person be?

Very. Used the familiar pattern that evening: got drunk, turned off my stupid, neurotic head. But it rarely lasts. Woke at three or so—sober, cursing myself. Read an old book, which I drag out often: Dag Hammarskjold's *Markings*.

Read Auden's foreword again, and came to that paragraph which had knifed me when first I'd read it. He's talking about Dag H: "To be gifted but not to know how best to make use of one's gifts, to be highly ambitious but at the same time to feel unworthy, is a dangerous combination which can often end in mental breakdown or suicide."

Definitely could have been written about me.

April 13: A Sunday. Woke very early—abruptly. These compulsive awakenings are lousy. One of the favorite fun-and-games of the depressive. No wonder I've loathed mornings most of my life. Though God knows Helen made them much better.

At breakfast, Mort's voice seemed far away, unreal. But after a while, gardening helped. Then I went to the tree. One weed to pull. I thought: Maybe if I change the label? It may not be permanent ink.

April 17: Morning—heard the pheasant off and on: love and grief-memory. Spaded up and prepared the marigold-zinnia bed. Still hurts, but it's bearable. Time, the healer, eh? I wonder. Toured the joint: lily of the valley starting. (My sister Sadie: "Oh, Ruthie, I love them!") Yes, certain flowers bring back certain people. But all flowers bring back Helen.

April 18: Morning paper—there's a new director at the Cleveland Play House. He's "very interested in new plays, new playwrights." I felt a little spark. But my rejected play needs one hell of a lot of work—and I have a book to finish.

Nevertheless, before settling down to that book, I finally sent away for the PEN list of grants for writers. Known about it for weeks, but couldn't seem to work up the—what, hope? Today, the Play House spark, I suppose. But I need a fire in my soul, not just a spark.

April 20: A Sunday; Mort's cutting grass. The day is warming.

At ten, Edna came out to help me with the outdoors. She does that often; a city gal has fallen in love with the country—and that pleases me. I've known this friend over thirty years—since WPA days, when we met and shared our young poems and discovered we both loved Keats.

I supervised her ritual planting of BBs in the wedding bed. She's been doing it for the past three years. Ever since she suddenly cried: "Could I plant some bachelor buttons? I love them. When I was a kid, and had to live summers with my aunt, she always had them in her yard, but I wasn't supposed to touch them." Enough said. And of course Edna picks "my own flowers" when they're in bloom. Nice to know I can still pass it on.

April 23: Finished the outline. Except I'm not sure how the book will end. In novels, I've always known, down to that last scene. But this one? That'll depend on what happens with "transfiguration," I'll bet. What a strange experience fòr the writer *and* the person. It's Helen's book, yes; but, triggered by her, it's become a kind of autobiography, too. Can I pull it off (as Ed used to say)?

April 25: The sword lower and lower: but I'm still afraid to start the actual writing. Went out and hoed my head off.

Eleven in the morning: Started! Lined up first batch of notes. Slow, so slow, I wrote five pages in that first notebook. Then ran out—fast. Spent the rest of the day gardening. You rotten coward.

April 26: Set alarm; up at six. (Mort, quietly: "The new book? That's good." And we kind of smiled.) At my desk by eight, all chores settled. I fought through quite a few pages. No smile! By the time I got out with tools, my heart was pounding and I felt perspired. If this book turns wholly into catharsis, I'll break into a million pieces. But it mustn't! Helen has a lot to give—to a lot of people.

And what about this, for truth? Is it just this book that panics me—or am I being scared, too, by all the rejections of the past six years? Who's going to answer that?

I cursed, out loud. Myself, of course. Then I did the whole marigold-zinnia bed. Went too hard and close with the book, but I had a rather marvelous picture of Helen laughing, her hands full of seeds in the soup bowl. Nevertheless, I was so goddamn relieved when I finished pasting down the last of the seeds.

Cut to May: Report from me to the Me:
Worked every day on the book with panic-runs out to plant, weed, hoe. Pain, pain: the past joy and woman and family and seasons coming to life in my own words.
Planted: all I should have.
Drinking: not bad. Meaning only when Helen rears *too* alive.
Gone back to work after the dinner dishes several times, and written into the night. Haven't done that for a long time. Feels good, right in the midst of the heart-banging. No word about the novel.

A Saturday. Mort (back from Chester): "The rotohoe can't be repaired. Shall I buy another secondhand one?" I'd been expecting that report, but I know his money situation. So I decided to use the old one-horse shay. Knew just where it was, upstairs. Carried it down, trying to leave the memories upstairs.

Once, I'd done more than a third of an acre with this one-wheel push tool. The young gardener, the young poet; even my weeping over writing had been young. It makes a difference! Poetic torment belongs to the young. Middle-aged anguish about writing has failure and fear crammed all through it. Well—big laugh—the one-horse shay works for the middle-aged gardener, too. Feels so damn peculiar to be using it right now. But then, the whole book is a thickly clotted mixture of such feelings. Levels—what an unwritten poem.

Wrote for hours, but with necessary run-respites. Robin news: every time I've walked past the front hedge of lilacs, for days now, a robin has come squawking out at me. I finally investigated—from inside the house. Found the nest: on the stone coping outside of the west window of the TV room. Very sloppy nest, straw and junk dripping down onto the brick, but Ma is sitting on it firmly. Fine. Easy to watch for eggs and babies from in here—without getting pecked by worried parents.

The frogs sound marvelous—quite an orchestra. They started Sunday night; I heard them at midnight, when I drove home from a movie and a friend's apartment. Tonight, the whole joint belongs to the flutes, violins, and bass baritones down there, as I read in bed. Memory is so many seasonal things.

Mail: new pictures of the twins. They finally look like real kids—instead of little, weak blobs. Wish I could see them. Wish somebody would offer me a plane ticket to Chicago. (Mort's been twice.)

But would I go? Those twins, Helen's dream-twins, this book: sounds like it could be a killer.

Continue to write a lot, but have to flee often. Out the desk windows: the grass is blue with the violets. Great patches—the way Helen loved it. Goes with the book. But Christ, what doesn't! She is alive as I write about her.

Mail: my agent sent me a query brochure re plays she'd received from an outfit called Office for Advanced Drama Research, University of Minnesota. They have Rockefeller funds suddenly, and soon "will be able to work with selected theaters throughout the country." Will consider any *unproduced* plays, work with playwrights, et cetera, et cetera.

Hey! I wrote the director at once. An honest letter describing my play, the background of its writing, the awful length. And that I hoped, some day, to rewrite and cut, submit to the Cleveland Play House (a line or two about my other play being done there, and the year). Now don't hold your breath, babe.

May 18: Worked book most of the day. Sometimes, when I rip away from the desk, I feel bone-bruised. Robin news: in the TV nest, a mass of gently heaving blobs when parent flies off for a while. It'll be interesting to see the blobs turn into kids—the way the twins did on snapshots.

When Mort came home for dinner, he told me that Aunt Amelia is dying: the doctor's report today. Wish I could have ten minutes of real talk with her about flowers. Leave my gardener friend with color and fragrance.

May 20: Haven't been able to write for two days. That word, *able*, must be a phony; surely, I could have forced it. Only real poetry can't be forced. I think. But how do I know? Maybe even Keats had to force something like "sick for home, in the alien corn."

I feel pretty bleak. I suppose Aunt Amelia brings back Helen— in a dreary way. This woman is in her nineties, and still hanging on. Uncle Hugo was almost ninety when he died. That fifty-four of Helen's death...

But—afternoon: there are all of a sudden three Johnny-babies. Strewn, fat round brown little beauties, all over the orchard area. All right, Old Lady, you still have the whip hand. To make *me* smile?

Eight-fifteen in the evening. Phone—nurse: Aunt Amelia is dead. Mort ran to his car. I thought: Rest in peace, old gardener. I'll go see Aunt Hattie tomorrow. Can't tonight, can't. Later—life's so damn odd!—on FM: *Death and Transfiguration.* For the first time since this music had come to me with a book title. When it ended, I went to my desk and was able to write. Jesus.

Cut to June: I'm back into the book—deep. I never look at what I've written the day before. Just keep crawling ahead. The TV baby robins look like live guys big as a parent—but still with open mouths waiting for food to be brought. Yes, I'd love to see the twins—let's face it. But it was wonderful to see Barbie and Martin for a day—at the memorial services for Aunt Amelia.

Frost, last night—in early June! What an awful spring. Goes right with my spirit. Quite a bit of stuff frozen: dahlia foliage, asparagus. And I suppose the lilacs got it.

Later: mail to go with the limp, blackened asparagus: ''...most careful consideration, but have decided that we just couldn't get the kind of sales on this novel that would please...'' And my agent: ''Jo, I honestly don't know if I can get this book sold, but I'll do what I can. The market for novels is so tough these days...''

Yeah, the ''disciplined'' writer got drunk. No, no excuse: if you're going to hobble along on wine-crutches, you'd better *know* you're a cripple. Oh, Christ, why not call a friend, go to a movie, fight with normal help? But no: the pattern of rescue, in this concentration camp, is drinking. And to be alone with death thoughts.

Later, half-drunk: I can't go on blaming my emotional mess on her death. Sad, sad: ''Oh, *toi*, did I do such a lousy job on you?''

No, dear, honestly you didn't. I guess the candidate for rejection-despair was well jelled long before I met you. When my beautiful crutch (no, not this dirty, wobbly wine-crutch; no comparison!) broke, I took the flop of the century. Oh, dear crutch, neither one of us knew you were that. Or did you, possibly, wise one? And hope that I'd heal, eventually—and put that cane aside for good?

Three-quarters–drunk: I think, very dully, of suicide. Completely new way of handling that old ''must I?'' No passion about it, whatsoever. Strange. I'd always sorrowed about the desire, fought it with fury even as I yearned for it. Shouldn't an enormous thing like suicide have emotion pounding through it?—tremendous waves of it, like music?

Horrible night. Waking often. Nightmares. Up early—my heart slamming instantly with that disgusting, numb way in which I had contemplated killing myself. But what really frightened me was: no longer safe with a new piece of work? No longer insistent on finishing a book? And especially this one!

Rushed out as soon as Mort left. Ran to the Helen-tree. There was one cluster of tiny ''roses'' open. So lovely. Finally took a whole breath. Discovered a new robin's nest—top rung of my honeysuckle trellis. Walked around the dam twice, then all over the place. Watered things. Weeded. Worked with the one-horse shay for a long time. And at last got to my desk, exhausted all through my soul, instead of my body. But I picked up a pencil.

Later, mail. Forwarded from the publisher in London to mine in New York to my agent to me:

> Dear Miss Sinclair:
> I have just read your book *Anna Teller,* for which I wish to thank you for writing.
> I am sixty-two and suffering from angina and have just lost my husband. At times I have felt defeated, but your character who of course dominates your book has given me encouragement. I am apt to forget that she is only a figment of your imagination, but I'm sure you must have met someone like her.
> Anyway, thank you again for your help. All good wishes to you.

I felt the most marvelous gratitude. Thought: See what a book can do? Why do I forget! Wrote my English fan an answer of honest thanks.

Four-thirty: the TV robins are gone; happy summer, kids. Inside blackness has lifted an inch or two. Thanks, whoever.

The entire farm is in. I set out the nine leftover cherry tomato plants in the perennial bed. No room elsewhere; and they're pretty as shrubs, growing, so what the hell.

Nighttime therapy, past week or so—clinging like a leech to Frankl's book. That quote he uses to prove that God preserves all your tears: ''Thou hast kept count of my tossings; put thou my tears in thy bottle! Are they not in thy book?'' Beautiful.

And this, says the author: ''Suffering is supposed to enoble—
to make one more conscious, more sensitive to the beauty, brevity,
of life.'' Please!

Cut to July: Very tired, but quite alive. Very conscious that I'm
fifty-six, and: ''When I have fears that I may cease to be before my
pen has gleaned my teeming brain....''

Mort patient and gentle, as usual (oh, yes, you get taught deep
by a Helen—anybody close to her). Regular letters from Barb and
D have helped a lot; they are deeply interested in my progress on
the book.

July 9: A Saturday. Four down—and how many to go? (Agent:
she'll resubmit, in a day or two.) This rejection says practically nothing: ''...and unfortunately, we do not think that this manuscript
is quite right for our list, and therefore, regretfully...''

The words are as wooden as that suicide thing I went through.
No Bach, no Keats. Made me think, for a rather blinding moment:
And this new book?—any use in writing it? Who the hell would even
know what I'm trying to say about life and death?

But I kicked that to pieces by going out to earth. Tied the cherry
tomatoes in the perennial bed to their stakes. Extremely lush growth;
must be the years-enriched flower earth. (Mine feels absolutely arid
today.) Edna came out for a few hours to help me. Set her to weeding the catnip row, while I replanted sunflowers. We have a million slugs this season—worst I've ever seen. They've eaten even
sunflower seedlings, usually the hats—leaving pathetic-looking bare
stems. Sent Edna home with roses, peonies, iris, morning glory
buds—which will open in her city apartment. Bach—Keats.

Four-thirty. Hot and humid. Mort's in town. Worked on the
book for about an hour. Badly. On the porch: I feel as stale as a fourth
rejection of a fifth rewrite. And what's all *that* about? Do I really
believe in the book, or has the entire thing turned into simple stubbornness on my part?

I watched the hummingbirds at the bergamot. As usual, I
thought of Helen convalescing from the sympathectomy. Pain,
pain—and yet whenever I came down to help, she was looking out
at the South Woodland lilies. Smiling, even as she waited for it to
be time for the morphine. ''Look, Ruthie. Hummy's there.''

Something smacked at me. Is the novel that important because I wrote it while she lay dying—and afterward? Is that why I can't and won't put it away (let *it* die)? Could that be even one nutty piece of the creative death question?

No answer. I thought of Frankl's concentration camp woman, watching her tree. Helen watching Hummy. Pain of all kinds, but you watch life eternal. If you're a certain kind of person.

I stumbled to my tree. After a while, I went back to the desk. To a piece of work. *My* life eternal.

July 12: From the Office for Advanced Drama:

> Dear Miss Sinclair:
> You have indeed written a major and very interesting work, in "The Survivors," but I am afraid that I must return it to you. In its present state, it is too big for us, or for the theaters which we work with.
> If the Play House indicates interest in the play, please let me know. I mention this because I'd really like to see the play if the Play House decides to do it.
> Cordially

I read the letter again. "Major and very interesting." How about hanging on to that, instead of to "rejection"?

Didn't work too well. So I went out and planted more Van Goghs. To touch a season of hope again, to touch poor mad Vincent with my kind of love for his genius, loneliness, unhappiness—and his insistence on working. (*Don't think of his suicide.*)

Cut to August: Writing every day (after a few hours of gardening). The levels continue to merge—to half kill me. It's like writing of now and then, feeling now and then. When I get to the strokes. . . Yes, I wonder if I'll be able.

But the tomato plants in the perennial bed make me smile. They're so tall and full, loaded with fruits. Jack-the-Giant-Killer stuff. Two of them almost touching the lowest branches of a locust tree. Reaching for sun? Me, too!

The fall insect sounds have started. A sudden wave of whirring sound all through the air. What a short season. Mail: my agent has submitted "Approach" to an old publisher friend: "Now remember, Jo, it's summer, a bad time in the business, so it'll take a while." I shrug. But does the soul shrug?

Days and days: wrote for hours; tried to see people, Fannie, a few movies. Tried to be a professional writer at work. Depressed much of the time, but I keep working. This week: no liquor for four days. And I keep reading—long stretches of sleepless night—the Frankl book. Like rewriting—the meaning glimmers and fades, glimmers, almost peters out. Not quite.

Eight glories in bloom—the wall's starting to look blue. Later, weeded and tied tomatoes. Corn: ears on six (more coming). For the kids' visit, next week. Good.

August 20: Feel better, finally. Is it the soon-to-come pieces of her—the family? Made up all the beds for the visitors. EJ wants to sleep in ''Gramp's room,'' is mad about Mort. That means making up Helen's bed. Still not good. Did that fast, and ran. But I didn't ''hear'' the bell. Thanks!

Next day: shopped. Including boughten apples—time to break Muffy in on the Johnny game; and the five-in-one tree has only a few this season.

Sunday: The kids came. Of course, Mort has taken his one week's vacation to coincide with this visit. Day and evening very good. Much talk, laughter, the incessant chatter of children, lots of food (tastes so different with a horde of ravenous eaters around). Rie came out, too. Love that Dutch accent; gives me a different whiff of world.

When I got to my room that night, Helen had not yet pounced on my heart. Read Frankl: the glimmer quite bright.

The Week of the Visit: Mort is painting gutters. Barb's cooking a lot; D studying and working for big stretches of the day in the TV room. Everybody goes swimming in the afternoon—except me. That's really when I manage to work best. (I joined them once.)

Yes, Muffy adored the groundhogs sitting up and eating apples. EJ only partially interested. Climbed up to peer into the hole of the WELCOME WRENS house, but very shruggish at the still-for-rent fact. After all, he's a big boy now! Much more interested in cutting grass on the sitting mower; he's a whiz at it. But still ardent about harvesting, and even does the one-horse shay; and I'm glad. I think I really passed that one on.

Yes, I got drunk (three times) but disappeared into my room

before it got too bad; and was careful of my talk and actions when the little ones were around. Lay psychiatric diagnosis: a big combination of Helen and her daughter and grandchildren, time lost, and the depression—which seems to be triggered by almost anything. For example, Barbie's voice is so much like her mother's!

Nevertheless, D and B and I had a chance to talk about politics, the war, sensitivity groups and behavioral therapy in general—evenings, on the porch (fireflies so wonderful). Mort plays Scrabble with them; and bridge, when Rie comes out. He reads bedtime stories to his grandchildren. Plays the piano and sings along with them; Barb often joins in. He seems to be so happy. Does he ever have sharp knives about Helen at a time like this? I can't seem to control it. Or a number of other things.

Like: the constant interruptions—and my work shot to hell. But why can't I simply relax and visit with beloveds? I see them so rarely, and I love being with them. But the book seems to have become more and more important.

That drinking. Sometimes the most feathery of things motivates it. Aside from the enemy daggers that come at me from daily life (from a letter of rejection, to a Bach melody, to Chippy running) and shove me into that first fatal drink, there is the "writer trauma" itself.

What else can I call it? The hours and hours of clutching at the so-called dream, its awful insistence on consummation. The hours of silence, when you're battling with the search for exactly the right word and the delicate feeling to make that word. The silence (which is so important) eventually turns explosive. You fight to stay quiet, in control; but the tenseness gets worse. Hours; pages and pages are filled. And then you start thinking: Is this any good?—will it make sense to readers? The time flies, and yet it's thick-mud-trapped.

But of course, there is no "aside from." Within those hours of writer trauma, the big enemies coil—always waiting to rear and pounce: the rejections over the years, the anxiety and fear that seesaw "belief" and "promise" until you're dizzy with the swiftness of that up and down. And so you start to drink. Emotionally, you're dying—again. So out comes the weapon. Christ, what a way to live.

August 29: Up very early, at desk long before Mort or the visitors woke. I got a good chunk of work done. Later, had coffee with B and D, then back to the writing. It's going well—God knows why. Only vaguely conscious of steps up and down (the storage space). Eleven-thirty or so: Barbie knocked on my door. Her eyes very excited. "Darling, want to see something special?" Led me into the garage.

I had to fight not to shout out the instantaneous slam through my head "No, God damn it! No, no!" The men had brought down the dollhouse, and an enraptured Muffy was putting things into all the rooms: dishes, stove, chairs, beds.

It's a large, expensive toy. Each room is perfect (even wallpaper), each piece perfect (including sinks, toilets, lamps). Even shingles on the roof. Open at the front—so that a child can play house in any of the rooms. Helen's parents had had it built for her when she was five.

Barb had played with this dollhouse. When I first moved into the Shannon place, the spectacular toy had still been in her bedroom, taking up much of it. Now her daughter. The talk: some day, when B and D bought their own house, they would have it moved there. And why not? A generations thing, for sure.

Helen's dollhouse—out of the blue. Almost as if my book had spewed it out. Her grandchild was clapping her hands with joy, Mort was laughing, Muffy's parents were smiling with love, even EJ interested. Of course, I smiled and pretended excitement, but I had been attacked with a vengeance. I thought miserably: Am I really the only one with a ghost in this garage? But I must be so sick. There's no *reason* to be tortured by this. These are normal people; everybody but me knows how to bury their dead for good, the right way. God, why do I continue to be struck down?

I watched everybody's happiness. These generations, lovely (like a wedding gown worn by mother, daughter, granddaughter)—I can see that so clearly. But Helen, Helen, they didn't let you finish out one part of your life, little girl-owner of this dollhouse. The fates— they wouldn't permit you to see this little one and her joy in your childhood plaything. They wouldn't let you finish out your span of generations. That's what I can't bear today.

September: House is empty. The dollhouse is back upstairs, and the original child-owner is buried in peace again for the moment. I fill many pages in the current notebook. Mornings, the wall is almost all blue—the dew on the open flowers seeming to make a deeper hue, a color so exquisite that all the senses have to take joy.

Nights: reading William Gibson's *A Mass for the Dead*. Fine job— real poetry of people and emotion. Goes with *my* book.

Days. Chippy comes to my feeder stump, where he fills his entire head with seeds. He's a smile. He goes with my book, too.

I feel better. The steady writing and gardening? Very little liquor, too. The mental ward—how it fluctuates in tempo.

September 16: Restless. Where's that damn novel? Working so long and tense these days on the new book that often my right hand aches from clutching the pencils. Okay, that part's good. Window: a lot of baby robins leeching at their parents for worms, squawking and freckled. A smile. Still putting boughten apples out. Johnny sits up like Ragsy, eating his apple. A smile. The tree? Beauty, eternity.

September 20: Five down, and—ah, at last—none to go. This rejection: ''. . .respect the honesty of the emotion. . .all the ardent labor that obviously went into. . .but sentiment becomes maudlin, drama becomes melodrama. . .most stringent cutting and other disciplining might convert it into a publishable. . .but not for us.''

My agent—poor kid: ''. . .and Jo, I don't think I can get this ms. off the ground. Couldn't you go ahead with your present book— and then, perhaps, go back to this one? I shall hold the ms. until I hear from you.''

There are times when you feel unreal in a particularly numb way, I suppose. This feeling had to do with a closing, an ending. I felt very alone as a writer. As I had felt alone—for six years—as a person. This was the last rewrite; I knew that. I think. If there ever is a last to anything in the life of writer or person. Chippy was eating. He jumped down, ran toward the slope. The seasons were in order, but everything else smelled and tasted like the end of the world.

I went out—very fast. Used the one-horse shay for a long time. Half succeeded in turning off my head with the slogging work. Then I sat on a bale of straw and smoked.

Helen's tree kept pulling at my senses. A strange thought came. That novel—it's been like a series of strokes, hasn't it? You get felled—then you come out of the rampant part, slowly out of paralysis. Learn to move that arm again, to walk again. Now, new hope. You're alive; you're rewriting. She's alive; washing clothes, finally, even baking a cake. Then—crash—another stroke; another rejection. Again and again: she comes out of it; another rewrite begins; woman and book still alive. We all believe again: This is the last— she's made it, for real—so will the book!

But the final stroke comes, anyway. And the death. Woman, book. Another thought: There were five strokes; this is the fifth version of the book. Fate? No. Just coincidence, kiddo.

I went to the tree. And I could go on quietly with the rest of it: I suppose it would be easy to think—in my kind of still-crazed emotions—that I'd die, too, in the writer's way, unless that book was published. Maybe even to believe that, with publication, some kind of meaning would go into her dying after all the phony rescues and hope.

Talk about creating a triple-locked door into your own prison!

I touched the tree. An apology, of sorts. There should be a book of much more meaning than one blurted out in sickroom and hospital, and within the sickness of the soul that followed her death.

September 24: Despite my honest dialogue with the tree and with the Me, I haven't been able to work on the new book since the announced death of the old one. The outdoors has had me; so has depression. Today, earth won. Chore by chore—and I finally ended up at the wall of blue. I hadn't had strength enough to look at it since the rejection. I sat on the planter coping, looked at the front doorway. The woman in the wheelchair was smiling. Her eyes were loving me and the flowers. Quite as if she were saying: Wasn't this wall always a promise? And any Poem as deathless in the heart as this beauty and color?

And then, at last, I could think with less despair of the book waiting on my desk.

Rest of the week: Worked six hours plus, every day. Didn't leave the desk except for brief garden forays, and house chores.

Evening reading: caught up with a lot of back copies of the *Times*. In one, the rejected author gets some stupid but great pleasure: Hemingway's estate and bibliography all set; and there are four unpublished novels—and plenty of short stories never published. Hemingway! He probably had sense enough not to rewrite a million times, but I notice he didn't throw any of it away.

Out to dinner once, and a movie, during this week of work,

Cut to October: A Saturday. Mail: the two boxes of the novel ms. Had a bad twinge—even though I knew it was on its way home. Opened the boxes. Automatic: I'll have to retype the first few pages—they look pretty shopworn. Then thought: Why? Thought it was dead?

Wry smile: Because you're probably going to try and rewrite this book, Jo Sinclair. Some day. Some year. You're the type. You don't throw away pieces of your Self. You never have. So I suspect you ain't about to start now.

Turned a page—and another inch of pain came up from that dedication:

> For my sister Fannie
> —who made this book possible

How I wanted to give her this—from my heart.

I put the boxes away. Came back to my desk; slight wave of nausea when I looked at the makings of the new book. Couldn't write. A stone trying to create delicate heartbreak? So I drove into town, to a friend. Turned off my head there.

Cuke and pickle beds frozen last night. Nothing else touched. The Old Lady, cynical joker. I should give a damn—because I'm back on the book. Have been writing, hard. Often, that drowning; always good when it happens. Everything else is wiped out. Wonderful respite.

Worked in the morning from eight until eleven. Then took down the wren houses, and cleaned them. No field mice to startle me this fall. I miss them, see them rushing off in all directions, and Ragsy taking off after one, hear Helen's wonderful laughter.

Back to work: half past twelve until four. Got very tired in the spirit: I'm getting closer and closer to the Journal of Death. Went out and cultivated a few beds of flowers. Wondered, as I tried to touch Helen and strength in this way, if my soul would stay Helen-touched enough to be able to finish this book. Couldn't answer—even when I went to the tree.

A Sunday. Spent Friday and Saturday in town, with friends. The truth: I fled the book. Today, Edna is due out to help me autumn-clean; all day. The sword of the death journal is still hanging.

Next day: No choice: at eight-twenty, I was at my desk—shoving myself into the section I've been dreading so long. Wrote until noon. Terrible morning. Already, she is so alive on this slow, inevitable road to death that my chest hurts. Ah, but if she were here, I know she'd say very quietly: "You'll do it."
Talk about levels!

Morning paper: war news stinks; but there's an original play on TV this evening. Free theater. I won't look at the Vietnam stuff—can't stand it. Yes, I would still love to write for TV. Wonder if I ever will—to any avail.
At desk by nine. It's a struggle—to get the right start on this section. The entire tie should be nature, of course—the joy of the spring blooming and the beginning of the winter ice forming in the wrong season (the Old Lady suddenly hating and punishing us mortals).
Late afternoon—out to pick Mort's dinner corn (a little bit of the evergreen left). The one burning bush is half-red, top down (the other bush died, and I still miss it). Not yet the flaming color it turns eventually—but red enough for me to think: Book, burn in me like that!

Next morning: I finally started *really* writing what I consider the heart of this book. Holding my breath; I have to look up often. Early afternoon—out my desk windows: a Ma cardinal eats sunflower seeds, then hops to ground from the ash to feed a (very red) baby—bill to bill. Baby is full of twittering infant-sound, and his tail quivers as he's fed.
Memory picture—first spring out here: new wren babies, about six, being taught to fly. Landing on the porch screen, scrabbling, screaming baby noises, clinging and climbing awkwardly up and down the big chunk of screen for about a half hour. Helen, laughing and laughing: "It reminds me of Barbie learning to walk. She had to have a yardstick in her hand—or she'd fall. Oh, *toi*, aren't babies of all kinds fascinating?"
Dived back into the writing.

Mail: Royalty statement—*Anna*—eighty cents. One copy sold in six months. But then, looking out the window, a blue jay flying into the Helen-tree, perching there. Helped.

October 13: It must be Helen-renewed in the book, in me: finally looked through the brochure of grants for writers that I've been avoiding. Here's one: the ANTA–Robert Bishop play contest (unproduced plays). Deadline: November 1. Wrote at once, airmail, for information. ("What have you got to lose, dear?")

Worked well all morning. Chippies entertained me, anytime I looked up. Temperature dropped to forty from seventy in the night, but no hard freeze. Tossed out four apples; nailed a fresh Russian to my feeder stump. Get fat, everybody—hibernation time cometh.

Early afternoon, back at my desk. Jesus, now it starts. Right now, my hands feel that convulsion of her leg. Suddenly I have tears in my eyes. Every moment in now, in today, I know what happened eventually, that year. And yet I have to write this as if I do not know. Possible? Later: I tie up that night of her first stroke—those bleak, night hallways of the hospital. All of me is a clenching.

Out!—before you start actually sobbing. I smell the marigolds I'm picking against the radio-announced freeze for tonight. On that other level, it's spring, but all flowers inside of me are dying.

Five-twenty-five: I went back to the book. I had to. I'm crazy. Chippy is running back and forth in front of my desk windows—"chip-chipping" like a little musical instrument. I can see either his tail or ears on each trip. Johnny is sitting up, eating an apple. In the notebook, the woman is so sick—while all of the outdoors today, which she gave me, is so healthy. I'm a mass of twisted, spiritual levels.

The rest of October: A welter of almost constant hurt and the chores of the changing seasons and writing—and drinking. The month has turned into a season of memory, for sure. And to write memory of this kind is intolerable punishment. I can't bear to go to my desk in the morning—and I can't bear staying away. Is it even possible to write about hope and recovery, when I know today that it didn't work out?

In October, survival comes two ways: stretches of hard gardening for pieces of the day when I run from the desk; drinking for night. By afternoon of the writing day, I hurt in every piece of me that can hold pain. By four or four-thirty, I'm on my knees.

Yet the season goes on, and the old, not-to-be denied merging with a new one starts. Oddly, it's comforting; it's therapy with a vengeance—Helen's old, old gift returning to me when I need it most. The burning bush is aflame from head to toe. Chippy disappears on cold days, comes back on mild ones. The first really hard freeze; and then, for days, I can clean up for winter 1969 between pages and pages of summer 1963.

I read, many evenings and nights—when I'm not too blurred. Sometimes, I go back to *Markings*—to try to touch a tormented man who learned how to survive. Often, I try to touch back to my own meaning by rereading Frankl's conception. I even force myself out some evenings—friends, a movie or concert. Nothing stays a lasting weapon for the next day.

But always, that next day, I'm back at my desk. Keep thinking, so often, of Jacob wrestling with the angel. I will not let you go unless Thou bless me. Yes, but who's going to bless me?

November: The month came in on a literary note. A Saturday: Mort brought in the mail. There was a newly published anthology, with an old magazine story of mine in it. Author's copy. Ha!—first I knew about it. Nobody had bothered asking my permission, let alone paid me for reprint rights. Nevertheless, it was a good-looking book for something called *Tales of Our People—Great Stories of the Jew in America*. I found the page for credits; discovered permission had been granted for my story by *American Judaism*—the magazine in which it had appeared—so this editor was in the clear.

I laughed. Okay, I won't sue them. Me (feeling better and better): Hey, look. You're in with Benet, Ferber, Miller, Roth, Shaw. What do you want for nothing?

After Mort had examined the book and said nice things, I took it into my room, turned to the right page: "The Medal" by Jo Sinclair. I stared at that page for a long time. Then I read a few paragraphs. It had been a long drought, a ravenous hunger: the look of the print screamed that at me. A lousy anthology, an old story—but it felt like bread and water today.

And then, suddenly, I laughed as I thought: Well, well, finally a new "add to" for all the *Who's Who* copy to edit. Placed the book on the shelf with the other nine anthologies containing stories by Jo Sinclair, went back to my desk. But my head couldn't put away the look of the printed words. A book—how it made life out of manuscript.

Suddenly I saw Chippy running, heading for the spills under the locust tree feeder. And I grinned. It wasn't really winter. Chippy knew much more about changing seasons than a dumb mortal. The mortal—who had laughed more today than she had in a very long time—went back to writing about the immortal seasons of the spirit in a courageous woman.

Now, here's a question for the Boston deus ex machina (waiting to gobble up all my published and unpublished work): that new anthology—with its first glimpse in years of a piece of my work in a published book—is that why I applied for two grants? (The ANTA play contest turned out to be dead—lack of funds.) Because I did that, very soon after the anthology was put on my shelf.

The quiet inside continues. It's not elation, or even eagerness. But it's a good stillness, and you go about your world with purpose and speed. Worked most of most days; oh, the pain was there, but I could write it. For one thing, Helen was getting better in this notebook. And even though one part of my head on today's level knew she had to die, I was able to write as if she never would: a professional, disciplined the right way in her craft.

Raining. Crow sound. I love the way those birds herald the entrance of both spring and winter. Worked all day, with very little interruption. Still going well.

Mail: letter from Barbie. This one spoke of D's sabbatical coming up in June of next year, and they are planning to take the kids and Rie to Holland for a few months; and hadn't I better get to Northampton for a long visit soon? Because after Holland, it might be the West Coast (sensitivity training stuff) for the rest of the sabbatical—probably thousands of miles from me and Novelty, Ohio. "Please? Especially because you've decided not to come for Christmas, darling."

B and D were finally going to have their own Christmas—in their own home. They'd been coming here for years over that holiday— years of Helen, and after Helen. Mort and Rie were going there this year.

I'd written them why I was staying home, and of course they both understood. (I wonder if I'll ever be able to bear Christmas—the right way.) I doubt if I'll get to Northampton. Money, sure, and it's time they stopped paying for my visits. But mainly, I want to stay with the book.

At my desk: I feel very close to Helen today. In this notebook, she's smiling and full of hope, so courageous. Each new and relearned movement of walk and motion and chore is being embraced joyously by her. And, on my level this year, this day, I too am trying hard to relearn. The steady writing, the grant letters I sent out to the creative world—that's hope, isn't it? Helen shaking out a freshly laundered sheet—laughing at the way her hand and arm are able, again, to do their share of life's work. Today, some kind of paralysis has left me, too.

November 18: Wrote a lot, between chores. But: teeter-totter! By mid-afternoon, started feeling depressed. Damn it. Plain tired? Or Helen-in-the-book ganging up on me? Plus I miss the gardening badly. Thought: Crutch, crutch!—well, I have wine in the house. Looked out at the tree. A redheaded woodpecker flew past, to the ash feeder. I looked down at my work. That's what it is, of course: in this notebook, Helen is about to have her second stroke.

God, God, how can I? Heard: "Oh, *toi*, did I do such a lousy job on you?" And thought: Damn you, she went through that stroke. All you have to do is write it.

So I did. And I did not get drunk that night.

Been writing full days. Sometimes I jump up and run, almost crying, from my desk. But I always come back. Today: twenty-six degrees. Chippy at the feeder. Go under, kid—it's time. The birds are all fluffed out fat with the cold. At nine-twenty, snow—heavy. Skip the tour? The more I get written, the quicker I'll get through this unbearable part. Helen's in the hospital again—very, very sick.

Stayed with the writing an hour or so, then I was wandering— my heart banging, as if the levels had actually clashed. Had to go out. The air, the snow, made me feel a little better. Toured the joint, briefly. Then watched the tree for a while. Thought: Helen, I sure would like to talk for an hour or so. To you, not the tree. Like: Do *you* think a person should attempt a book like this? Be able to write it? I'm not a stone. I'm not a masochist, either—you know that. Should a human being torture herself this way? Wrestle with Jacob's angel and half suspect it's some kind of demon, wonder who will win? And this notebook, especially—the levels are murderous. How come I'm living the same month as that year? And friend, I feel so weak this month, this year. Nobody to be strong for, to switch roles for. Just me. And I never could do miraculous things for myself.

I put a hand on the tree—a moment. But Helen, this book is not for me. It's for—I hope!—a lot of people who have to know there are women like you in this world. Touching you, in this book— Jesus, it could give them so much in their hearts. Isn't that why I have to do it? No matter what happens to me? And anyway, dear, the book is for you, too. So maybe I will pull it off. A kind of switch of roles, after all?

Looked around. The snow was lovely, the new season fresh, eternal—so clean. I walked the east go-down, and around the dam. Helen no longer hurt in me—quite as if I *had* talked to her. And Ragsy was around—my old dam companion in all seasons. She didn't hurt, either. Somehow, the levels had straightened out. When I went back to my desk, memory and torment channeled into work that seemed, again, so meaningful. Thanks, whoever!

Evening: for one more small evidence of the hope I'd touched again at the tree, I read the carbons of those two letters asking for grants. The National Endowment for the Arts, in Washington, D.C.; and a private foundation, in Boston, for ''middle-aged, well-established writers on hard times.'' Well, ain't that Jo Sinclair? I thought with wryness that was half a smile.

I'm almost positive the National Endowment is out for individual grants. Anything I've read in the *Times* lately says Congress has slashed that outfit a lot. But: What have you got to lose, *toi*? All right, friend. I'm going to try like hell to go on trying. Okay?

Cut to December: I'm deeply back in the book. Good! Writing six and seven hours a day—torment pushed back, as if Jacob is winning that wrestling match, after all. Fifteen to eighteen degrees; putting out big doses of suet and peanut butter to warm the birds. Cardinals by the fives, making their winter sounds, instead of songs. Seasonal substitutes are lovely.

Mail: one down; and no point in being bitter about money spent for war and going to the moon, instead of the arts.

National Endowment for the Arts to applicant:

> . . . In reply to your inquiry about our program of individual grants in creative writing, we can offer almost no encouragement at this time. As you may know, we made grants in varying amounts in fiscal 1968 to 75 writers throughout the coun-

try. However, because of severe cutbacks by the Congress in
our funding for fiscal 1969...

Odd!—I grinned. Thought: Screw you, Congress. But it serves
me right—holding out my hand like a phony beggar. I've never liked
begging for me, or been good at it. It's different when you beg for
others—have you forgotten?

I crashed back into work. In the notebook, I'm learning to give
Helen her shots. I'm damn good at it—and I'm helping my friend.
To hell with money.

December 23: Marvelous, fantastic: been writing steadily. Even
though the second answer came like another blizzard, to match the
season and the no from Washington.

Foundation (for middle-aged, et cetera) to applicant:

> ...and after reviewing your book, *Anna Teller*, the trustees
> of this Foundation feel they cannot be of assistance to you.
> However, the new book you outlined for us sounds as though
> you should be able to find a publisher for it who would give
> you an advance...

Me (to inner Me): In other words, do it yourself. And might as
well laugh, too. Because since when did *you* become a beggar? Writer
or carpenter, babe, make your own dough. Put up or shut up, as
my niece would say.

And I filed my application carbons and the answering letters
in the box that would go to the Jo Sinclair Collection at Boston
University. Laughed. These ought to pep up my morgue!

Today, at my desk, I think: As long as I'm able to go on working. That's all that counts. The letters didn't even depress me. And
that is damned interesting for a patterned kid like me. Have I somehow buried a word called *rejection?* Not too long ago, that's exactly
what my guts would have labeled those no-letters. Strange as hell!
Because why, all of a sudden, do I know that the only thing that
really matters is this book—to finish it as honestly and as well as
I can?

On the other hand, nothing is "all of a sudden." Better know
that, too. Mr. T. S. Eliot, you're quite a poet. I'll take a piece of that
stanza I love so much—for a piece of some kind of answer to the
Me at this desk today:

In order to arrive at what you do not know
You must go by a way which is the way of ignorance.
In order to possess what you do not possess
You must go by the way of dispossession.
. . .And what you do not know is the only thing you know
And what you own is what you do not own
And where you are is where you are not.

Levels, again? Maybe even therapy. As Eliot would say, in that same poem: "The wounded surgeon plies the steel / That questions the distempered part."

This whole month of December—so much of it goes with that Eliot poem. All of a sudden, something kicked me in the soul. Only it couldn't have been all of a sudden. And I still don't understand the enormous, strange thing that happened. Yeah: "You must go by a way which is the way of ignorance."

Enormous; though I was completely unaware of it until a signal went off in me like—what?—a time bomb, I suspect. Time surely must have played a hell of a big part in this thing. Do many tremendous changes occur that way, I wonder? Had the hidden change already started months before that night? A year or two before?—and I ready, but not knowing it, for the smash-second of signal to disclose that change?

New questions—but very uncertain answers. Yeah: "And what you do not know is the only thing you know."

All I do know for sure is this: one evening (alone in the house), I was watching TV—one of those rarely performed original scripts, and a good one. Near the end, one of the people in the play said to another: " 'Therefore choose life.' That's from *Deuteronomy*, sir."

What they call the shock of recognition? I soaked in that phrase; I'd read it often, heard it many times over the years. But maybe a person has to be ready before she can recognize a particular music. Or maybe the old, old wound must be clean of the last vestige of poison—in order not to reject medication. That evening, those words hit me like a pure-new message. "Therefore choose life."

When I went back to my room, I was still dazed, thinking: What, what? Choosing life—rather than the dying ways. Choose? Well, I suppose it *is* a choice. Yours. Not somebody else's.

I stared out my desk windows—at the night, at the tree I could not see. And my mind opened even more. Listen! Isn't that what

transfiguration could be? Not a book sold, a play produced—as proof
that you're still a creative artist. The choice within—yours: to live.
And—you better face this!—did you ever actually *choose* life? You
waited for it, or death, to choose you.

As kindergarten-easy as that? So simple? So clear-cut? So abruptly? Or have I really been ready for months, years? Still, it's incredible. Wonder if it'll last. After the long torment about creative death?
After that endless search for the magic ingredient which was to van-
quish any death? Hers—mine. How could anything be that simple?
(As simple as finally—years late—nodding quietly to "that which
the earth covers over *must* be forgotten"? My God.)

Can I? *Me*? But yes or no, at least for one night, this one hour,
look at the changed meaning of that word, *transfiguration*, which
had assumed such an unearthly aura. This is like being given a translation from a language I haven't been able to read. Down from the
Christ-and-cross heights—never for me, even in deepest grief and
pain. The translation concerns a small person and readable earth;
seasons changing with no mystery; elementary explanations of
mourning and loneliness, of the depression over hard, honest work
gone wrong for many reasons.

As I tried to dig more deeply into this new mass of thoughts,
it seemed to me that the pattern of transfiguration must surely have
begun to shift a long time back, without my knowing it—but the
last of its changes of shape and meaning may very well have come
under the impact of those letters saying no.

And then, could this have happened? I watched that TV play,
the letters and God knows what else scrambled inside of me like
pieces of a jigsaw puzzle. And when somebody on the air said:
"Therefore choose life," it could have been somewhat as if those
pieces came together—to make a whole picture. And maybe I *can*
call it transfiguration? It looks like a down-to-earth picture for an
ordinary human being who happens to be a writer. It looks like solid
meaning.

Whatever happened—as simple, as amazing, as that—seemed
to be a very honest piece of awareness. Not knowledge—oh, no,
nothing that certain. But even to be *aware* of such an important
could-be?

In bed, I read the entire Eliot poem that starts: "In my beginning is my end." And finishes with: "In my end is my beginning."

But I read over, several times, the words that were so exact for what had happened to me that evening:

> Home is where one starts from. As we grow older
> The world becomes stranger, the pattern more complicated
> Of dead and living. Not the intense moment
> Isolated, with no before and after,
> But a lifetime burning in every moment
> And not the lifetime of one man only...

Inside me, quiet thanks for fine poetry. ''...the pattern more complicated of dead and living.'' Yes. But understanding that very complication, at last, has created for me some kind of new, simple pattern of working and living. At least for this night. Amen.

The next morning, I fed the birds, toured the joint, and went to work. Wrote my book most of the day, grateful that the new pattern was holding.

December 24 through 26: Wrote, wrote, wrote. The new pattern still holding. Thanks, whoever.

December 27: Early—out the windows: a fairyland of falling snow, and the whole world already buried in soft white. Lots of bird action and colors at the clogged feeders with their tall hats.

This is the anniversary of Helen's death. The tree, the beauty of the season, the story of her life in these notebooks—but no desire to cry, to curse. Is it possible that the new pattern can hold this strongly? Will it continue to? Don't know yet—any of it. But I didn't wake heavy and black. I thought of her at once, of course, but with stillness.

Radio: In this area, we are having the coldest and snowiest winter since 1963.

Continuously fascinating—those two levels. Today, even the harshness of the winter goes with the book—the six years a bridge of some kind. And today, it all seems very natural. Is that what awareness does?

Outside: as I unclogged and loaded the feeders, whisking off all the hats, then put out plenty of suet and peanut butter, several chickadees flew near my head, scolding, urging. A laugh—a good one. It was still snowing hard; it must have been all night, because the stuff I walked through hit me halfway up my legs and got into the tops of my big boots.

Wondrously lovely everywhere I looked, as I struggled through those rearing white waves. And my head was full of fragments out of the Frankl book. It's that kind of a day: a meaning-time, a soul-time. In and out of my head, bits written by that man who "started" in prison (and am I coming out of mine?—that's what it feels like): "There is only one thing that I dread: not to be worthy of my sufferings." Quote Dostoyevski. Another writer. But a major writer. And you must know damn well by now that you're minor, kiddo. Better try for the closer stars, I'd say.

I pushed through the great drifts, to the narcissus bed; had a picture of one of the poeticus in late April bloom. Looked over, beyond the forsythia: the west groundhog holes are covered high. Bulbs and sleeping Johnny-babies, waiting for a new season. For how long have I been dormant?

Walked on—fighting the marvelous weight and pull of the snow—toward the tree. And thought: I have not been worthy of my sufferings. Definitely. The tears, the drinking, the awful bouts of depression, the near-suicidal hours, the helplessness to move out of myself-in-chains. But my suffering *was* honest. Frankl: "If there is a meaning in life at all, there must be a meaning in suffering."

Past the perennial bed. The rose bushes are almost hidden— just the top branches of two or three showing above the drifts. Frankl: "Spiritual freedom—which cannot be taken away—that makes life meaningful and purposeful."

Even in prison, he meant. Any concentration camp—especially the one you put yourself into—is what I mean. Therefore choose life. Will I ever know why it took me until now to be able to touch words like that? Doesn't matter. Use them, and know quietly that tomorrow they may be unusable again. But maybe they'll stay?

I walked—actually battling the snow. Got to the tree a little breathless. But the wind has swept a lot of the snow toward the east go-down, and most of the tree is unobscured; I can stand close.

No weeping. And the label I pinned to this haw? No. Touch the tree, not the death.

Some of the branches of her tree had been layered by snow, intricately, as if the wind had sculptured the white perfectly; other branches were bare. The combination was lovely. I thought: What *is* transfiguration? Will I ever be sure? Could it possibly be an awareness of the meaning of one's own self; being able to live with that meaning? Being able to bear acknowledging a small talent, perhaps, rather than the great Poems you've always yearned to write—and she promised you would?

I'm not sure—of any of it. But I suspect something: a small poem can be as beautiful as a small flower. Give quite a bit to people.

I felt sort of stunned. Though I knew that the years of pain and tormented anticipation of my own kind of death had not been a waste, or anything but my honest reaction to her death and my life after it, I realized that a certain phase of my agony was over.

No miracle—oh, no. That was part of the awareness, too. There was no certainty that today's new gateway would stand. I knew damn well, here at the tree, that nothing was ever wrapped up. That later, or tomorrow, I could be hopeless again, without belief. But I did know that today was happening.

I started for the house; for the book waiting on my desk. My head going right on: This tower *has* narrowed. Will I actually have to leave in order to choose life honestly? Today, I know something else: I've been frozen emotionally to this house, this land. The financial bind was a phony; I could have gotten the money. But know the rest of it: the tree will live, no matter what I do. And she will, in me, for as long as I'm alive.

When I got back into the house, I felt as if I'd been on some far, deeply enriching journey. The stillness continued when I got to the desk. In the notebook: I'm giving her shots for the dizziness. Christmas is coming—and the family.

I wrote steadily. The two levels, the juxtaposition and merging of years and days—astounding. But not surprising. Nothing is, anymore. Just the way the new pattern holds in me.

Around ten o'clock, Mort and the kids phoned from Northampton. Then EJ and Muffy came on; the air crackled with excitement. Nobody mentioned Helen, but of course that's why they phoned. And so early on her day.

Out the windows (as I listened and talked): two male pheasants under the ash feeder, eating spills. How dull and muted the colors of a winter pheasant. But remember how, in early April, the brilliance comes back into them? And sap rising, the first crocus knifing through even half-frozen earth.

I began to write again; after a while, went in deep. Until the phone: Martin. He, too, calling on this day of his mother.

Then lost in the writing again; plucked up briefly by phone calls from my sister, several friends. Nobody saying her name—all expecting me to be the usual for this anniversary—sad, black, possibly half-drunk.

And I thinking: How long will this pattern hold? I had liquor in the house, in case it didn't—suddenly. But I kept drowning in the writing.

When finally I looked up, my hand cramped, it was almost three o'clock. Went to put drops in my eyes, to get some coffee and a lunch sandwich. Then I was writing again—steadily, in control, though all of it was coming back in such vivid detail: the beginning-death in her, the fear in me.

Writing and writing; all of it good. But those two levels—quiet as I thought I was—apparently fought each other in me. All of a sudden I'd jumped up, gone fast to the kitchen, to the utility room, then into the living room.

I was all right. It was just that I was so frantic to *do*. But to do what? Try to save her again, all over again? I knew better today— but that other year of the notebook was aching in me.

Near the front window, I watched the standing feeder—the birds drawn to it, and under it; the line of them sitting on the snow fence. I looked at the spot where the bleeding heart lay dormant—until its next season. I thought: Be still, Helen. Be at peace in me. I won't let you die over and over. I promise.

When I went back into my room, I desperately wanted a drink; and all of me did not want to drink. Sat at my desk, looked out. The pheasants were gone. A Hairy at the suet in the ash, chicka-dees flying back and forth. The snow so beautiful; her tree so beautiful.

I didn't go back to the book. The entire day must have been a stealthy earthquaking of those levels—within the quiet, good hours of work. I felt the impact now, and the urgency of those new ques-tions I'd been able to ask myself. It was snowing hard again. I visual-ized a bird in the tree, very red against all that white as it darted to another branch. A living bird in her tree.

And found myself writing; no, not the book; I had taken a fresh pad of paper, pushed the current notebook to one side. Slow—so slow—but out of my heart, at last, came that poem.

Woman into tree:
May all the seasons float or whirl or dance
About you always—eternity of rhyme and bridge.

May the sun come at times like laughter,
The moon gentle you and tender you
For all the nights to be;
And stars there—always stars—to cool the heat,
To jewel the harshest black.
In every summer, take peeper sound for talk
Those summer days, and summer nights
More instruments to hear:
The owl who calls and makes you smile;
The frogs upon your visioned dam,
Reflected in your pond,
Their drums and flutes a mirrored echo in your pond.
For fall, take all the tree-toad song.
For winter, stillness wrap you round with snow and cloud,
Or wind sometimes to make the sudden cry
That turns the silence into fugue.

Woman into tree:
I give you back the seasons of my heart,
This earth insistent on replenishing its hope
To grow the tallest dream, the smallest dream
You told; and thus I give you back the song,
The poem new and old as all green spring.
I give you back the life you pointed out.
Much as I fought to blind my Self,
It is in me—that life to take,
Like promises you made that bird would sing
And bloom would show
And all the Poems would be.

Tree, woman into tree:
Now live forever—and let me free
To live.
I give you to the seasons,
To the life of those who come to touch,
To smile at all the birds within your green.
I give you, and take you with me
Into all the seasons of my soul.
I give you to me,
The lover of trees and dream and song.

Now tree, now soul,
You touch eternity.

I felt shaky with gratitude. It had been so long coming; I had
wished so bitterly for one new poem.

Thought: How to make a life-day out of a death-day?

I wanted to cry; the shivering was all through me by then. Got
myself a drink—had it in sips. Medicine, not turn-off. No, I didn't
want to turn off this head. When I read the poem again, it felt like
some kind of acceptance, finally, of grief and memory. And of
myself—alive, and wanting to be. A strange feeling.

Wandered around the house for a while, thinking of how the
new pattern had not changed back yet, or smashed—though it was
evening, and almost an entire day had gone past mourning into
work, into honest questioning of myself—and even into poetry.

A good talking to Self: It's okay. I do realize that nothing is ever
wrapped up in a neat bundle of what-will-be. But don't I really know
a few certainties today? Yes, spring will come, and the tree leaf out—
no matter where I am. The book will be finished. And, though my
heart will ache for what was, and what could have been, don't I
know that I will walk again into the poems of all my spiritual
seasons?

I went back to the desk. To work. To my life. I wrote for a long
time. Wrote until the feeling prickled at the back of my neck. I had
been attuned to this moment all day: it was ten minutes of ten, as
I looked out the window.

I said, out loud: "Therefore I choose life. Please. All right, we'll
see. I want to try—please?"

There were tears in my eyes. I thought of the liquor ready for
me if I needed it. I thought: Will I be able to do it? At my age—with
my emotional background?

My eyes came away from the tree I could see only in my heart.
I went back to work. On my new book.

Bibliography—Jo Sinclair

Novels

Wasteland   New York: Harper & Brothers, 1946. Paper edition. New York: Lancer Books, Inc., 1961. Reprint. Philadephia: The Jewish Publication Society, 1987.

- $10,000 Harper Prize Novel Award, 1946; Book Find Club Selection; Honorable Mention, Ohioana Library, 1946
- Published in Great Britain; translated into French, Hebrew, Italian, Norwegian, Spanish, and Swedish; transcribed into Braille
- Optioned for a play by Bernard Hart via Dramatist Guild of the Authors League of America, 1947

Sing at My Wake   New York: McGraw-Hill Book Co., Inc., 1951. Paper edition. Garden City, N.Y.: Permabooks, 1952.

- Published in Great Britain; translated into French

The Changelings   New York: McGraw-Hill Book Co., Inc., 1955. Reprint. New York: The Feminist Press at The City University of New York, 1985.

- Certificate of Honor and the Harry and Ethel Daroff Award, the Jewish Book Council of America, 1956
- Certificate of Recognition, Brotherhood Week, the National Conference of Christians and Jews, 1956
- Best Book of Fiction by an Ohioan, Ohioana Library, 1956
- Nominated for the Pulitzer Prize in Fiction by Edward C. Aswell, editor-in-chief, McGraw-Hill Book Co., Inc., 1956

Anna Teller   New York: David McKay Co., Inc., 1960. Reprint, New York: The Feminist Press at The City University of New York, 1992.

- The 1961 Literature Award of the Cleveland Arts Prize; Best Book in Fiction by an Ohioan, Ohioana Library, 1961
- Published in Great Britain

Plays

On the Streetcar: a one-act play produced by the Cleveland People's Theater, 1935

Listen to My Heart: a one-act play produced at Cleveland College of Western Reserve University, 1939

Jesus Was a Dream: a three-act play commissioned by Karamu Theater, Cleveland, 1940

The Long Moment: a three-act play produced by the Cleveland Play House, 1951; Fellowship House, Cincinnati, 1951; and the Venzuella Jones Repertory Group at Saint Martin's Little Theater, New York, 1952

The Survivors: a three-act play. Winner of the Luci and Harry Wolpaw Playwriting Grant, Jewish Community Centers, Cleveland, 1969

Jo Sinclair's short stories, articles, and poetry have appeared in more than twenty-five magazines and journals, including *Esquire, Harper's, Reader's Digest,* and the *Saturday Evening Post.* Her work has been anthologized in twelve volumes since 1938, most recently in *America and I: Short Stories by American Jewish Women Writers,* edited by Joyce Antler (Beacon Press, 1990).

Sinclair's work has also been the subject of television broadcasts, including *At Mama Bufano's* (1952), an adaptation of a story originally published in *Cosmopolitan,* and *We Can't Be the First!* (1956), winner of second prize for drama in the National Playwriting Competition in Civil Rights sponsored by the Fund for the Republic. *All of Us Were Healed* was produced in 1942 for Station WHK in Cleveland, and Sinclair was commissioned to write several drama series for radio, sponsored by the American Red Cross (1943), the Jewish Community Council in Cleveland (1947), and the Cleveland Chapter of the Conference of Christians and Jews (1948).

"The Jo Sinclair Collection" is housed in the Twentieth Century Archives of Mugar Memorial Library at Boston University.

New and Forthcoming Books from The Feminist Press

Anna Teller, a novel by Jo Sinclair. $35.00 cloth, $16.95 paper.

The Captive Imagination: A Casebook on The Yellow Wallpaper, edited and with an introduction by Catherine Golden. $35.00 cloth, $14.95 paper.

Fault Lines, a memoir by Meena Alexander. $35.00 cloth, $14.95 paper.

I Dwell in Possibility, a memoir by Toni McNaron. $35.00 cloth, $12.95 paper.

Intimate Warriors: Portraits of a Modern Marriage, 1899–1944, selected works by Neith Boyce and Hutchins Hapgood, edited by Ellen Kay Trimberger. Afterword by Shari Benstock. $35.00 cloth, $12.95 paper.

Lion Woman's Legacy: An Armenian-American Memoir, by Arlene Voski Avakian. Afterword by Bettina Aptheker. $35.00 cloth, $14.95 paper.

Long Walks and Intimate Talks. Stories and poems by Grace Paley. Paintings by Vera B. Williams. $29.95 cloth, $12.95 paper.

The Mer-Child: A Legend for Children and Other Adults, by Robin Morgan. Illustrations by Amy Zerner and Jesse Spicer Zerner. $17.95 cloth, $8.95 paper.

Motherhood by Choice: Pioneers in Women's Health and Family Planning, by Perdita Huston. Foreword by Dr. Fred Sai. $35.00 cloth, $14.95 paper.

The Princess and the Admiral, by Charlotte Pomerantz. Illustrated by Tony Chen. $17.95 cloth, $8.95 paper.

Proud Man, a novel by Katharine Burdekin (Murray Constantine). Foreword and Afterword by Daphne Patai. $35.00 cloth, $14.95 paper.

Women Writing in India: 600 B.C. to the Present. Volume I: 600 B.C. to the Early Twentieth Century. Volume II: The Twentieth Century. Edited by Susie Tharu and K. Lalita. Each volume: $59.95 cloth, $29.95 paper.

Prices subject to change. For a free catalog or order information, write to The Feminist Press at The City University of New York, 311 East 94 Street, New York, NY 10128.